Determinants of Learning

Esmor Jones and Tony Brazendale

Ward Lock Educational

ISBN 0 7062 3355 7 casebound
0 7062 3356 5 paperback

First published 1974

Set in 10 on 11 point Linotype Plantin
by Willmer Brothers Limited, Birkenhead
for Ward Lock Educational
116 Baker Street, London W1M 2BB
Made in England

Contents

For Sara and David

Acknowledgments

The publishers and authors would like to thank the following for permission to reproduce copyright material:

Allen and Unwin Limited, E. and J. Newson *Four Years Old in an Urban Community*; J. S. Bruner 'The course of cognitive growth' © 1964 American Psychological Association, reprinted by permission; A and C Black Limited, Francis Lewis . . . *And Softly Teach*; Curtis Brown Limited, J. Kirkup *The Only Child*; Eyre and Spottiswoode (Publishers) Limited, S. Mays *Reuben's Corner*; Faber and Faber Limited, G. H. Bantock *Education, Culture and the Emotions*; N. A. Flanders and *The Journal of Experimental Education*, Table 1 'Interaction, analysis and training'; Granada Publishing Limited, A. B. Clegg *The Changing Primary School* London: Chatto and Windus Educational; William Heinemann Limited, R. Church *Over the Bridge*; Mrs Jules Henry, J. Henry *Essays in Education*; Dr W. Labov, 'The logic of nonstandard English' *Georgetown University Monograph on Language and Linguistics*; Peter McPhail, 'Adolescence: The Age of Social Experiment'; Manchester University Press, C. Lacey *Hightown Grammar*; The Merrill-Palmer Institute, F. Harrison 'Relationship between home background, school success and adolescent attitudes' *Merrill-Palmer Quarterly* 14, 1968, 331–344; National Association for the Teaching of English, John Dixon 'Growth through English'; Nelson, London, L. A. Stenhouse *Culture and Education; New Society*, D. White extract from 'Brum's mobs'; Penguin Books Limited, S. Turvey in R. Fraser (ed) *Work* (Pelican 1968, © Penguin Books 1968), M. Morse *The Unattached* (Pelican 1965, © Mary Morse 1965), L. C. Taylor *Resources for Learning* (Penguin Education Special 1971, © L. C. Taylor 1971), C. Hannam *et al Young Teachers and Reluctant Readers* (Penguin Papers in Education 1971, © Charles Hannam, Pat Smyth and Norman Stephenson 1971), Tyrrell Burgess (ed) *Dear Lord James* (Penguin Education Special 1971, © Tyrrell Burgess and contributors 1971); Pitman Publishing Limited, London, John Holt *How Children Fail*; Laurence Pollinger Limited, M. Mead *Coming of Age in Samoa*; Carl Bereiter and Siegfried Engelmann *Teaching Disadvantaged Children in the Preschool* © 1966, reprinted by permission of Prentice Hall Inc, Englewood Cliffs, New Jersey; Routledge and Kegan

Paul Limited, S. Isaacs *Intellectual Growth in Young Children* London: 1930, D. Hargreaves *Interpersonal Relations and Education* London: 1972, *Social Relations in a Secondary School* London: 1967, B. Jackson *Working Class Community* London: 1968.

Foreword

Colleges of education are changing rapidly. Clearly, it will not be long before all new entrants to the teaching profession will be graduates. As a consequence, the old concurrent courses are on the way out. This is not necessarily a matter for grief; the mixture of main subject and education courses was a little bit like French dressing. The two elements did not always mix well. The problem now may be that the colleges will attempt to imitate inappropriate university patterns. In pursuit of academic respectability, courses will be remote from children and classrooms. There is no need at all for this to happen. The study of children and their needs will always be intellectually demanding as well as stimulating and relevant.

This book is offered as an attempt to marry theory and practice in a relevant way. It has long been realized that the social sciences have much to offer the teacher; the trouble has been that sociology and psychology have all too often been presented to students as disparate disciplines. What have the social sciences to tell us about children growing up and children learning? What have they to say about the relationships of the classroom? If these questions are to be answered, if only tentatively, then we must unify, not atomize.

The material in this book, whether discussed in the main text or presented in extract form, is highly selective. It is impossible in a single volume to cover all the research into cognition, learning styles, social surveys, classroom behaviour, emotional problems and so on. Indeed it is not even particularly desirable to do so. Therefore personal preferences have inevitably dictated to a certain extent what we have included, though throughout we have attempted to include material that strikes us as significant and useful. Often, introductory texts tend to *reify* processes. Look, for example, at the chapters in almost any standard college text on memory or personality. Textbooks also tend to deal discretely with sociological material—there are sections on the family, the peer group, the school whereas all bear simultaneously upon the child.

We believe it is more worthwhile to attempt, however imperfectly, a synthesis of some of the more interesting findings. We feel it is asking too much to leave the making of links to the students; they have enough to do in acquiring their new role. They need all the help we can give in making early classroom experiences productive. The book is, of course, unashamedly theoretical. But we hope that it will help students, who only too often find theory well removed from teaching practice reality, to look at children with a deeper understanding.

We have one further criterion. We believe books on education should be readable. There is no need for scholarship to be lost in the mists of jargon. Far too much work in the social sciences is written in an arcane dialect. There is little the sociologist or the psychologist has to say that cannot be expressed in plain English.

We take joint responsibility for all that is said in the book. Of course, there has been a division of labour. Tony Brazendale wrote the first two chapters and Esmor Jones the last two. But all four are the product of joint discussion.

Finally, we would like to thank our students. Their open comments, their expressions of need and their ideas have made a vital contribution.

Chapter 1: 'The child is father to the man'

Both the Jesuits, and the behaviourist psychologist Watson who declared he could make any infant into any adult, are in surprising agreement with the poet William Wordsworth on this point. Whatever each child may bring with him from his parents in the form of a genetic 'blueprint', it is generally acknowledged that he is also a product of the society, the family, into which he is born. 'Children are seen and not heard', we used to say. 'Manners are caught, not taught' is another genteel phrase from the past which hints at the force of home, school and neighbourhood in making us what we are. R. D. Laing and other psychiatrists associated with him have urged us to look again at the way the family makes some of us over into its own image.

If early experience and environment are felt to be so important, then clearly one's membership of a particular family and subculture will affect how one learns as well as what one learns. Professor Illsley, a sociologist in Aberdeen, has 'taped' the speech of middle and working-class three-year-olds by attaching a signal transmitting device to them for twelve hours a day. He and his team found that not only did middle-class toddlers ask *more* questions than working-class ones, they also asked different *kinds* of questions.

Irrespective of social class, learning is obviously dependent on maturation. Learning to tie shoelaces, for example, ultimately depends upon the development of the appropriate neural structures in the brain. In addition, of course, practice and play with string, wire and Christmas cracker puzzles all provide the necessary 'training'. But *no* amount of practice alone could enable a year-old baby to tie up shoes; the skills are heavily dependent on physical development. Nose-blowing on the other hand, is less obviously dependent on the state of readiness of the nervous system. Yet unless the child can 'read' nose-blowing instructions from a patient adult—an ability again reliant upon the physico-chemical development of the nervous system—there will be no learning. Maturation is therefore one of the required conditions if learning is to take place.

Social learning, as our Aberdeen three-year-olds showed, is even influenced by social class at a very early age. Other forms of social learning, also involving language, include such things as, for example, learning how to be teacher's pet, or learning to avoid answering questions in class. Most early social learning takes place in the family and involves learning to share, to obey, to be punctual and to tell the truth. Psychologists tend to differ from sociologists in this, in that psychologists have traditionally studied a feature of learning (for example, does the child learn to comply because his mother is a source of pleasure to him?), whereas sociologists have usually preferred to analyze social learning and to see if this varies between social groups or ethnic minorities. Perhaps a better way of putting this would be to say that most psychologists think of 'learning' as that activity which singles out living from non-living organisms. Even the lowly flatworm has learned to wiggle down a forked 'maze' provided it is rewarded with a waterwell.

Of course everyday experience would suggest that human learning is slightly more complicated than the models of animals learning such as dogs salivating to a bell, or monkeys tapping ratchets to obtain a peanut suggest. Nevertheless, because of the ease and speed with which learning can be observed and tested in animals, and because past learning can be controlled, animals have proved almost too convenient as 'subjects'. Learning in deliberately simplified environments suggested to psychologists of the past that *all* learning was subject to the same laws. Thus the learning of cues by which a hungry rat finds his way through a maze to a food trough is seen as analogous to that by which an organist learns a Bach fugue. This *stimulus-response* school of psychology became known as the behaviourist school because it claimed to focus on observable behaviour to the exclusion of everything else. In the USA it has largely been associated with the names of psychologists such as Thorndike, Hull, Tolman, Watson and Skinner.

The influence of Behaviarism upon academic psychology in America and elsewhere has been immense. It has confronted tough theoretical problems such as language-learning with ingenuity, but it has also attracted a good deal of criticism in postulating internal and presumably unobservable stimuli and responses in mental activity such thinking, for example. Some psychologists now consider behaviourism to be intellectually exhausted as a means of theorizing about human behaviour. We can understand this better if we look more closely at the behaviourists' experiments. In Pavlov's famous set of experiments, the dog was rewarded after hearing a bell tinkle by the sight and smell of food. In one sense, the bell signalled 'food-on-the-way'. The behaviourists have developed this simple conditioning experiment further by requiring the animal (cat, monkey or pigeon) to *do* something (press a bar or tap at a lighted panel) before being rewarded. Thus Thorndike (1921) placed a thirsty cat in a box and observed how long it took the cat to escape from the box to the saucer of milk visible outside. He noticed that gradually useless bits of 'random' behaviour were dropped from the cat's repertoire of responses until the cat was no sooner in the box than he had negotiated the catch to escape. Skinner (1953), in work with pigeons, sought to show that, provided a particular response is in the animal's repertoire, carefully timed and spaced rewards or 'reinforcements' can be delivered so as to shape the pigeons' behaviour. Skinner would set target behaviour (in one experiment the target was 'to be able to play ping pong') and selectively reinforce those bits of the animal's behaviour which conformed in any way to the target. He first reinforced any steps the pigeon took towards the ball, gradually holding back rewards until the pigeon had to do more and more to gain the grains used as reinforcement. More and more refined responses were shaped in this way until only a hit in the right direction would count as a piece of gamesmanship worthy of reward.

According to Skinner, all behaviour, human and infra-human, can be shaped by the principles we have described. Isn't a salaried worker 'reinforced' by his monthly pay cheque ('fixed-interval' reinforcement)? And again, isn't the piece-worker reinforced by receiving wages proportionate to his work output (fixed ratio reinforcement)? Basic to the conditioning experiments of Pavlov and of the American behaviourist school is the notion that reinforced behaviour will be repeated, while non-reinforced behaviour will be dropped from the set of responses. Of course, the $S-R$ learning model deliberately excludes *unobservable* behaviour from consideration. Thinking, imagining, planning, indeed consciousness itself all suffer from this exclusion. Input is observable; output is observable—the rest is not amenable to scientific study. It is only a short step from this to refusing to allow any 'internal' operations the right to exist.

Meanwhile, other branches of psychology, such as the study of child development, set about the task of gathering and recording data on the physical, motor and emotional development of children in considerable isolation from behaviourism. As a result, child study was tacitly allowed to take into account the whole organism, and this inevitably led to an awareness of the fact that social and emotional development are inseparable from motor and cognitive development. Its antecedents were the baby-biographies which educated Victorians, (Darwin was one) kept of their children's early years. In Switzerland, of course, another student of childhood, Jean Piaget, was independently charting the mental and physical development of his own three children by meticulous 'experiment' and notetaking.

Of course, child study carried out by academically-trained psychologists was inevitably preoccupied with learning. The major theoretical interest of child development in the 1930s lay in the attempt to apportion the determinates of behaviour between *maturation,* on the one hand, and *learning,* on the other. Identical twins, and contrasted ethnic samples (white versus non-white children) were used as subjects in these studies. One interesting 'experimental design' was revealed by the child-rearing practices of the Hopi Indians in the USA. Some Hopi women were still, in the 1930s, carrying their infants on their backs in cradleboards between birth and 15 months. Before 15 months white American children were crawling and taking their first tottering steps. Despite the lack of opportunity to 'practise' walking, the Hopi infants displayed neither retardation nor any other difficulty when allowed to walk at 15 months of age. Similar findings were noted for other motor behaviour when twins were used as experimental and control 'subjects'. Stair climbing, buttoning, and other motor skills were found to develop at the same stage even if one twin was given premature practice. This did not occur, however, when one twin was taught specialized skills such as swimming or skating. In general, however, the position seemed to be that a child will only exercise motor skills when he is ready. Special opportunities, or their absence, before the appropriate neural and muscular structures are activated have, apparently, little lasting effect.

Two other justly famous social surveys which have been subsequently hailed as landmarks of 'learning in the community' must be mentioned here. Although the first was carried out in Samoa by a social anthropologist, and the second in England by two British psychologists, the fact that they both pursued novel ways of studying social learning, (more precisely, *socialization*,) merits them an important place in socio-psychological investigation. While Margaret Mead, the anthropologist, was engaged in field work in Samoa among adolescent girls, John and Elizabeth Newson were surveying Nottingham infants. Miss Mead (1943) writing in 1928, speaks first:

> What we wish to test is no less than the effect of civilization upon a developing human being at the age of puberty. To test it most rigorously, we should have to construct various sorts of different civilizations and subject large numbers of adolescent children to these different environments. . . . We should vary one factor, while the others remain quite constant and analyze which, if any, of the aspects of our civilization were responsible for the difficulties of our children at adolesence.

As this was a utopian dream, Miss Mead tells us she spent most of her time with the girls of the Samoan island community, studying most closely the households containing adolescent girls. 'Speaking their language, eating their food, sitting barefoot and cross-legged upon the pebbly floor, I did my best to minimize the differences between us.'

This investigation was carried out in 1925. In 1963, thirty-eight years later, the Newsons, two Nottingham University psychologists, set out to obtain home interviews with over 700 mothers of one-year old Nottingham children, during which they questioned mothers about how they handled their babies during the first year of life. In this sociological investigation, the Newsons (1965) claimed that they were 'trying to find out what parents actually do, what sources of advice do influence them, how they actually feel about their children and how they react in practice to all the situations which naturally arise in the handling of a young baby.'

Clearly, both Mead and the Newsons employed field work to dig out the information they were interested in. Their basic methodology, that of data collection and classification, was also utilized by the American child psychologists of the 1930s. For, in the collection of data about mean walking ages, or the rules and routines of adolescent Samoan girls, or the upbringing schedules of Nottingham mothers, we see the same attempts to *codify* behaviour. There is no formulation of hypotheses to be tested. The aim of all these rather different investigations is classification—clarification, if you like—rather than understanding. By understanding, I refer to the need to build models which will present simple and clear examples of the systems they represent. Of course, classification is essential before experiment can begin. It is notoriously difficult to 'model' human behaviour, and examples from our cousins, the primates, have been instructive rather than directly transferable. Attempts to programme computers to play draughts or chess are only now beginning to shed some light on how the brain processes and stores information. It is, then, small wonder that the early hopes of the psychologists who sought to study simple learning in lab animals under drastically over-simplified conditions should have been dashed. The stimulus-response model which informed this early work did not prove durable in subsequent attempts to unravel the complexities of *human* learning 'when information is being processed through a number of sensory channels into perceptual, linguistic, and attitudinal organizations' (Apter 1970). If one adds, for good measure, the further complexities introduced by a number of variables which exist in the world outside the laboratory, the task seems almost insuperable.

Ironically enough, it was a sociologist, Basil Bernstein, and not a psychologist, who provided us with the vocabulary—the ABC almost—in which to talk about socialization. Initially, these notions of Bernstein, basic though they later seemed, triggered off a whole new way of articulating ideas about language, social class and educability. It was not until psychologists, however, seizing on Bernstein's brilliant formularization, applied his generalizations to the way in which children are brought up, that the fruits of Bernstein's original proposition were reaped.

The distinguished American linguist, Noam Chomsky, was also writing (and being 'translated' into lay terms) during the decade 1960–70, and his influence on our views of the nature of language was immense. His seminal work provided yet another insight into the role of language in the developmental process, and his work had implications for Bernstein's hypothesis which the latter has now accommodated. It is to language-acquisition itself that we must first turn.

It had been an important contribution of the child development researchers of the 1930s to catalogue and codify the number, type and rate of growth of word utterances. Yet in some ways, this important task served to obscure one salient factor about the language of the infant. This is that 'the infant learns fast . . . needs relatively little practice at

13

talking and . . . soon uses language in a consecutive manner' (Sluckin 1970). Such a suggestion poses a problem for the behaviourist who has traditionally held that the one-year old babbles, emitting a repertoire of meaningless sounds. Some of these sounds are shaped, by contiguity, to an important 'reinforcer' in the baby's life: the mother. Mother's interest in her child leads her to 'recognize' sounds the baby makes, and to comment on them or repeat them. Possibly, by selecting 'mama' from the speech-play of the child's 'ma-ma-ma-ma ba-ba-ba-ba', and repeating it, the child learns to give his mother a 'name'. The behaviourist would suggest, further, that because the mother hugs the child or plays with it while she talks with it, her voice acquires a reinforcing quality or property *which the infant seeks to reproduce in subsequent babbling*. The infant's vocal reproductions thus come to have secondary reinforcing properties. His own babbling, shaped (i.e. corrected) by mother, becomes self-reinforcing, and in time, highly selective. Gradually, it might be argued, sounds or *phonemes* not found in the infant's speech community are dropped from his repertoire and only those which mother can respond to—make sense out of—are retained. For the behaviourist, however, certain difficulties remain.

Two-word utterances, or *holophrases*, such as 'milk all gone', 'doggy all gone', etc, are typically produced by children in their second year. These holophrases are not only a kind of compressed sentence; they display a knowledge of grammatical rules. 'Allgone' is the pivot on which naming words are hung. The pivot word 'allgone' functions, of course, as a verb in the utterances quoted. It is, to put it mildly, difficult to see how this all-purpose word and the way it is used could ever have been learned through contingencies of reinforcement. After all, the child has not heard his parents use language in this tightly compressed, elliptical way. Nor, for that matter, has any four-year-old gardener who proudly proclaims: 'I've digged up all the flowers,' ever heard the past tense of 'to dig' formed in this way.

One can, of course, explain such an utterance by making the inference that the child has somehow acquired a rule: 'the perfect of verbs like to dig, to hop, to hope, to suck, etc is formed by adding "ed" to the main stem.' This explanation implies that children are capable of inducing rules from the linguistic data presented to them by their environment. No one would seriously contend that parents teach their two-year-olds to speak by parroting rules, however!

Chomsky has conceptualized language as having a 'generative grammar'. This generative grammar is an explicit description of the internalized rules of a language as they must have been mastered by a 'speaker/hearer'. It does not set out to be a model of performance. Obviously, the person who hears and transmits may have no notion of the grammatical rules belonging to that language. Chomsky (1965) explains his position on language acquisition as follows:

... the child approaches the data with the presumption that they are drawn from a language of a certain well-defined type, his problem being to determine which of the (humanly) possible languages is that of the community in which he is placed. Language learning would be impossible unless this were the case. The important question is: What are the initial assumptions concerning the nature of the language that the child brings to language learning, and how detailed and specific is the innate schema (the general definition of a 'grammar') that gradually becomes more explicit and differentiated as the child learns the language? For the present we cannot come at all close to making a hypothesis about innate schemata that is rich, detailed and specific enough to account for the fact of language acquisition.

Other workers (Sinclair de Zwart 1969) have suggested that the 'sensorimotor' schemes of the first 18 months of life, in which the infant builds upon his innate reflexes, are co-ordinated to provide a necessary precondition for language acquisition. One instance must suffice. She quotes the following example of Piaget's:

J. around 1:6 knows better and better how to take advantage of adults to get what she wants; her grandfather is especially docile in this respect. The term *panana* (grandpère) is used not only to indicate her grandfather but also to express, even in his absence, her desires; she points to what she wishes to have and adds *panana*. She even says *panana* to express a wish to be amused when she is bored.

Arguing that these productions almost certainly prepare the way for further verbal acquisition, de Zwart points out that these verbal schemes show a detachment of a kind from the subject's own actions and a desire to communicate by way of sound-complexes used by the other partner in a verbal exchange.

As Chomsky has pointed out, linguists are concerned with the study of the rule-system of language, and sociologists with the study of the social rules which decide for us how we are to behave in a given social context. 'Behave' is used here in the sense of what option we shall exercise. For instance, a young police constable in the north of England may address a working-class middle-aged man who is blocking other spectators' view at a football match as 'cock'. However, if later in the day a young man of his own age approaches him at the station Enquiries desk, the policeman may refer to him as 'squire' before the enquirer's middle-class accent proclaims to the policeman that the man is of higher socio-economic status than himself. He may then drop 'squire' in favour of 'sir'—or leave off any such title! Bernstein and his fellow sociologists at the London University Institute of Education have made use of the concepts of social

15

context, and social role allied to membership of social class, as a tool to elucidating how we come to select the speech variant we do.

Bernstein (1971) argues that all children have access to restricted codes (by which he means speech which is not normally accessible to outsiders). His example of a married couple leaving a cinema and talking about the film helps here: ' "What do you think?" "It had a lot to say." "Yes I thought so too—let's go to the Millers, there may be something going on there".' The form of the social relationship—that of a close marital one, for example—dictates the form the communication will take. Assumptions can be left unspoken, or transmitted by gesture or other non-verbal signs. 'The unspoken assumptions underlying the relationship are not available to those who are outside the relationship.... These are limited and restricted to the speakers. The symbolic form of the communication is considered yet the specific cultural history of the relationship is alive in its form.' How does this apply to children's use of language? Bernstein (1970) brilliantly illuminates the socialization process by suggesting that middle-class children not only share this 'communalized role' (equally that of husband and wife, mother and baby, or pub 'regulars') but also have access to a role which working class children seldom experience because of the constraints placed *upon* working-class children by their confinement to a single social situation.

Thus, when middle-class and working-class five-year-olds were given a series of four pictures which told a story, which the children were subsequently asked to reproduce, there was a marked discrepancy between the way in which each group responded to the invitation. The first picture showed some boys playing football, the second the ball smashing the window of a house, the third a woman looking out of the window, and a man making an ominous gesture, and the fourth depicts the children moving away.

Bernstein gives us two model stories, as related by a middle class and a working class child respectively:

1 Three boys are playing football and one kicks the ball and it goes through the window the ball breaks the window and the boys are looking at it, and a man comes out and shouts at them because they've broken the window so they run away and then that lady looks out of her window and she tells the boys off.
2 They're playing football and he kicks it and it goes through there it breaks the window and they're looking at it and he comes out and shouts at them because they've broken it, so they run away and then she looks out and she tells them off.

Without having the cards in front of us, we could not make much of the working-class child's account, because it does not make the meaning explicit: there seems to be no realization that the meaning has to be made 'public' to others who haven't got the pictures in their mind's eye. It is,

Bernstein argues, a question of *role*: working-class children do not perceive the set of pictures as a 'public' occasion for explication because they have not been socialized to manage the necessary role relationships which such contexts require. The public, elaborated speech variant that the middle-class child is able to produce on the occasion cited, is available to the child because he has been enabled to 'code-switch' precisely as a result of having been socialized in a certain way.

Figure 1 Realization of the regulative context

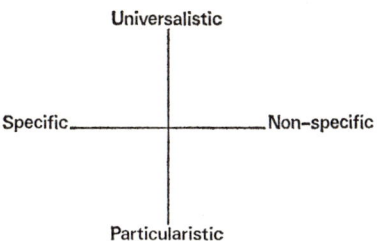

Bernstein borrows Halliday's (1969) formulations to arrive at four critical contexts of socialization:

1 The regulative contexts: these are authority relationships (e.g. home, Sunday school), in which the child rubs up against the 'moral order' and the power that this has to keep him in line.
2 The instructional contexts: here (as, for example, in informal guessing games with mother or nursery teacher) the child learns about the objective nature of things and persons, and picks up skills of various kinds.
3 The imaginative or innovating contexts: the child (as in painting or dancing) is encouraged to re-create or 'play with' the elements of his world in whatever way he likes. Fantasy and 'let's pretend' games would also fit here.
4 The interpersonal contexts: here the child is made aware of how others—and he too—feel. 'Telling off' and explanations of bad temper, or 'instruction' as to how to make reparation for destructive acts, would no doubt find a place here.

It is Bernstein's contention that 'the critical orderings of a culture or subculture are made substantive—made palpable—through the forms of its linguistic realizations of these four contexts—initially in the family and kin.' If these contexts employ mainly 'restricted' speech variants, then Bernstein (1970) postulates a different mode of communication (*context-bound*, for instance) from contexts which are realized in elaborated speech variants where the communication is thought of as *context-free*. The former mode, or 'deep-structure', is held to be based in *communalized* roles, the latter to be based in *individualized* roles. By

17

individualized roles, Bernstein seems to mean those roles which spell out to the child being disciplined that he is being given a rule which,

1 has some demonstrable grounds for being invoked,
2 may be adjusted to the issue in question in the light of special circumstances,
3 can be modified and applied with a degree of refinement to the particular issue, the intentions of the child and the circumstances and requirements of the situation (see figure 1, page 17).

This is the point of the exercise: the middle-class child is not merely confronted with commands, unvarnished orders, or given short shrift, as is the case in a restricted code situation. Instead there is the chance to question, to ask for explanation, to offer justification. *The role options* which the mother or father proffers to the child are—it is held—actually contained in the middle-class parents' use of an elaborated speech variant. As Bernstein says, 'all children have access to elaborated codes and their various systems of condensed meaning, because the roles the code presupposes are universal. *But there may well be selective access to elaborated codes because there is selective access to the role system which evokes its use.*' [My italics]

By way of contrast, developmental psychologists have appeared to ignore the extraordinarily powerful tool which linguistic (or speech) variants offer us as ways of understanding how a child becomes a member of his family/community. Instead, they have seen the process of socialization both less ambitiously but perhaps more concretely. It is envisaged as proceeding—by a progressively widening circle of socializing agents—in the contrasting developmental theories of Robert Sears and Jerome Kagan, for example. But whereas Sears's (1969) developmental position rests on essentially three developmental phases—the phase of rudimentary behaviour, the phase of family-centred learning and the phase of learning which takes place outside the family learning—Jerome Kagan (1969) looks instead at target-behaviour. He asks: what are the desired behaviours which Western (American) society sets its children? Whereas, for Sears, socialization proceeds from the infant outwards, Kagan appears to be interested in the *mechanisms* rather than in the *agents* of socialization. Some examples will make this more concrete.

According to Kagan the major psychological entities to be socialized include:

1 the acquisition of desired behaviours, such as skills of reading, arithmetic, cooking, social poise,
2 the inhibition of undesirable behaviours, such as aggression, destruction, crying, dependency, incontinence,
3 the acquisition of culturally approved values, for example, sincerity, altruism, ambition,

4 the suppression of undesirable values, for example, hate, narcissism, sexual infidelity.

He sees the accomplishment of socialization as taking place through *four* basic mechanisms: the desire for recognition and affection, the motive to avoid unpleasant feelings caused by punishment, identification, and a general tendency to imitate the actions of others. He suggests that reward and punishment, combined with observation, foster the acquisition of 1 and 2 above, while identification with a model is likely to mediate the acquisition or suppression of value-systems. Do class-*differences* permeate these agencies of socialization in view of the use middle-class parents allegedly make of linguistic labelling?

Robert Sears, by contrast, appears more interested in *stage-specific* behaviour. His first, rudimentary stage depicts the first 10 to 16 months of life. The infant is seen to be handling inner drives which beget tensions. In striving to reduce these tensions, brought about by the need for food, elimination and personal warmth, opportunities for interaction with the caretaker-mother crop up continually.

Socialization proper doesn't begin until the child is in the second half of his second year and lasts until school. *Secondary* rather than *primary* drives are becoming the springs of action. Now the child can recognize cues: the refrigerator signifies 'appeasement-of-hunger'. Dependency is weaned. Competition with others for parental approval is the order of the day. Punishment does not alter behaviour but tends merely to change the relationship between punisher and punished. Punishment is played down in Sears's account of socialization. Sex roles are learnt at about four years. Sexual modesty, toilet-training and the formation of 'conscience' are all products of this stage too.

In his third phase, the wider social environment—especially school and the peer group—takes over the job of socialization. The child carries over into this new arena the patterns of positive and negative attention-seeking from the earlier mother-child relationship. Dependency on family lessens and is transferred to teacher and peer group.

Kagan sees socialization proper as beginning at age three, a little later than Sears. In Kagan's own words, 'Dependency, aggression, sexuality, and task competence are some of the major behavioural areas around which the child has to negotiate during the three years from 3 to 6.' He concludes later, that 'the preschool years are characterized by a symbolic labelling of the self.' Interestingly enough, Trasler (1970) suggests that the higher incidence of delinquency in working-class males may be due to the absence of the labelling which middle-class mothers provide for their children. A child learns to attach a label to his own behaviour or feelings, which gradually becomes an internalized rubber stamp; the working-class child, Trasler suggests, is not given this wealth of dis-criminatory verbal tags. Future internalization of rules is thus hampered. The process of socialization, then, is handled within class subcultures as the culture's 'code' permits. The depiction of past behaviour, the description of present circumstances and the prediction of future contingencies are all handled by one's linguistic code. The middle-class child is warned, scolded, reminded, informed, about events past, present or to come. It is suggested that the child *introjects* these convenient markers with the memory of the experience they denote. As Kagan puts it, 'an awareness of how *right* or *wrong* one's attitudes and wishes are is as important in defining what is a person as his physical appearance or overt behaviour.'

However, it must be said that psychologists are by no means in agreement as to how to *conceptualize* infancy and the attendant socialization. The concepts are still fairly global and when they are broken down sufficiently to be amenable to laboratory experimentation, the very artificiality of the laboratory makes inference from laboratory findings difficult. Part of the difficulty lies in the inability to build a model of human socialization. Lacking a 'hypothetico-deductive system'—in which the model is derived from the theory and compared to the system under investigation—the study of socialization has had to work on the raw material and has consequently been theoretically barren, seeing socialization only too often as a one-to-one, mother/child relationship.

Other schools in psychology have sought instead to employ a clinical frame of reference in child-study. Such theories have traditionally sprung from doctors who have worked with disturbed child patients or psychotherapists without medical training. There are many distinguished child psychologists who have worked with children as teachers, analysts or doctors. The work of Melanie Klein, Anna Freud and Susan Isaacs is world-famous. Certainly the work of D. W. Winnicott, a paediatrician who became a child psychiatrist, is of particular relevance here.

Winnicott's theory of the development of the self-concept in the infant is one that appears to be incapable of experimental testing, in or out of the laboratory. There is no reason, however, why we should reject Winnicott's work out of hand for that reason. It is based on clinical expertise and judgement and while it may need correction if we are to be able at some point to check its assumptions, it is very much better than nothing and has the feel of plausibility about it. In some ways, Jean Piaget's massive work on the child's processing of information is equally vulnerable, since he has used the clinical method extensively in his work with very young children, including of course, his own children. While Piaget was interested in cognitive growth and Winnicott in emotional development, they both used 'abnormal' children as subjects in their work and we may therefore consider their methods together.

Winnicott treated children who displayed symptoms of emotional disturbance, symptoms displayed in a less severe form by the 'normal' child. Winnicott's child-patients either displayed these disturbances in excess, or simply failed to surmount them. Piaget's sample included not only his own but other, middle-class Genevan children: children, then, of abnormal or exceptional intelligence and all from culturally-rich professional homes. Just as the child therapist will encounter a disturbed child first through the medium of paints or clay, so Piaget set up encounters with objects (a rattle, a pencil, etc) and after noting the child's reaction, placed the objects in another position. Again, when studying children at an age when they were able to give verbal explanations, Piaget would affect ignorance of whatever was being investigated in an attempt to discover what concepts, or 'rules', were entertained by the child. He recorded children's replies to questions such as 'What makes the wind blow?' or 'What are the rules?' (for a game of marbles). In analogous fashion, the child therapist uses the paintings, doll-play or model-making of the young child who cannot verbalize his conflicts. As Erikson in *Childhood and Society* observed of children's play in the clinic: ' . . . seemingly arbitrary themes tend to appear which on closer study prove to be intimately related to the dynamics of the person's life history.' In the first, Piagetian situation, the clinical approach is structured and the child responds (or fails to respond) to the 'manipulations' of the therapist; in the therapeutic encounter, however, the position is less clearly formulated and the therapist has to rely much more on the toy-, motor- or verbal-behaviour of the child. Social scientists like Margaret Mead have actually lived with the subjects of the investigation whose behaviour they were observing. The Newsons, we recall, interviewed the parents of their subjects. No doubt at a later stage, the Nottingham children, now aged 10, will be interviewed about their upbringing in person. Both workers were thus able to communicate the 'flavour' of their research and add the richness of clinical observation to their statistically-presented findings.

The relatively unhelpful academic models of the learning process—at least until the appearance of D. O. Hebb's *The Organization of Behaviour* (1949)—have not noticeably impeded attempts to investigate the ways in which children make sense of the outside world, whether at the breast, in the crib, nursery or playground. The fact that children have to be socialized into certain universal experiences—toilet-training, for example—makes cross-cultural comparison feasible and suggestive. Nor have cross-cultural/subcultural studies been confined to sociologically-biased investigations. Piagetian tests of conservation, for example, have been administered to Chinese children in Hong Kong, coloured children in the West Indies, Adenis and European children in Aden, and Senegalese city and bush-dwelling children in Senegal, West Africa.

By conservation, Piaget refers to the ability, first displayed at age five or six, to begin to reason independently of misleading visual cues. The classical experiment he carried out required the child to pour lemonade from one of two jars of similar volume, containing equal amounts of lemonade, into a taller narrower vessel. Children who had not learned to 'conserve' quantity typically declared that the tall jar contained more lemonade than the remaining squat jar: despite the fact that they had just acknowledged the amounts of lemonade in the first two jars to be the same.

21

Investigation into child-rearing and development seems to proceed at two levels, characterised by different interests: at the global level will be field work by social anthropologists interested, say, in Bantu child-raising practices; or sociologists investigating the learning of sex-roles in a South Yorkshire mining community. Work at this level of generality will provide ideas, hunches and leads which the social psychologist, who prefers to work in a tighter, less descriptive style, will want to follow up. It is true that sometimes even psychologists will do 'global' work, as in the study of the 'fatherless' families of fishermen in Tromso (Norway) and Genoa (Italy) by co-operating teams of psychologists who administered doll-play 'projective' games to the children, as well as interviewing mothers. But this is the exception rather than the rule.

Psychologists have begun to move from experimental situations in the child laboratory—with its one-way mirror, its toys and its play space—to the family itself. Sceptical of studies which purport to measure the interactions of only two participants, as if children were typically brought up by one (female) adult only, they have engineered introductions into the family and their role has been that of 'participant observer'. Recent work has included attempts to discover what mothers, rated as 'good' or 'above-average' by professional judges, actually do with their children which differs from that which 'below-average' mothers do. This kind of small-scale investigation is often open to statistical treatment since it attempts to contrast one child, or set of children, with another.

More recently, the focus for much academic and applied work has been the acquisition and development of language. This thorny problem has involved psychologists interested in machine intelligence, learning theorists, linguists and sociologists, as well as developmental psychologists. Notwithstanding the immensely complex issues raised by any theory of language-acquisition (such as Chomsky's, for example), the centrality of language to thinking and learning has already been demonstrated by the failure of compensatory education projects which have specialized in providing working class children (in particular American Negro children from the ghetto) with 'enrichment' programmes such as zoo visits and lots of adult attention. Indeed, Bereiter and Engelmann (1966) argue powerfully for positive discrimination of an *academic* kind for deprived children: the teaching of logical thinking, no less! They point to the fact that blind children barely lag behind sighted children in IQ and attainment, whereas deaf children are on average 10 IQ points behind, and are typically 2 to 5 years of attainment in arrears. This demonstrates, they argue, the critical importance of aural (linguistic) experience to the pre-school child.

A programme of training in the structural and logical use of language is presented in their book. W. Labov (1969), a linguist who has been carrying out sociolinguistic research in Harlem with working class black children, argues that the social context in which Bereiter and Engelmann obtained their test findings was inimical to their arriving at any other conclusions than they did. Particulars such as the employment of 'large, friendly, white interviewers', the middle-class nature of the formally structured interview situation, and the fact that interviewers did not employ Nonstandard Negro English (NNE), were cumulative, and adversely affected the linguistic performance of the subjects interviewed by Bereiter and Engelmann and their associates.

Labov asserts that the misconceptions held by Bereiter and Engelmann as psychologists were compounded by the almost mute behaviour of their black interviewees. These misconceptions with relation to 'illogicality' or lack of 'grammaticality', for instance, were formed during the interviews and were later recognized for what they were: cultural misperceptions on the part of white, standard English speakers who had no linguistic training. For example, 'They mine' or 'Me got juice'—utterances of pre-school ghetto children noted by Bereiter and Engelmann as betraying 'illogical' or 'nonconceptual' thinking—betray nothing of the sort. As Labov points out, the former phrase is a contraction which follows the same regular rules found in standard English construction. 'Me got juice' does not, as Labov demonstrates with a good deal of evidence, indicate an inability to recognize the differential use of personal pronouns.

A change in social context soon brought about change. When a skilled Harlem-born interviewer found difficulties in eliciting verbal responses from the eight-year-old brother of a local teenage gang member who had been admirably vocal, he decided to try and alter the atmosphere of the interview and make it more like a party. He, as a black, was already able to speak NNE dialect. By sitting on the floor (thus reducing height discrepancy between interviewer and subject), and passing potato crisps round to the subject and his best friend (another deliberate change had been to include a third party), the atmosphere became more matey than formal. When the interviewer began by introducing taboo local playground slang, the interview was assured of success. A wealth of verbal material, in terms of sheer production, was so easily elicited that talk of 'verbal deficit'—the alleged source of black working class children's poor school performance—was confounded. Bereiter and Engelmann, of course, had seized on precisely this absence of verbal production as illustrating the need for teaching 'deprived' ghetto children formal English! In fact, as Labov's taped extracts of interviews demonstrate, these children normally perceive the test interview as a formal, threatening situation and clam up.

Verbosity, then, isn't in question. What, however, of grammaticality? Bereiter and Engelmann's programme of remediation involves question-and-answer with particular attention to getting their young clients to observe elaborated Standard English speech. Thus, to the question, 'Where is the squirrel?' the reply, 'In the tree' is disallowed despite the fact that we all use such short, elliptical forms continually. Labov points out that none of the preschool subjects responded with 'The tree' or 'Squirrel the tree' or 'The in tree'—utterances whose grammaticality (or lack of it) is *not* in doubt.

Labov concludes: 'Given the data that Bereiter presents, we cannot conclude that the child has no grammar, but only that the investigator does not understand the rules of grammar.' Labov goes on to comment that the investigators believed themselves to be teaching the black child an entirely new language, whereas they are, in fact, merely teaching him to produce minimally different forms of the language he already possesses. This conclusion is strikingly close to that of Bernstein's, and of course to Chomsky's, who, as we saw earlier, has usefully distinguished between competence and performance. In the wholly alien encounter with a white, or middle class Negro, interviewer, these urban American black children from the lower working class were unable to manage the role, and hence the language.

It has not been possible within the limitations of space to touch on work-in-progress into the constituents of socialization in the very young infant, nor on the social-reward theory of Bandura and Walters (1969). We have concentrated on language because this field is not only crucial to all learning later in life, but its acquisition, and interconnected social role correlates, are vital to the understanding of how subcultures order their environment and interact with the external world.

SECTION 2

The study of infancy has been actively pursued since the baby biographies kept by middle class Victorian parents a hundred years ago. Gesell's *Infancy and Human Growth* (1928), Susan Isaacs's *Social Development in Young Children* (1933), Carmichael's *Manual of Child Psychology* (1946), and Jersild's *Child Psychology* (1933) were all products of that decade's interest in the maturation-versus-learning argument. They presented research that appeared to show both development and intelligence as fixed 'givens'. Human beings were depicted in such a way as to make the task of parental child-rearing and school curricula that of providing the optimal conditions for the unfurling and unfolding of the pre-set organism.

Both Froebel's mystical view of the child as analogous to a plant requiring only the right soil to 'grow' in, and the American educationalist G. Stanley Clark's contention that the individual child's life-history recapitulates that of the human species, provided philosophical warrant for such a position. Freud, too, was already being misrepresented into portraying all parental 'discipline' as undesirable repression, which, if abolished, would enable children to grow up untrammelled by trauma and tradition. Socialization and education should, like careful pruning and delicate watering, merely allow the child room in which to grow.

Parents were not to overstimulate children by too much love and hugging; teachers were not to intervene in the pupil's legitimate maturation. The time would arrive when this or that child was indeed 'ready' to learn to read, to write and to study. But, so the doctrine went, the child was self-paced. It would affront his nature, as well as prove wholly ineffective, to step in and attempt to speed up or improve upon nature.

Oddly enough, it was the psychologists writing from a Freudian rather than an experimental background who launched the assault on the normative study of children. In this section, we shall examine the infant from three viewpoints.

First, we shall review the development of the inner life of the infant proposed by D. W. Winnicott (1964), contrasting it with the findings of developmental psychologists such as Dennis and Dennis (1940), and Dennis (1960). His research, allied with that of Spitz (1945, 1946), put forward the concept of 'the facilitating environment' which had been largely responsible for the abandonment of the notions of fixed development (if not of fixed intelligence) by most contemporary psychologists. In this first section, we shall have to consider exactly what constitutes 'mothering' or 'caretaking'. Is it the provision, for example, of 'stimulation', or alternatively, the delivery of a 'reward' by mother in instrumental learning terms? Or, yet again, is mothering simply the attachment formed by the infant to a stimulus-figure, somewhere after the age of six months, akin to the 'imprinting' on to moving objects by the young of other species at sensitive periods after birth?

Secondly, we shall have to consider that behaviour which sets man off from the other animals: his verbal behaviour, or language. While we shall not try to do more than examine briefly some of the more promising research in this area, we shall have to try to relate these formulations to the current preoccupations of educational psychologists and sociologists. These workers, while insisting that linguistic competence is the birthright of even the most deprived child, seek to differentiate between working class *context-bound* speech and middle class *context-free* speech, so as to sensitize teachers to the contexts they create in the classroom in which to transmit 'the principles and operations' deemed worthy of being passed on to the next generation.

Finally, we shall have to scrutinize the infant with the eyes of the physical anthropologist. Any account of the origin of speech must be speculative, but an informed and intelligent guess has been hazarded by Suzanne Langer, the philosopher, who has reviewed the suggestive evidence from brain-damaged patients and from the study of our primate relations, the great apes.

First, however, let us examine D. W. Winnicott's speculative account of the baby's development from a creature unaware of any sense of self, to that of a recognizably human infant. Winnicott, as a child analyst, sees the pre-school infant's emotional development schematically as a movement from 'double dependence', where the infant in the first few months is himself unaware of his dependence, via 'dependence', where some awareness exists and the baby can let the environment know when affection is needed; through to 'independence', which essentially signifies freedom from mother. Winnicott conceives of this development as involving a number of structures. These include such components as integration, personalization, psyche, soma and mind—all technical terms for the ways in which the infant is thought to apprehend his environment.

Thus the infant, he suggests, first gains a sense of self by experiencing himself as the agent in rage (or temper tantrum), or in the excitement of feeling. *Integration* of these feelings gradually becomes a settled fact. Thus when regression, which is no more than a loss of what has been painfully acquired, is perceived by the analyst, we may speak of *disintegration*, presumably an extremely harsh and painful experience for the infant. Two other important concepts proposed by Winnicott for understanding the infant's developing sense of self must be mentioned. They have to do with the infant's body-image and his sense of reality. As Winnicott explains, the *psyche* (or sense of self) has to be integrated with the *soma* (bodily experience in general) if future mental health is to be at all secure. Lack of adaptation, Winnicott suggests, may otherwise lead to a rather tenuous linkage of 'myself' with 'my body'. A good mother will therefore always wake the infant up gently to allow the return of the psyche to the body. If not, one might assume that physical frustrations wouldn't be registered with the right kind of incisiveness by the infant. He would feel 'lost', since his body would not *belong* to him in a concrete sense.

Winnicott reserves the notion of *mind* for the functioning of those parts of the brain which develop later than those areas controlling the primitive psyche. 'Mind' seems to be employed by Winnicott partly in the sense of long-term memory, a process which, incidentally, is thought to involve the 'proteinization' of cells in the cerebral cortex of the brain. One imagines that often a mother will unwittingly fail to adapt to caretaking demands from her child. Provided, however, that the infant's intellectual processes can account for and thus allow for such failures, the infant can tolerate these failures. This requires the infant to have some internal 'representation' of a *continuing mother*, and resembles Piaget's mental images thought of as developing at about 18 months. Winnicott's use of 'mind' goes beyond the chemistry of memory-traces, however. He seems to regard it as synonymous with *empathy*: somehow the infant, via the growth of 'mind', manages to 'feel for' mother and can take over part of her functions. He begins recording events which are stored away, available for retrieval at some later date. An important contribution to our imaginative grasp of what it must feel like to be a language-less creature entirely dependent on an external being for comfort and nourishment is provided by Winnicott's notion of *object relationships*. These are yet a further component of the inner life of the infant. They begin, says Winnicott, in relation to part objects such as the breast. This (the breast) requires the infant to 'create' his world. 'The infant reaches out, and the breast is there and the breast is created.' Now this notion of object-relationships is extremely important, since the process of integration already referred to allows the part-object gradually to be felt as a whole person. 'Breast' becomes 'mother'. Again, once the infant recognizes that reality 'out there' consists of a *whole* object or *caretaker* (note that the peak age for smiling is 4 months, and for smiling exclusively at mother, 6 months) it is *ipso facto* in a position to be truly dependent. In a way, this is the start of a sense of dependence, containing, paradoxically, the seeds within it of a later need for independence, for standing on one's own feet. Erik Erikson (1965), an American child analyst, refers to the dependent stage (his 'oral-sensory' stage) as that time during which the infant learns the basic sense of trust and mistrust. This sounds very much like Winnicott's concept of 'mind'. The beginnings of independence are consigned by Erikson to the succeeding 'muscular-anal' stage. In this stage, not normally reached until about 20 months of age, at the earliest, the child learns and acquires the muscular control to hold on to or release his faeces. He is now ready for potty-training. This location of libido, an instinctual energy thought of as 'sexual' in the broad sense of 'pleasurable', in the anal zone is thought to characterize all the child's dealings with the world at this time; so that, at best, Western society's emphasis on too early and too rigid toilet-training impairs its children's progress through this mode. Erikson asserts that 'the sphincters are only part of the muscle-system with its general duality of rigidity and relaxation, of flexion and extension.' He explains that the rapid development of the entire muscle-system at the age of two gives the child a suddenly enlarged power over the environment ' . . . in the ability to reach out and hold on, to throw and to push away, to appropriate things and to keep them at a distance.' He declares that the child obtains a sense of inner goodness from unforced evacuation; a sense of inner badness if his sphincter muscles let him down! Autonomy and pride, then, balance doubt and shame. Indeed, Kagan (1969) specifically links the stigma of 'you are dirty' or 'you are bad', applied by parents to a child soiling himself, to the growth of the child's self-concept. The parent's reactions towards the child and their verbal labelling of him gradually take a hold. Parents are seen as god-like figures: what they say is unquestionable. Their negative evaluations become part and parcel of the child's view of himself.

Winnicott appears to be alluding to Erikson's notion of a shift of libido from the mouth to the anal zone, when he comments that the satisfactions which are of such immense importance to the infant in his first year of life result from just such instinctual impulses, in a word, spontaneity. But this spontaneity must be surrendered if the caretaker-mother is to be boss. Immediate gratification has to give way to delayed gratification. In a short but important discussion of infants' possessions, Winnicott goes on to point out how teddies, rag dolls, and bits of cloth work as *symbols*, notably standing for the breast. Only gradually do they stand for babies or for mother or father. These dolls and pieces of soft cloth are seen by Winnicott as 'transitional objects' which mediate between the infant's self and the outside world. When integration and personalization are fully attained, however, such part-objects are dispensed with, only to be returned to, along with thumb-sucking, at times of loneliness, sadness or anxiety.

It is perhaps less difficult for us to conceive of the symbolic use children may be making of 'objects' if we recall the Harlow and Zimmerman (1959) study attachment in monkeys. One of their findings concerned an infant monkey reared in isolation and fed from a wire-frame 'mother' with an artificial teat. When a similar wire-mesh 'mother' covered in terrycloth was placed in the cage, the baby monkey would happily feed from the wire-mesh figure but spent much more time with the terrycloth mother. Wooden spiders placed in the cage provoked anxiety, causing the infant monkey to run and cling to the terrycloth mother. It has been suggested by subsequent researchers that if a young monkey is to develop normally, it must have some interaction with an object to which it can cling in the first months. Another monkey is the best caretaker, but a terrycloth substitute mother does at least allow the infant to cling, and is therefore better than a wire-mother, even one that gives a permanent supply of milk.

In attempting to assess the worth of the clinical, analytical evidence we have been surveying, it is a little disconcerting to learn that studies carried out on samples of children from birth onwards seldom reveal any significant personality differences which could have resulted from differential child-rearing treatment, such as how the children were toilet-trained, for example. Nevertheless it may be that these upbringing treatments do not get 'picked up' by the tests employed by the psychologist, either because these tests are relatively crude paper-and-pencil affairs, or because the interviewee suppresses or distorts information. Nevertheless, the importance of the very young child's inner life for later learning is supported by hard evidence from an interesting chance 'experiment' provided by the social services.

In a series of experiments conducted just after World War II, R. A. Spitz administered Hetzer-Wolf baby tests to 'Foundling House' and 'Nursery' children. The design of Spitz's experiment was, as we have said, provided by an accident of social welfare planning. The Foundling House housed 61 infants who were cared for in a routine impersonal way after their mothers ceased to attend to their needs at about 3 months. The Nursery children were, on the other hand, cared for by their mothers—delinquent girls—who were housed next door in a penal institute. The social-class status of the mothers was generally higher in the Foundling Home than in the Nursery and this doubtless contributed to the quality of care. The results are easily summarized. The mean developmental quotient (DQ) for the Foundling Home children dropped from 131 points to 72 points over 9 months while that of the Nursery infants rose over the same period from 97 to 100 points, with a 'peak' of 112 points in the fourth and fifth months. Spitz attributed the decrease in DQ in the Foundling Home to lack of mothering. All the illegitimate infants in the Nursery were, of course, tended by their mothers, the delinquent girls. Spitz designated the DQ drop by the term 'hospitalism' and subsequently drew attention to a childhood syndrome which he called 'anaclitic depression'. This took the form of weepiness, withdrawal, loss of weight, *decline in DQ* and susceptibility to infection.

This research has been criticized on the grounds that the baby-tests employed may well have been invalid for technical reasons; it has also been suggested that the reported lack of variation in stimulation, toys and light may be more important in contributing to developmental decline than any lack of a strongly emotional-personal relationship with the mother, as Spitz implies. However, Kagan, in a discussion of 'attachment' behaviour in monkeys and human infants, suggests that the human mother's provision of food, alleviation of pain and tactile stimulation, in addition to acting as a stimulus-figure for the scanning, vocalizing, sucking and manipulating of the baby, suggests a view of attachment which is akin to the attachment process in sub-human primates. If attachment is based on the hypothesis that every organism is equipped with a special set of responses that can be elicited at birth, then we can immediately place human infant behaviour in this wider spectrum. The infant of any species emits these responses to the first appropriate and available stimulus in his environment. This stimulus is, through mother-baby interaction, likely to provide the source of attachment. Thus there are, according to Kagan, three mechanisms which will lead the child to value a caretaking adult: reduction of discomfort, the receipt of pleasant sensations, and the attachment process, in which the adult becomes the stimulus-object for the infant's early behaviours.

J. McVicker Hunt (1961) in his *Intelligence and Experience* cites work by Dennis and Dennis in which sheer poverty of environment seems to be the cause of stunted development. In the case of Dell and Kay, fraternal twins reared from 2 to 14 months by the researchers, the twins were given an excellent diet and every physical comfort, but they had little opportunity to explore the nursery environment and received minimal social stimulation. Over 50 items of behaviour they showed retardation in motor activity such as reaching, grasping, sitting alone and standing with support. The evidence from the relatively recent work on attachment would, of course, legitimately allow one to conclude that the minimal social stimulation was the key to the results.

Dennis and Najarian's work in the Lebanon supports this interpretation. Babies brought up in a Creche with better-than-average material comforts but minimal mothering were compared on tests with babies in a Well-Baby Clinic. The Creche children's mean DQ score on the Cattell

Infant Scale was 63 points against the Clinic children's 101 points. Since the children were all between 3 and 12 months, and matched for social class, the highly significant DQ difference led the researchers to conclude that learning had a more important role in infant development than psychologists had ever begun to imagine. We should perhaps stress the clear absence of proper mothering in the case of the Creche infants in explanation of these discrepancies in score. Results quoted by Dennis from an even more impersonally-run orphanage in Teheran force one to conclude that motor development cannot proceed in the absence of maternally-delivered stimulation, if crucial neural/physical structures are to develop properly.

In McVicker Hunt's words (1961):

> Deprivations of experience have been found to make a difference in the rate at which infant organisms develop behaviourally. The more severe the deprivations of experience, the greater the decrease in the rate of behavioural development. Moreover, the effects of deprivation of experience may show most plainly when the experiences . . . are quite different from the performances measured. This last fact suggests that the earlier investigators saw experience, learning and practice in too narrow a fashion.

Whether or not one chooses to interpret delay in sitting, walking and talking as a function of caretaking behaviour, or simply as stemming from a lack of visual-motor stimulations, it is clear that the inner life of an infant, however well-cared for materially, depends on the kind of attention mothers (or mother-substitutes) normally provide in human society. If experiential richness is lacking, psycho-physical development will lag behind. Whether the resulting damage is permanent or not is not yet clear.

Of course it is without question the mother who is uniquely well-placed to induct the child into the speech-community of which she is already a member. As we indicated earlier, the picture of language-acquisition has been radically re-drawn after the attack to the behaviourists' position mounted by Chomsky. Let us briefly review the field.

The generalizing and focusing functions of language in the formation of concepts in the infant has long been recognized (Luria 1971); moreover, by labelling acts or wants as 'good' or 'bad' (Trasler 1970), it has been argued that the relatively elaborated language of middle-class mothers (and fathers) enables the child to internalize the depiction of certain acts as 'stealing', 'taking what belongs to you', etc, because the labelling is not done arbitrarily—some explanation is given.

While these questions are central both to concept-attainment and the acquisition of morality, we need a theory to explain, quite simply, how a child acquires 'the ability to produce and to understand an indefinite number of sentences that have not previously been heard. The comparative ease and rapidity with which young children learn their mother-tongue remained completely mysterious as long as both the learning organism and the verbal behaviour to be learned were thought to be as amorphous in structure as associationist theory supposed them to be' (de Zwart 1969).

Noam Chomsky's salient contribution to this debate stemmed from his training as a linguist: he turned our attention away from a system of elements ('bits' of verbal behaviour that may or may not get reinforced) to a system of rules. Chomsky's grammar is an explicit description of the internalized rules of a language as a child hearing and speaking that language must have mastered them. As Chomsky describes it, 'a speaker must select an hypothesis regarding the language to which he is exposed that rejects a good part of the data on which this hypothesis must rest.' In more simplistic terms, the young child, who is a fast learner, requiring little practice at talking, soon finds himself able to use words in sentences that he may never have encountered before. Somehow or other the child learns by himself to make sense of his own language and thus constructs the rules according to which his language functions.

Suzanne Langer, in *Philosophical Sketches* (1962), makes some interesting speculations on the origins of speech, noting that man was already man, with social intentions, when he began to speak. But, if we are in fact defining man by his ability to use symbols, rather than making noises to communicate like the birds or beasts, then we are putting the cart before the horse. Man was, she insists, an *animal* when he learned speech. She examines classical neurological evidence from brain injury to make the point that such brain damage typically reveals that speech functions are not uniformly deranged: some aspects of verbal memory, for instance, are untouched. Names of living objects and persons' names may be retained, even while an inability to assign a name to inanimate objects is found. Or inability to understand spoken language in such patients may co-exist with unimpaired ability to understand printed or written language. If separate, discrete losses take place, she argues, then it is possible that these are distinct abilities that may have developed independently in the prehuman brain during the hundreds of thousands of years of prehistory. Noting that widely differing animal species possess some, but not all, the requisites for speech, she observes that none of them were biologically so well equipped for the development of speech. Here again, they had some, but not all, of the necessary physical attributes.

Langer singles out the visual system as the critical factor in the pre-human hominid's development of language. She suggests that the capacity to develop visual imagery in the humanoid brain and the role it assumed in an exciting social magico-religious dance triggered off what we call speech.

Her speculative argument is technical. Our ancestors' brains, she suggests, were bombarded with stimuli which could not be relayed to the muscles to produce overt responses for there were simply too many stimuli. As a result, many of the stimuli—including countless visual stimuli—got no farther than the association areas of the brain: they finished in the brain. Remarking on the way in which we selectively ignore much of the data which arrives at the eye (the afferent branch of the brain's optic nerve), she nevertheless insists that some of the images we receive on the retina—and we receive many, for we find 'focused gazing' pleasurable—are subsumed into larger compound 'visualizations'. It is clear she insists, that we habitually produce mental images without even trying—as in dreams. Dreams notoriously throw up symbols, and don't we strive to make sense out of the inverted, casually-unconnected chains of images which we 'watch' during sleep in all their vague, spontaneous and exciting variety?

Langer cites four characteristics which are likely to have enabled such images to take on the quality of symbols. First, the brain must produce a prodigal supply of images: if imagination is to be of some moment, it is important that a large number of the images thrown up be redundant: excess energy on the brain's part is required. Secondly, images so aroused must be capable of modifying each other: images fuse and mesh, some colouring and dominating others, so that vision is abstractive, stressing this image, and playing down that one. The third characteristic is the fact that images derive from 'percepts', the sensory data which is transformed by the brain into the 'seeing' we report. No one tells us that what we report as 'out there' *is* out there. We make the inference intuitively. Langer declares that it is this recognition by the perceiver of the external source of what he sees—that he recognizes images as representations of the visible world—that is the basis for public importance underlying symbolism. We can refer to our images, and expect that others will understand and share what we say we are seeing. Finally, we are open to a host of impressions from the past. The sight or sound of a singer or a song will call up a whole sequence of memories in the mind's eye. Even the smell of salt water will recall to us the first seaside trip we ever made or the first boat we ever sailed on. Images are also triggered off by internal stimuli: in daydreaming, we find ourselves in a private world of mental events prompted by an association of which we were entirely unaware. This ability and receptivity of the imagination allows images to cut free from direct sensory percepts and to float in our own inner world. Whatever the original stimulus was is of no account. The image can stand for, or *symbolize*, something other than the original stimulus which released the flood of fancies.

In the pre-human hominid of which we are speaking, however, we have still to explain how one image should hold or dominate another— whether the 'prompt', or stimulus for it, was internal or external. For Langer, this can only be answered by linking imagery with emotion. As we can observe in the imagery of sleep (dreaming), we find one or two images recurring within the dream or from one dream to another. The particular image insists on being recognized—it is highly emotionally charged. Man's speechless ancestor was equipped with the '. . . power of elaborate vocalization, a discriminative ear that heard patterns of sounds, the nervous mechanisms that controlled utterance . . . and the tendency to utter long passages of sound in gatherings of many individuals.' These traits, allied to high-grade mental activity issuing in visual image-making, set the scene for speech to appear.

Langer's anthropology is less well established than her suggestive psychology, but her novel ideas, though impossible to 'prove', are not beyond reason. Indeed her argument is tightly structured and works as follows. If communal ritualistic dances were held to mark an 'occasion', then they were very likely accompanied by shouts and cries. She draws on an interesting speculation of Donovan's *On the Festal Origin of Human Speech* (1891), that vocalizing accompanied primitive dance; meaning might have accrued initially to lengthy vocal sequences which were gradually broken or condensed into separate parts, each with its own assigned sense. Langer's contribution lies in the role she assigns to imagery. It can be assumed that the steps and gestures of the dances (whether mime or merely athletic) would be known with the vocal accompaniments to all the members of the primitive tribal horde—just as we know how to dance a conga and remember the vocal accompaniment of 'Aye, aye conga'. It is probably enough that the song accompaniment would become increasingly split off as the dance becomes more elaborate. At high points in the festivities, special shouts or calls would have been made.

Images—private, of course, to each celebrant—must have been evoked at these high points by the vocalization, and these images would recur in the over-heated brains of the actors each time the tribal dance was performed. Eventually, Langer thinks, these images became embedded in the well-known sequence of the ritual dances. Watching children play Ring a Ring a Roses today, for example, we can recall in advance, without difficulty, the elaborate exclamation 'ALL FALL DOWN' even though we may not have played the game since childhood. Out of season, so to speak, a snatch of the festival song would spontaneously summon up an image of the dance's activity in the way that 'ALL FALL' evokes in us the linked hands and lowered bodies of our circle, ready to crash to the floor at the word 'DOWN'. In our early forebears, the evoked image would be there, private certainly, but a private picture of a public celebration. The things imaged are public things: the sounds accompanying and calling up the images are public property too. Just as the sounds of the dance—the climaxes—affect everyone by raising up images at roughly the same point in the dance, so the images locked away in the individuals as private scenes stand as 'equivalent symbols' for the turning-points in the ritual. Observers of football match supporters can of course see the same thing when Liverpool score at home; away from the match, children in Liverpool playgrounds can be heard chanting L-I-V-E-R-

P-O-O-L and no one doubts what they are signifying! When these vocal 'bits' are uttered out of context—as they are in Liverpool and elsewhere —meaning attaches to the utterance. Another being *understands*. Again, if our Liverpool children are playing ball in the street, the L-I-V-E-R-P-O-O-L chant makes their game the richer. It is given a larger-than-life flash of colour. Likewise, if our anthropoid ancestors refer in gesture to an object—totem pole, stone circle, or whatever—out of ritual context, so to speak, any vocal element of their reference is unambiguously seen as referring to that object as if it were physically present. Sounds originally employed for communion, says Langer, are now there for communication. Perhaps long portmanteau words were formed and condensed from the ritual shouts, until these rich block-busters of speech were cut down and made more specific. Eventually, (and inexplicably at present), the phonetic repertoire became 'synthetic', and words were built up into sentences. As sound was increasingly utilized for communication, images were dropped out: they were not necessary. With the advent of written pictures or 'ideographs', even hearing was by-passed or superseded.

Speech was, in short, assembled from the key activities of sight and hearing: it took upon itself the office of communication, and no doubt physical gesture and sign-language gradually fell from the hominid's repertoire of communication. Speech had arrived and was henceforth increasingly indispensable.

SECTION 3: READINGS

Socialization

1 From *Four Years Old in an Urban Community*
To a far greater extent, the working-class wife must expect to find her major satisfaction in being the indispensable provider and minister to the needs of her husband and children. By way of compensation, the role of 'our Mam' is accorded high status value. Her children are thus a proud possession, a symbol of status in themselves, and an extension of her own personality. If 'the mester' is a king in his own home, 'our Mam' is certainly the queen, and in the ideal working-class family the roles are mutually supportive.

It seems to be generally true that many working-class women find the role of Mam highly satisfying in and of itself. She is the one person on whom the whole household depends for succour and comfort; the sure anchor to which husband and children cling. Even at work, the sandwiches made up by Mam will often be preferred to anything the canteen can offer; and children at school or in their first jobs will rush back to her during their lunch break for a quick cup of tea and a chat. The total helplessness and dependence of the young baby epitomizes her relationship with all the other members of the family; and, despite the disinclination towards breast feeding, her nurturant role is highly valued.

Consequently, babies are for being picked up, petted and made a fuss of. They are to show off with to the neighbours, to be dressed up in their finery and pushed out in opulent and immaculate perambulators for all the world to see and admire. At the same time, the antics of babies are regarded as a rich source of potential amusement for other adults. Thus they are often teased and stimulated in a way which would be looked at with disfavour by middle-class mothers. Many of these interviews were punctuated by the mother's efforts to put the baby through his repertoire of tricks and social graces, whether by tickling him, enticing him to walk, or by exciting him with the false cry of 'Daddy's coming!'

By contrast, the convention among middle-class mothers seems to be that one blatantly shows off one's children only to relatives and very intimate friends; on other social occasions, references to the child's virtues are made in careful understatement, and it is the visitor who is expected to initiate any admiration. In general, during a social call, the baby is left to get on with his own pursuits on the floor, and the mother ignores him unless he demands or provokes her attention. This is probably connected with the fact that so many middle-class mothers seem to see the period of infancy in particular, not as a time of fulfilment, but as an abnormal and in many ways deplorable interlude in an otherwise sane and well-ordered life: or at least, this is the impression which, again, it seems conventional to put forward. Ideally, the middle-class woman has a tasteful and well-run home into which it is possible to invite visitors at any hour. Once babies arrive, however, the reality frequently includes piles of dirty and malodorous clothes in the kitchen, toys all over the house, a rackful of steaming nappies hiding the fireplace and dribble (or worse) on the living-room carpet. Under these conditions she may find it difficult to reconcile her self-image as a mature and sophisticated woman with her role as a housebound baby-minder, nappy-washer and domestic slave. The resulting state of conflict and frustration may be shown in a variety of ways. She may live nostalgically in the past, remembering her early adult life, when she was still at work, as a time of gay adventure and unfettered freedom. Alternatively, she may see the humorous side of her present predicament, and put it to social use by telling funny stories against herself: how the elderly visitor, arriving unexpectedly, was guided deftly past the unemptied potty behind the front door only to come upon the toddler admiring her naked stomach in the hall mirror; or how the cake for a party, collapsed when its baking was interrupted by the baby, was filled up with chocolate icing and passed off as a special new recipe. It is easy to understand why the young middle-class mother, in conversation with other adults, will often adopt a tone of mock callousness towards her children: 'I've decided I just can't stand babies', 'You can have mine any time you like', and so on. Publicly, at least, her aim is to get the babyhood stage over as soon as is reasonably possible, in order to return to the civilized state she fondly thinks of as normal.

35

2 From *Four Years Old in an Urban Community*

For almost as long as children have been considered worth studying separately from the total man, the phenomenon of play has engaged the attention of philosophers and psychologists. Its function has been variously explained. Spencer saw it chiefly as the means by which the surplus energy of childhood was discharged. Groos explained it in terms of instinctive modes of action through which both animal and human young developed and improved their skills in preparation for their mature role. G. S. Hall believed that the child tended to repeat in his individual history activities typical of the evolution of the race: 'The best index and guide to the stated activities of adults in past ages is found in the instinctive, untaught, and non-imitative plays of children. . . . In play every mood and movement is instinct with heredity. Thus we rehearse the activities of our ancestors, back we know not how far, and repeat their life work in summative and adumbrated ways'.

Freud put forward a view more closely related to the child's individual emotional needs, seeing in play both the compulsion to repeat life experiences, in order to gain emotional mastery of them, and the rehearsal of adult roles, the attainment of which is, he says, 'a wish that dominates them the whole time'; and Melanie Klein and others developed this into a conception of play as the symbolic acting out of wishes and ideas almost exclusively deriving from infantile sexuality. Margaret Lowenfeld, while drawing much from psychoanalytic ideas, refused to be bound within so narrow a framework, and saw the child's play as his 'work, thought, art and relaxation (which) cannot be pressed into any single formula'; she continues, 'It expresses a child's relation to himself and his environment, and, without adequate opportunity for play, normal and satisfactory emotional development is not possible'.

Although students of child development have differed in their conception of the precise role of play, there is, then, a fundamental agreement that here is a phenomenon deserving very close attention because it seems to serve important biological functions for the child's growth towards maturity: in particular, in that it facilitates both conceptual development and social and emotional learning. And it is clear from our conversations with mothers that the majority of them would share, whether as a reasoned or as an intuitive conclusion, this view of play as something of positive value to the child. Play for most mothers is not merely an amusement to occupy the child and keep him out of their way: those who have watched their children at play (and this includes nearly all mothers) usually seem aware of some educative element, in the broadest sense of the word, which is present perhaps more obviously at this than at any other age.

Off-licence manager's wife:
He keeps saying, 'Mummy, will you come on this bus, it's sixpence at this end'. 'Course, you have to join in if you have the time. We do try to take

an interest in that sort of thing, because we know that it's his mind at work all the while and he's learning all the while.

3 From *Four Years Old in an Urban Community*
The most striking finding is that mothers in Class V are far less likely to participate wholeheartedly in their children's play than are other mothers. It might be thought that this result could be due to the larger average family size with which Class V mothers have to cope; but the result holds regardless of the number of children, and cannot be adequately accounted for on this basis. An alternative explanation is that these mothers often have a somewhat more formal and tradition-oriented conception of the maternal role, which does not include coming down to the child's own level in play: thus Mrs Allingham, ... who considered herself too old for that sort of thing at 26, was also the wife of an unskilled labourer.

Fairground worker's wife:
I think it's because I never was a child, really—with having to be grown-up so early in life. I had to do all the family washing when I was eleven. ... I don't remember much about my childhood really—I remember all the cooking, and things like that.

Many were very definite that they felt too old for this sort of play.

Pipe inspector's wife (aged 42):
I don't play with him. I mean I'm old to muck about, sort of thing, and I'm not a young mother, really, am I? I mean, I had my first when I was 29, so I mean I wasn't young then, was I? As I said, I think they get on your nerves a bit when you're older—'cause I mean, I used to look after children when I was in my teens, and I mean you've got patience then, but you haven't when you're older.

However, it would not be true to suggest that the sample divides into younger mothers who play and older mothers who do not. In a random sample, approximately one mother in four is aged 36 or more; but the proportion of this age-group rated as wholeheartedly participant is still very high: 62%, against 66% for all ages combined. It is not possible to show any significant overall relationship between maternal age and degree of play participation; perhaps we really need a measure of being young in heart rather than young in years. Mrs Allingham looked surprised at our question, and answered with a laugh, 'Oh, no! I'm too old for that now!'; but Mrs Denison found the question entirely serious: 'I like to join in games with her. I want her to feel I'm interested in them. I love to play with her—I'm still a child really, when you come to think about it'. The truth is that Mrs Allingham, at 26, is in fact a year younger than Mrs Denison: the moral of which is that a mother is as young as she feels.

Lorry driver's wife:
Oh, she has a baby and she picks it up and puts it down, sort of thing. (And this baby isn't a doll ...?) Oh no, it's in her mind; she wraps it up and puts it on the settee. I have to carry it about in my arms—I'm as daft as her!

It is, as we have suggested, the working-class section which produces a minority group of mothers who will tend to laugh at the child, to snub his imaginative flights, and generally to act in ways which are aimed at pricking the bubble of his illusion. In this working-class group there is often also an underlying current of anxiety. It is they who feel that there might be something disturbing about the mental health of a child who seems to this extent out of touch with reality; who distrust an imagination which, they believe, might later lead the child into plain dishonesty; or who regard the child's stories as already constituting a threat to their control of his behaviour. A few examples from this group will illustrate the disquiet which fantasy can generate.

Miner's wife:
He's got a ... I'll tell you what it is—it worries me sometimes—he's got a vivid imagination; and it goes on and on and on until he *lives* it; and sometimes, these imaginary people, you have to *feed* them with him, do you see what I mean? It worries me.

Fitter's wife:
He'd make up stories like 'I was at school today, and my teacher smacked me and made me go in the corner', and things like that. It got so bad that I tried to stop it, because I didn't want him to go from an imaginary story to a downright lie—because there's not much difference between the two.

Miner's wife:
I've said to him, you know, 'That's never happened, you're imagining things!' I've told him, I've said 'Now, that's *wrong*—you've got a vivid imagination'.

Railwayman's wife:
Do you know, she *talks* to herself rather a lot—yes—I can't really *name* what she talks about; she talks to her dollies a lot. And she answers herself back as well, sort of thing, you know: it worried me, that did. But then I told a young woman round here, she said her child did it, so I didn't bother any more.

The mother who is able to enter the child's imaginative world and who is willing to accept his fantasies at face value will almost certainly act as a stimulus to the production of further fantasies, or to the elaboration of those he already has. Not all mothers are enthusiastic about these manifestations of imagination, however; and it is here that we find another subtle but definite difference between middle-class and working-class, especially lower working-class, wives. The middle-class mother typically welcomes and encourages fantasy play, taking it seriously as a normal and delightful phase of childhood, something to be respected and indeed treasured for as long as it lasts. She tends, too, to see it both as pleasing evidence of the child's present creativity and as a talent to be fostered as the basis for a future imaginative facility. Thus fantasy for her is not just a part of the magic of childhood, to be shared with delight, but the promise of a poetic sensitivity which might all too easily be stunted by an adult's indifference. 'I don't want her to grow up too much—I think it's very, very good, imagination, at this age', said a teacher's wife, herself a fashion designer; and a mother who had worked as an untrained teacher echoed her: 'She hasn't anyone in particular, but she talks to her toys and has very, very good imaginary games'. The middle-class mother of the little boy who owned two garages with lions and elephants in them said her reaction was just to 'string along with him, I don't prick him like a bubble, because I think it's a marvellous thing to have an imagination, and you can almost *see* the things—you can almost believe he's telling the truth!' The wife of a shop-owner said that her little boy's imagination was 'not yet' as strong as his sister's, with the implication that this was something that would eventually come with practice as they played together, and added 'I fall in with them, because to encourage their imagination like that, it's quite a big thing, isn't it?'

Almost every middle-class mother agreed with this; one of the very few with reservations was a clergyman's wife, who in this and all other areas of behaviour was particularly concerned to make her children aware of the exact import of their actions, usually in a moral frame of reference. She explained, 'Well, we have a family formula—"is this real, or is it pretend?"—and if it's pretend, well, we talk about it, but we talk about it as "your pretend".'

4 From *Four Years Old in an Urban Community*

We had expected that many mothers would be less inclined to explain about the father's role in reproduction at this age; but we had not anticipated the number of those who would be reluctant to explain how the baby emerged. This was considerable, and indeed we wished afterwards that we had deliberately asked for mothers' attitudes towards imparting this particular information. The quotations below illustrate various points at which the mother decides to stop short; the first was in fact classified as 'would not tell'.

Wireman's wife:
I think I should make a little tale up, you know—it's a seed planted, and it grows and grows, and eventually it's *brought about*. I don't think I should actually tell him. I wouldn't say *where* it grew, or anything like that.

Lorry driver's wife:
The little girl (then 5) asked me when I had the last one, 'How do they get out?' I can't think of anything to tell her. I said 'I'll tell you when you get a little bit older'—but, I mean, how can you explain that to a kiddy of six? You can't really, can you? (You think she wouldn't be able to understand?) Well, it isn't that. But I should imagine it would frighten a little kid of six.

Labourer's wife:
Well, he knew the baby was *there*, and he kept saying 'How does it come? How does it come?'—and of course I just ignored him.

Clerical officer's wife:
He knows they're in Mummy's tummy, you know. But I haven't told him Brian's (husband's) part in it. I've just told him there's a seed. But I haven't told him Brian's part, because he's the type that would want to practise, I'm sure! He so wants to get down to the bottom of everything.

The mother who wants to tell the truth but at the same time does not want to tell the *whole* truth often snatches gratefully at fortuitous circumstances that let her out of her dilemma; thus we had several instances of mothers who had had Caesarian operations who were glad to be able to say that they had 'had an operation', which was apparently a more palatable admission than the baby's more normal means of exit.

Cabinet maker's wife (social work trained):
He's not quite sure how they come out, he keeps asking me how they do; and I say, 'Well, the doctor and the nurses take them out for Mummy', you know, and try and pass it off like that. (You don't want to explain that yet?) No, not just yet, where they actually come from; out of the tummy, yes. But he thinks they've got to cut open your tummy to get them out—which they did with Janie, so it was all right, I could say 'Yes, they did with Janie'.

Other mothers were similarly relieved to escape from having to tell the child at all; 'He did once ask', said a surveyor's wife, 'My friend had just had a baby, and before I could think of an answer, he said "Did he come from the hospital?" and I said "Yes". So I let it slide. It was true, she *had* had him in the hospital, so I thought, well, I'll let that go for now'. Another child had been told (by no less an authority than the midwife's little girl who lived up the road) that when enough pennies had been saved up, the midwife would bring a box with the baby in it; '—so neither of them's asked any more—they think you save pennies, which you *do* really, don't you?'

The fact that the mother chooses not to tell the child the truth of where the baby is before birth does not necessarily imply that she will tell him a direct lie. She may simply ignore the child's questioning or make it plain that the subject is taboo—'Don't be rude!'—or she may honestly postpone the conversation—'I can't tell you that now, when you're as big as Michael I'll tell you all about it'. Another ploy is to say that it costs a lot of money to have babies, thus *implying* that they are bought, without actually spelling out the lie. Other mothers fall back on Heaven: 'He thinks he comes from Jesus, and I let him accept that'; 'I'd say that Almighty God sent them'; 'I'd say "It's up to God", that's what I should say'. A bricklayer's wife had substituted Heaven for her husband's less vague explanation:

I always tell him they're from Heaven, God, you know. They kept asking their Dad, and their Dad was at work one day, and Andy said 'Miss Evans has got babies, hasn't she, Mum, why don't you get one?'— that's the baby-shop (*sic*) on the corner! I said, 'Oh no, love, she doesn't have babies'. He said 'Well, me Dad said so'. Well, I didn't know *what* to say then, without contradicting my husband, so I said 'Well, God makes little babies'. And now Andy keeps asking God for another little baby— now he knows where they are!

Means by which mothers avoid telling their children where babies come from: by social class

	(percentages of total class groups)					
	I & II	IIIwc	IIIman	IV	V	All (random)
	%	%	%	%	%	%
Mother would not tell yet	12	27	55	47	75	46
Avoids telling without falsehood	4	8	14	7	9	11
Gives false explanation	8	19	41	40	66	35

The 'little tales' which mothers told their children varied a good deal both in originality and in plausibility. Traditional 'past fairy-tales' are certainly not extinct: 'I say the same as everybody else tells them—the stork!' said a dustman's wife, and a miner's wife who had answered our query as to whether Gwen knew with an astonished 'No!—I hope not!', assured us: 'They come by Santa Claus or the stork'. A labourer's wife, like several other mothers, had 'bought Edna from Woolworth's—she's always thought that, and I don't think she'd take it into her head that we got her from anywhere else'. All of a nylon winder's children had been 'born under a goosegog bush', a lace machinist's wife found her two sons in the back garden, and a metal polisher's wife specified that she had found Una's baby sister 'under a cabbage patch': 'She said "They don't though, Mummy, they come out of your tummy", and I said "Who told you?" and she said "The little boy next door" '. As is appropriate in a Welfare State, however, most of these babies seem to come on the National Health: 'The Clinic nurse brings them'; 'You have to order them from the hospital'; 'The midwife brought it in her little black bag'. Those who lament the decline in traditional folklore may be heartened to learn that new myths can be generated in a modern social context. A number of Nottingham children know perfectly well that a baby arrives in the form of a large egg, packed in a brown cardboard box and delivered by the nurse or handed out at the clinic; eventually, after a period of incubation, the midwife comes to the house in order to break the seal and take out the newly-hatched baby.

5 From *Four Years Old in an Urban Community*

The classless society in Britain is still a long way off. Men may be born equal; but, within its first month in the world, the baby will be adapting to a climate of experience that varies according to its family's social class. How far these experiences are built in to form a basic personality structure which is recognizably different for different occupational groups, and how far such structures are self-perpetuating in the following generation, we are not qualified to say; much, of course, must depend upon whether the basic structure includes among its characteristics the inclination to accept or to reject adaptation and change. The increase in social mobility offers rewarding opportunities for research here. It is not possible, with the data we have, to make a comparison between, for instance, first- and second-generation professional-class families; but the findings of Jackson and Marsden on the attitudes of professional men born of working-class parents might lead one to expect such a group to adopt the stricter aspects of middle-class upbringing methods, while rejecting their more permissive attitudes. This is pure speculation; but it is an investigation which could be made, and especially at such a time as this when we know that both social mobility and class differences in behaviour are high.

6 From *Coming of Age in Samoa*

From birth until the age of four or five a child's education is exceedingly simple. They must be house-broken, a matter made more difficult by an habitual indifference to the activities of very small children. They must learn to sit or crawl within the house and never to stand upright unless it is absolutely necessary; never to address an adult in a standing position; to stay out of the sun; not to tangle the strands of the weaver; not to scatter the cut-up coconut which is spread out to dry; to keep their scant loin cloths at least nominally fastened to their persons; to treat fire and knives with proper caution; not to touch the kava bowl or the kava cup; and, if their father is a chief, not to crawl on his bed-place when he is by. These are really simply a series of avoidances, enforced by occasional cuffings and a deal of exasperated shouting and ineffectual conversation.

The weight of the punishment usually falls upon the next oldest child, who learns to shout, 'Come out of the sun' before she has fully appreciated the necessity of doing so herself. By the time Samoan girls and boys have reached sixteen or seventeen years of age these perpetual admonitions to the younger ones have become an inseparable part of their conversation, a monotonous, irritated undercurrent to all their comments. I have known them to intersperse their remarks every two or three minutes with 'Keep still', 'Sit still', 'Keep your mouths shut', 'Stop that noise', uttered quite mechanically although all the little ones present may have been behaving as quietly as a row of intimidated mice. On the whole, this last requirement of silence is continually mentioned and never enforced. The little nurses are more interested in peace than in forming the characters of their small charges, and when a child begins to howl, it is simply dragged out of earshot of its elders. No mother will ever exert herself to discipline a younger child if an older one can be made responsible.

If smaller families of parents and children prevailed in Samoa, this system would result in making half the population solicitous and self-sacrificing and the other half tyrannous and self-indulgent. But just as a child is getting old enough for its wilfulness to become unbearable, a younger one is saddled upon it, and the whole process is repeated again, each child being disciplined and socialized through responsibility for a still younger one.

This fear of the disagreeable consequences resulting from a child's crying is so firmly fixed in the minds of the older children that long after there is any need for it, they succumb to some little tyrant's threat of making a scene, and five-year-olds bully their way into expeditions on which they will have to be carried, into weaving parties where they will tangle the strands, and cook-houses where they will tear up the cooking leaves or get thoroughly smudged with the soot and have to be washed— all because an older boy or girl has become so accustomed to yielding any point to stop an outcry.

Language

7 From *Teaching Disadvantaged Children in the Preschool*
These observations are quite limited, being based on intensive work with only 30 disadvantaged Negro preschool children and on less intensive work with perhaps 50 more. However, there are no other data currently available that go much below the surface in describing the nature of language deprivation.

The speech of the severely deprived children seems to consist not of distinct words, as does the speech of middle-class children of the same age, but rather of whole phrases or sentences that function like giant words. That is to say, these 'giant word' units cannot be taken apart by the child and re-combined; they cannot be transformed from statements to questions, from imperatives to declaratives, and so on. Instead of saying 'He's a big dog,' the deprived child says 'He bih daw.' Instead of saying 'I ain't got no juice,' he says 'Uai-ga-na-ju.' Instead of saying 'That is a red truck,' he says 'Dar-re-truh.' Once the listener has become accustomed to this style of speech, he may begin to hear it as if all the sounds were there, and may get the impression that he is hearing articles when in fact there is only a pause where the article should be. He may believe that the child is using words like *it, is, if,* and *in,* when in fact he is using the same sound for all of them—something on the order of 'ih.' (This becomes apparent if the child is asked to repeat the statement 'It is in the box.' After a few attempts in which he becomes confused as to the number of 'ih's' to insert, the child is likely to be reduced to a stammer.)

If the problem were merely one of faulty pronunciation, it would not be so serious. But it appears that the child's faulty pronunciation arises from his inability to deal with sentences *as sequences of meaningful parts.* Even a sophisticated adult will have difficulty pronouncing a very long word if he is unable to deal with it in parts (the reader might take a try at EMPIANASROFLALILIMINLIAL, reading it aloud once and then trying to repeat it from memory). In the Cognitive Maturity Test, children are called upon to repeat sentences of varying degrees of complexity. The severely disadvantaged child will tend to give merely an approximate rendition of the over-all sound profile of the sentence, often leaving out the sounds in the middle, as is common when people are trying to reproduce a meaningless series—this in spite of the fact that the words themselves are often very simple, like 'A big truck is not a little truck.'...

For instance, after dozens of repetitions of 'His father said he could have candy or a cookie,' the child may come no closer to rendering the last three words of the sentence than 'a-uh cookie.' It will then become evident from questioning that the child does not understand that a choice is involved. But if the child is unable to produce *or* differently from *and,* he is in a poor position to learn the difference.

8 From *The Logic of Nonstandard English*

The question is, by what mechanism does the colour bar prevent children from learning to read? One answer is the notion of 'cultural deprivation' put forward by Martin Deutsch and others: the Negro children are said to lack the favourable factors in their home environment which enable middle-class children to do well in school. (Deutsch *et al.,* 1967; Deutsch, Katz and Jensen, 1968.) These factors involve the development of various cognitive skills through verbal interaction with adults, including the ability to reason abstractly, speak fluently, and focus upon long-range goals. In their publications, these psychologists also recognize broader social factors. However, the deficit theory does not focus upon the interaction of the Negro child with white society so much as on his failure to interact with his mother at home. In the literature we find very little direct observation of verbal interaction in the Negro home; most typically the investigators ask the child if he has dinner with his parents, and if he engages in dinner-table conversation with them. He is also asked whether his family takes him on trips to museums and other cultural activities. This slender thread of evidence is used to explain and interpret the large body of tests carried out in the laboratory and in the school.

The most extreme view which proceeds from this orientation—and one that is now being widely accepted—is that lower-class Negro children have no language at all. The notion is first drawn from Basil Bernstein's writings that 'much of lower-class language consists of a kind of incidental "emotional" accompaniment to action here and now' (Jensen, 1968, p. 118). Bernstein's views are filtered through a strong bias against all forms of working-class behaviour, so that middle-class language is seen as superior in every respect—as 'more abstract, and necessarily somewhat more flexible, detailed and subtle'. One can proceed through a range of such views until one comes to the practical programme of Carl Bereiter, Siegfried Engelmann and their associates (Bereiter *et al.*, 1966; Bereiter and Engelmann, 1966). Bereiter's programme for an academically oriented preschool is based upon their premise that Negro children must have a language with which they can learn, and their empirical finding that these children come to school without such a language. In his work with four-year-old Negro children from Urbana, Bereiter reports that their communication was by gestures, 'single words', and 'a series of badly-connected words or phrases', such as *They mine* and *Me got juice*. He reports that Negro children could not ask questions, that 'without exaggerating ... these four-year-olds could make no statements of any kind'. Furthermore, when these children were asked 'Where is the book?', they did not know enough to look at the table where the book was lying in order to answer. Thus Bereiter concludes that the children's speech forms are nothing more than a series of emotional cries, and he decides to treat them 'as if the children had no language at all'. He identifies their speech with his interpretation of Bernstein's restricted code: 'the language of culturally deprived children ... is not merely an underdeveloped version of standard English, but is a basically non-logical mode of expressive behaviour' (Bereiter *et al.*, 1966, p. 113). The basic programme of his preschool is to teach them a new language devised by Engelmann, which consists of a limited series of questions and answers such as *Where is the squirrel? The squirrel is in the tree.* The children will not be punished if they use their vernacular speech on the playground, but they will not be allowed to use it in the schoolroom.

If they should answer the question *Where is the squirrel?* with the illogical vernacular form *In the tree* they will be reprehended by various means and made to say, *The squirrel is in the tree.*

Linguists and psycholinguists who have worked with Negro children are apt to dismiss this view of their language as utter nonsense. Yet there is no reason to reject Bereiter's observations as spurious: they were certainly not made up: on the contrary, they give us a very clear view of the behaviour of student and teacher which can be duplicated in any classroom. In our own work outside of the adult-dominated environments of school and home, we do not observe Negro children behaving like this, but on many occasions we have been asked to help analyze the results of research into verbal deprivation in such test situations.

Here, for example, is a complete interview with a Negro boy, one of the hundreds carried out in a New York City school. The boy enters a room where there is a large, friendly white interviewer, who puts on the table in front of him a block or a fire engine, and says 'Tell me everything you can about this'. (The interviewer's further remarks are in parentheses.)

[12 seconds of silence]
(What would you say it looks like?)
[8 seconds of silence]
A space ship.
(Hmmmm.)
[13 seconds of silence]
Like a je-et.
[12 seconds of silence]
Like a plane.
[20 seconds of silence]
(What colour is it?)
Orange. *[2 seconds]* An' whi-ite. *[2 seconds]* An' green.
[6 seconds of silence]
(An' what could you use it for?)
[8 seconds of silence]
A je-et.
[6 seconds of silence]
(If you had two of them, what would you do with them?)
[6 seconds of silence]
Give one to somebody.
(Hmmmm. Who do you think would like to have it?)
[10 seconds of silence]
Cla-rence.
(Mm. Where do you think we could get another one of these?)
At the store.
(Oh ka-ay!)

We have here the same kind of defensive, mono-syllabic behaviour which is reported in Bereiter's work. What is the situation that produces it? The child is in an asymmetrical situation where anything he says can literally be held against him. He has learned a number of devices to *avoid* saying anything in this situation, and he works very hard to achieve this end. One may observe the intonation patterns which Negro children often use when they are asked a question to which the answer is obvious. The answer may be read as 'Will this satisfy you?'

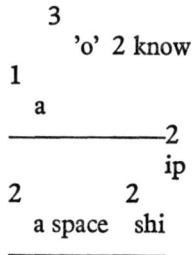

If one takes this interview as a measure of the verbal capacity of the child, it must be as his capacity to defend himself in a hostile and threatening situation. But unfortunately, thousands of such interviews are used as evidence of the child's total verbal capacity, or more simply his 'verbality'; it is argued that this lack of verbality *explains* his poor performance in school. Operation Headstart and other intervention programmes have largely been based upon the 'deficit theory'—the notions that such interviews give us a measure of the child's verbal capacity and that the verbal stimulation which he has been missing can be supplied in a pre-school environment.

The verbal behaviour which is shown by the child in the test situation quoted above is not the result of the ineptness of the interviewer. It is rather the result of regular sociolinguistic factors operating upon adult and child in this asymmetrical situation. In our work in urban ghetto areas, we have often encountered such behaviour. Ordinarily we worked with boys 10–17 years old; and whenever we extended our approach downward to 8- or 9-year olds, we began to see the need for different techniques to explore the verbal capacity of the child. At one point we began a series of interviews with younger brothers of the 'Thunderbirds' in 1390 5th Avenue. Clarence Robins returned after an interview with 8-year-old Leon L., who showed the following minimal response to topics which arouse intense interest in other interviews with older boys.

CR: What if you saw somebody kickin' somebody else on the ground, or was using a stick, what would you do if you saw that?
LEON: Mmmm.
CR: If it was supposed to be a fair fight—
LEON: I don' know.

CR: You don' know? Would you do anything . . . huh? I can't hear you.
LEON: No.
CR: Did you ever see somebody got beat up real bad?
LEON: . . . Nope ? ? ?
CR: Well—uh—did you ever get into a fight with a guy?
LEON: Nope.
CR: That was bigger than you?
LEON: Nope.
CR: You never been in a fight?
LEON: Nope.
CR: Nobody ever pick on you?
LEON: Nope.
CR: Nobody ever hit you?
LEON: Nope.
CR: How come?
LEON: Ah 'on' know.
CR: Didn't you ever hit somebody?
LEON: Nope.
CR: [*incredulous*] You never hit anybody?
LEON: Mhm.
CR: Aww, ba-a-a-be, you ain't gonna tell me that.

It may be that Leon is here defending himself against accusations of wrong-doing, since Clarence knows that Leon has been in fights, that he has been taking pencils away from little boys, etc. But if we turn to a more neutral subject, we find the same pattern.

CR: You watch—you like to watch television? . . . Hey, Leon . . . you like to watch television? [*Leon nods*] What's your favourite programme?
LEON: Uhhmmmm . . . I look at cartoons.
CR: Well, what's your favourite one? What's your favourite programme?
LEON: Superman . . .
CR: Yeah? Did you see Superman—ah—yesterday, or day before yesterday: when's the last time you saw Superman?
LEON: Sa-aturday . . .
CR: You rem—you saw it Saturday? What was the story all about? You remember the story?
LEON: M-m.
CR: You don't remember the story of what—that you saw of Superman?
LEON: Nope.
CR: You don't remember what happened, huh?
LEON: Hm-m.
CR: I see—ah—what other stories do you like to watch on TV?
LEON: Mmmm ? ? ? . . . umm . . . [*glottalization*]
CR: Hmm? [*4 seconds*]
LEON: Hh?

48

CR: What's th' other stories that you like to watch?
LEON: Mi - ighty Mouse . . .
CR: And what else?
LEON: Ummmm . . . ahm . . .

This nonverbal behaviour occurs in a relatively *favourable* context for adult–child interaction; since the adult is a Negro man raised in Harlem, who knows this particular neighbourhood and these boys very well. He is a skilled interviewer who has obtained a very high level of verbal response with techniques developed for a different age level, and he has an extraordinary advantage over most teachers or experiments in these respects. But even his skills and personality are ineffective in breaking down the social constraints that prevail here.

When we reviewed the record of this interview with Leon, we decided to use it as a test of our own knowledge of the sociolinguistic factors which control speech. We made the following changes in the social situation: in the next interview with Leon, Clarence

1 brought along a supply of potato chips, changing the 'interview' into something more in the nature of a party;
2 brought along Leon's best friend, 8-year-old Gregory;
3 reduced the height imbalance (when Clarence got down on the floor of Leon's room, he dropped from 6ft 2in to 3ft 6in);
4 introduced taboo words and taboo topics, and proved to Leon's surprise that one can say anything into our microphone without any fear of retaliation.

The result of these changes is a striking difference in the volume and style of speech.

CR: Is there anybody who says *your momma drink pee*?
⌠LEON: [*rapidly and breathlessly*] Yee-ah!
⌡GREG: Yup!
LEON: And your father eat doo-doo for breakfas'!
CR: Ohhh!! [*laughs*]
LEON: And they say *your father—your father eat doo-doo for dinner*!
GREG: When they sound on me, I say *CBM*.
CR: What that mean?
⌠LEON: Conger-booger-snatch! [*laughs*]
⌡GREG: Conger-booger-snatcher! [*laughs*]
GREG: And sometimes I'll curse with *BB*.
CR: What that?
GREG: Black boy! [*Leon—crunching on potato chips*] Oh that's a *MBB*.
CR: MBB. What's that?
GREG: 'Merican Black Boy!
CR: Ohh . . .

GREG: Anyway, 'Mericans is same like white people, right?
LEON: And they talk about Allah.
CR: Oh yeah?
GREG: Yeah.
CR: What they say about Allah?
{LEON: Allah—Allah is God.
{GREG: Allah—
CR: And what else?
LEON: I don' know the res'.
GREG: Allah i—Allah is God, Allah is the only God, Allah—
LEON: Allah is the *son* of God.
GREG: But can he make magic?
LEON: Nope.
GREG: I know who can make magic.
CR: Who can?
LEON: The God, the *real* one.
CR: Who can make magic?
GREG: The son of po'—[CR: Hm?] I'm sayin' the po'k chop God! He only a po'k chop God! [*Leon chuckles*]

The 'nonverbal' Leon is now competing actively for the floor; Gregory and Leon talk to each other as much as they do to the interviewer.

9 From *Intellectual Growth in Young Children*
A2. *Imaginative and hypothetical application*
16.10.24.   When the bonfire was burning in the garden, Christopher (4;1) said, 'Let's make the flames high! Let's make them go up to the sky!' George (4;1) remarked, 'If you do that, you'll burn God'.
11.2.25.   The children were speaking of 'going up into the sky', and Theobald (4;11) said, 'I'd like to see the birds and the fairies'; Frank (5;3) added, 'Oh, yes, and Jesus'.
24.2.25.   The children found some ice in the wheelbarrow in the garden, and broke it up, talking about it interestedly. Theobald (5;0) said, 'My hands are so cold, they'll melt all away'.
25.2.25.   Theobald (5;0) drew with chalk on the floor 'a mountain going up into the sky', and then walked along some lines saying, 'I'm going up into the sky'.
Frank and Dan were climbing on the window-sill, and Frank said he would 'push Dan's foot up'. Paul (3;11) said, 'Yes, we'll push Dan up to God'. Frank (5;4): 'Yes, and perhaps He'll kill him'.
30.4.25.   Mrs I. overheard Harold, Paul and Theobald talking in the sand-pit about Christopher, who is not present this week. They had evidently been discussing where he was, and one boy said, 'Perhaps he's dead'.
16.6.25.   There was some talk among the children about the effect of water upon the bonfire. Duncan (7;0) said, 'If you put water on, it makes

50

more blazes'. Mrs I. said to him, 'Let's do it and see'. He put some on, and saw that it put the flames out; but he went on to say, 'After it has dried, it makes more blazes—Auntie told me so. She said that once she nearly had the house on fire because she tried to put it out with water'. (Phantasy or mis-hearing?) Mrs I. suggested his trying further to see the effect, but he preferred to talk about it dogmatically.

19.6.25. The children had made a bonfire of garden rubbish, and Duncan (7;0) put an old tennis ball on to the fire, telling the others, 'It will make a smell—and perhaps it'll explode'. But nothing happened, as it did not fall into the hot part of the fire.

A3. Make-believe and dramatized knowledge

13.11.24. Harold (4;11) and Benjie (4;1) broke up a piece of the garden path with a hoe, saying, 'We're mending the road'.

11.12.24. The children were playing a game of 'shooting' with sticks as guns. Frank (5;1) suddenly said, 'I'm going to shoot Jesus—Bang! Bang!'—pointing his stick upwards.

26.1.25. Frank (5;3) invented a game and told the others how to play it. They stood round the room while one of the children spoke the following (Frank's composition): 'The beautiful snowy mountains, the sun and the moon and the stars; the sun is shining on the mountains; the sun melts the snow away; and then there are great waves on the sea, and the waves knock over the small boats'. At this, the one who spoke had to chase all the others and catch them. At first Frank was very shy about telling his verse, and whispered it first to Dan and then to Mrs I.; but presently he stood up and said it to everyone.

3.2.25. When they were making 'trains', Frank (5;3) said, 'In my train people sleep and have a wash. There is a big boiler, and the engine heats it up'.

5.2.25. Dan (3;9) ran round the garden as an aeroplane, 'finding its way in the dark, and going up off the ground, getting smaller and smaller'.

10.3.25. Paul (4;0) looked in the mirror, and said laughingly to Mrs I., 'There's another Malting House School, there's another one—I can see the room and the people'. Mrs I. said, 'It's a reflection, isn't it?' 'Oh yes—it's *really* the same school', he said.

17.3.25. Harold got a stick for a gun and said he was going to shoot Tommy when he had put some gunpowder in. He used sand as gunpowder, and then shot at Tommy saying, 'Bang, bang'. Frank (5;4) said, '*You* did not say, "Bang", did you?' Harold said, 'No'. Tommy said, 'Yes, you did'. Frank said, 'No, it was the gun that said it'.

B. Practical insight and resource

17.10.24. The children had been carrying water out into the garden in cans and jugs, and as there were some damp feet, Mrs I. said, 'No more to-day'. Tommy (2;8) was doleful when Mrs I. would not let him take more, and passing back through the schoolroom, he saw the vases on the tables, full of flowers. Without saying anything, he put down his can on the floor, and took each of the four vases in turn, lifting the flowers out, pouring the water into his can, and putting the flowers back on the table. He then walked out into the garden smiling, and saying to the others, 'Tommy has some water now!'

29.10.24. Benji (4;0) and Christopher (4;1) wanted to drag some large logs of wood from one side of the garden to the other; they took walking sticks and hooked them into projecting branches on the logs, and dragged them, with much pride.

8.12.24. There is a skylight window on the roof, and a cord hangs down from it. Harold (4;11) seeing this cord swinging, said, 'Oh, we could fasten an aeroplane on that, and it would fly'. He made one of the kind the children often make, fastening two or three bricks together transversely with plasticine, and hung it on the cord. The others watched it swinging, and presently each did the same, taking turns. They set the cord swinging freely and watched it with delight.

5.3.25. The children built up a large bonfire with sticks and shavings left by the carpenter. It burnt very clearly and they said, 'Let's boil some water on it'. They made a tripod with large sticks and hung a bucket on it with a string, and got a can of water hot. Later they stood cans on the fire itself. Harold (5;2) said, 'Now I'll be able to have some hot water to wash my hands with', and asked Mrs I. to help him carry in a bucket of warm water, and washed his hands in it.

21.4.25. Frank (5;6) suggested that they should make a tent on the lawn with some sticks. He told Mrs I. how to make it—'You put the sticks up, and put something over them, and then you have a tent'.

5.6.25. Duncan (6;11) told the others, 'I know how to take the piano to pieces', and showed them how to take off the front and the cover of the keyboard. The others crowded round and looked at the mechanism eagerly.

8.6.25. Duncan (6;11) again took off the front of the piano, the others helping and showing great interest in watching the hammers strike the wires when the keys were depressed.

15.6.25. The children made a large square 'oven' with the real bricks we have for building, and burned hay in it. They arranged holes in the bricks at the bottom, to create a draught.

16.6.25. The piano-tuner came, and Duncan (7;0) took the front of the piano off for him. He told the other children, 'I know how he does it'.

II. INCREASE OF KNOWLEDGE: PROBLEMS AND EXPERIMENT, OBSERVATION AND DISCOVERY

16.10.24. George (4;1) had a yellow purse. He put his finger into it, and said, 'It's like a glove'. Then he said, 'It's yellow—are gloves always yellow?' Mrs I. showed him her own, which were brown.

12.11.24. Some modelling wax having been dropped on a hot-water pipe, the children discovered that it had melted, and tried some more. When they found that all the wax would melt, whatever colour it was, they went on to try other materials—plasticine, wood, chalk, and so on, talking about it together and telling Mrs I., 'Plasticine melts. Wood won't melt', and so on. The whole of this was entirely spontaneous. (Ages 4;0 to 5;0).

21.11.24. Frank (5;0) saw Mrs I. opening the skylight window, and came to watch how it was done. He then asked if he could do it, and spent some time practising the way the two ropes had to be held for opening and shutting it, one left loose and the other pulled. The others all joined in this later on, with great interest.

28.11.24. In the garden Frank (5;0) recognized from the outside the skylight which he had enjoyed opening from the inside several times. He looked very pleased when he recognized it.

12.1.25. There was much excited interest in the bubbling sounds made by the hot-water pipes this morning. The children kept running to listen to them, and wanted to climb up so as to see into the cistern.

6.3.25. A piece of plasticine had rolled underneath the piano, and this led Harold (5;2) and Frank (5;4) to put more there, saying, 'Perhaps it will make the piano play differently'. They were reluctant to take it out again. Tommy (3;0) overheard this, and put some inside the piano, telling Mrs I. gleefully, 'I put plasticine down the piano, and it does not play the same now'.

16.3.25. The children were making sails for their boats, and fastening them on with string. Theobald (5;0) was much poorer both in planning and in constructing than the others were. He had to draw a sail before he could cut it, and at first made very small ones. He was very dissatisfied with his work when finished, and asked Mrs I. to help him. She took a rectangular piece of paper and cut diagonally across it, showing him how she did it. He was most interested in this, and in the middle of tying on the sails, he returned to it, and said, 'How do you put the triangular pieces of paper to make them square?' Mrs I. suggested that he should try to do it, and he experimented with them, but unsuccessfully. He walked round them to get different views, asking, 'How do you look at them to see them square?' He was not satisfied until Mrs I. showed him how to put them together in a square.

16.3.25. Paul found a wet box of matches with one live match in it, in the garden. Harold (5;2) tried to strike the match, but it would not ignite. He said, 'The box is too soft'.

23.3.25. The children found ice in the wheelbarrow, and took it out, breaking it with a stone. Dan (3;10) was holding two pieces in his hand, and they froze together. 'Look, they are stuck', he said.

21.4.25. The carpenter came to fasten up some trellis work, and Frank (5;6), when watching him said, 'Oh, he's cutting off a triangular piece of wood'—in a tone of great interest. There had been another carpenter in the school last term, and Dan (3;11) said, 'It's a different carpenter man'. Frank asked Mrs I., 'Did you want another one for a change?' and Dan: 'Do they live together?'

SECTION 4: QUESTIONS FOR DISCUSSION

1 Do you consider that pre-school education can be justified on the grounds that it promotes thinking (cognitive growth)? What evidence would you use to convince a sceptic?

2 'Underestimation of the potentialities of slum children and of ethnic minorities tends to be reinforced by too early and too frequent use of intelligence tests unsuited to their particular needs' (Kelsall and Kelsall 1971).

Can you give any other evidence which suggests that slum and minority children are, in general, woefully underestimated and misplaced by the educational system?

3 If the mother is as vital to a child's future mental health as the work of Bowlby (*Child Care and the Growth of Love* 1970) suggests, may not 'nursery education for all' be a slogan we ought to abandon?

4 Clearly children in the first four years of life have an invisibly potent inner life: what experiences, good or bad, can you recall from your own pre-school days? (Most people can recall events from their fourth year of life onwards.)

5 Imagine that you have been parachuted into a country whose script you cannot read and whose language is wholly unfamiliar to you. Describe your first days in the place, recording your attempts at conversation in detail. How did you cope in the end? What kind of working vocabulary did you require? How did you learn it? And how far was your experience, albeit imaginary, analogous to that of a child born into a particular speech community?

REFERENCES

BANDURA, A. and WALTERS, R. H. (1969) *Social Learning and Personality Development* New York: Holt, Rinehart and Winston

BEREITER, C. and ENGELMANN, S. (1966) *Teaching Disadvantaged Children in the Preschool* London: Prentice Hall

BERNSTEIN, B. (1970) Education cannot compensate for society *New Society* 26th February, 344–7

BERNSTEIN, B. (1971) 'Social class, language and socialization' in *Class Codes and Control* London: Routledge and Kegan Paul

BOWLBY, J. and FRY, M. (1970) *Child Care and the Growth of Love* Harmondsworth: Penguin

CARMICHAEL, L. (1946) *Carmichael's Manual of Child Psychology* New York: Wiley

CHOMSKY, N. (1965) *Aspects of the Theory of Syntax* Boston: MIT Press

DE ZWART, S. (1969) 'Linguistic contributions to the study of mind and future' in P. Adams (ed) (1972) *Language in Thinking* Harmondsworth: Penguin

DENNIS, W. (1960) Causes of retardation among institutionalized children *Journal of Genetic Psychology* 96, 47–59

DENNIS, W. and DENNIS, M. G. (1940) The effect of cradling practices upon the onset of walking in Hopi children *Journal of Genetic Psychology* 56, 77–86

ERICKSON, E. (1965) *Childhood and Society* Harmondsworth: Penguin

GESELL, A. (1928) *Infancy and Human Growth* New York: Macmillan

HALLIDAY, M. A. K. (1969) quoted in B. Bernstein (1970) Education cannot compensate for society *New Society* 26th February

HEBBS, D. O. (1949) *The Organization of Behaviour* New York: Wiley

HARLOW, J. and ZIMMERMMAN, A. (1959) Affectional responses in the infant monkey *Science*

ISAACS, S. (1933) *Social Development in Young Children* London: Routledge and Kegan Paul

JERSILD, A. T. (1933) *Child Psychology* New Jersey: Prentice Hall

KAGAN, J. (1969) in H. W. Maler (ed) *Three Theories of Child Development* New York: Harper and Row International

KELSALL, R. K. and KELSALL, H. M. (1971) *Social Disadvantage and Educational Opportunity* New York: Holt, Rinehart and Winston

LABOV, W. (1969) *The Logic of Nonstandard English* Georgetown Monographs in Language and Linguistics 22

LANGER, S. (1962) *Philosophical Sketches* London: Oxford University Press

LURIA, A. R. and YUDOVICH, F. (1971) *Speech and the Development of Mental Processes in the Child* Harmondsworth: Penguin

MEAD, M. (1943) *Coming of Age in Samoa* Harmondsworth: Penguin

MCVICKER HUNT, J. (1961) *Intelligence and Experience* Oxford: Ronald Press

NEWSON, R. and E. (1965) *Patterns of Infant Care in an Urban Community* Harmondsworth: Penguin

SEARS, R. (1969) in H. W. Maler (ed) *Three Theories of Child Development* New York: Harper and Row International

SKINNER, B. F. (1953) *Science and Human Behaviour* New York: Macmillan

SLUCKIN, W. (1970) *Early Learning in Man and Animal* London: Allen and Unwin

SPITZ, R. A. (1945) *Psychoanalytical Studies of Children* 1, 53–74

SPITZ, R. A. (1946) *Psychoanalytical Studies of Children* 2, 113–117

THORNDIKE, E. L. (1921) *Educational Psychology* New York: Columbia University Press

TRASLER, G. (1970) 'Delinquency' in H. J. Butcher and H. B. Pont (eds) *Educational Research in Britain 2* London: University of London Press

WINNICOTT, D. W. (1964) *The Child, the Family and the Outside World* Harmondsworth: Penguin

READINGS

1–5 NEWSON, J. and E. (1968) *Four Years Old in an Urban Community* London: Allen and Unwin
6 MEAD, M. (1943) *Coming of Age in Samoa* Harmondsworth: Penguin
7 BEREITER, C. and ENGELMANN, S. (1966) *Teaching Disadvantaged Children in the Preschool* New Jersey: Prentice Hall
8 LABOV, W. (1969) *The Logic of Nonstandard English* Georgetown Monographs in Language and Linguistics 22 Washington: University of Georgetown Press also reprinted in A. Cashdan and P. Grugeon (eds) *Language in Education* London: Routledge and Kegan Paul
9 ISAACS, S. (1930) *Intellectual Growth in Young Children* London: Routledge and Kegan Paul

Chapter 2: Language: the building of connections

Most children spend the years between learning to talk and going to school in and around the home. Boys as well as girls help with the washing-up, are sent on simple errands, take out milk tokens to the front door or run for the morning paper as it thumps on the mat. Boys play soldiers, dress in jeans and cowboy hats, wield sixshooters. Girls try their hand at knitting, perhaps, or are taught crocheting by granny; they learn to dress, undress and bathe their dolls. They may also, of course, join in the rough and tumble of hide and seek, 'Hit' (or 'It'), and give as good as they get.

The arrival of speech at about the age of two shortcuts all the 'training' of babyhood. Now, at last, parents can send messages swiftly: Pavlov's 'second signalling system', speech, does away with the need for lengthy instruction procedures based on the 'first signalling system' of conditioning. Learning replaces training. Messages transmitted through the medium of language can, of course, be ignored. The point is that a vast new universe awaits the child: *meaning* is about to enter his world. Not merely do mothers and fathers find themselves being asked incessant 'why?' and 'how?' questions but parents themselves are now able to employ the most powerful instrument of socialization: the human voice.

The enormous variety of dos and don'ts can be swiftly and efficiently communicated to the infant, permitting discriminations, exceptions to the rule and qualifications. Thus warnings (about strangers, rivers, safety matches and main roads) are given; instructions (what to say to shopkeepers, to people having birthdays, to neighbours when a ball has to be retrieved, to the ice cream man) are taught; rebukes (for fighting, sulking, tantrums, taking other children's toys) are explicit or potentially so.

The ability to talk, that is, to join two words, at age two is accompanied by motor development. Indeed, many motor milestones of sitting up, crawling, standing and walking unaided have already been passed: the latter at about 15 months. Bladder and bowel control are achieved by three and four years respectively. In passing, we ought to add that what counts as acceptability in continence will be largely determined by subcultural (or social class) attitudes and norms: 'dummies' (comforters) are a similar class-linked device to ease weaning, traditionally a working-class one.

Bowel and bladder control—Erikson's muscular-anal stage—is succeeded by the libidinal jealousies of the succeeding Oedipal, or locomotor-genital stage. Yet as early as the age of three, boys are choosing different toys and pursuits from girls: sex-linked roles are beginning to emerge. 'Masculine' games will be opted for by boys, and games and toys permitting speed, mobility, aggression or power will be preferred to girls' 'cissy' games. Girls may, indeed, spend their time indoors or at least play at games related to the home, including housekeeping, babies and looking pretty (or ensuring that the dolls do). Naturally, there will be exceptions which will depend on the masculine/feminine roles portrayed by the adults of the house: middle-class mothers may be more tolerant of 'milk-sop' behaviour in boys than working-class mothers. A particular mother may cling on to her child's babyhood, perhaps refusing to have her son's curls cut. Or, she may give her daughter the freedom *she* was denied as a child. The tendency for each culture to evoke different behaviours from boys and from girls and to proffer different attributes as desirable for each sex can be seen long before a child enters school. Boys are encouraged to live up to certain expectations: 'big', 'brave', and 'boys don't cry' are the labels handed to him by parents, teachers and grannies. Girls similarly aspire to be the 'good girl' their mothers enjoin on them. This labelling by 'significant others' is thought to be internalized by the child and assimilated into his developing self-concept. The cultural transmission of values in this way is commonly reinforced by the selection of toys available for boys and girls. Boys do indeed 'choose' guns, knives, trucks and model excavators, and girls dolls, beads, trinkets and nurses' outfits. But the cultural influences which predetermine such choice are powerful and include other children, advertisers, fond parents. In a sense, boys (and girls) could not be expected to choose anything else.

Accordingly, since sex-typing is culturally defined, children are rewarded for sex-appropriate behaviour, and are punished for defiance. Research—mainly American—suggests that the parents punish aggression and overt 'sexual' behaviour more consistently in daughters than in sons; passivity, dependency and the open display of fear are more consistently penalized in sons. Given the labelling process described earlier, children are made aware of what parents expect from them in the way of behaviour and, of course, it is gratifying to be rewarded for 'proper' behaviour. Finally, in most families there exist powerful and persuasive models in the persons of mother and father.

Men and women are seen by children to be *sui generis* in a whole host of visually vivid ways, including dress, physique, size, hairiness and genitalia. Vocal timbre, emotionality and gesture are other features which children will pick up through visual-auditory channels. Moreover, other salient differentiating cues are indicated by activities around the home:

men cut lawns, have workbenches, grease the car, attend to electrical fittings and do odd-job running repairs. Women cook, dust, shop, pay the breadman or milkman and exercise sole sway over the washing machine. We may note, in passing, that the advent of technology and the attitude-changes engendered by working wives is altering rigid role-playing. Men are now seen in laundrettes and supermarkets. Women may drive the 'second' car and, if working, may receive help in housework at evenings or weekends from their husbands. In short, the customary role-cues are less sharp than they were. In clothes, hairstyles and 'accessories', men and women, at least among the unmarried urban young, are converging in what must be an extremely confusing way so far as the child observer is concerned. Nevertheless, outside women graduate circles at least, the expectation that men shall be dominant and adventurous, women compliant and conservative, still predominates. As we have suggested, these cultural prescriptions are no doubt transmitted not merely by father/son, mother/daughter 'modelling', but from the models and ideal-types portrayed by filmstars, TV personalities, pop singers, etc.

Evidence is beginning to emerge, however, to confirm what many have long suspected: that many overt sex-differences in thinking, skills and overt personality must be biologically based. There certainly exists clear biochemical warrant for the observed higher level of activity in boys, for instance, but the licence boys traditionally receive for rough-housing and healthy disobedience makes the separate strands of nature and nurture hard to disentangle. Women in our society have been expected—perhaps owing to their dependent status—to resolve conflict or anxiety in a passive way, so no doubt women's alleged emotionality and little girls' hard-won concessions to sob or sulk, are similarly inextricably involved in origin. As to the abundant opportunities offered to girls to observe adult life at first hand, it is clear that they have a head start. Their proximity to mother may help explain in part their superior vocabulary and social skills throughout school life. For girls can learn women's work not merely through 'anticipatory socialization'—looking and learning—but by actually pitching in. The mysteries of cleaning, bread-making, knitting or shopping may all be painlessly made plain in this way. Boys are comparatively handicapped. Except for farmwork, construction work and the like, boys—especially, of course, middle-class boys—are unlikely to have any clear idea of what father does at work. Off to work before the children are awake perhaps, and only back home for the evening meal, father inhabits a world of men and activity which remains a closed door to most sons. There are obvious compensations for boys here, as girls seem to have learned. As Brown (1965) points out, not merely do many girls between 3 and 10 show a strong preference for masculine games, but 5- to 10-year-old girls may even express a wish to be a boy or a daddy when they are grown up.

If one turns from role-acquisition to the acquisition of concepts, one finds interesting differences between the sexes, but cross-class differences are now also markedly apparent. Girls, indeed, match their social prowess with a maturation 'setting' which is ahead of boys from birth and this may help account for their superior scores on reading and other attainment measures up to pubery. It is clear from the work of the cognitive psychologists under Jerome Bruner at the Harvard Center that language is a crucial link between the stage at which a child cannot conserve quantity, for instance, and the stage, typically reached between ages six and eight, at which he can. Language appears to be so important to cognitive development that if language is not available to 'encode' logical thinking, cognitive development will be halted.

Piaget, in his work, distinguished broadly between *pre-operational* (birth to age seven) and *operational* thinking (age seven upwards); he observed an important subdivision at about the age of 11. He postulated a final stage of *formal operational thinking* which many will enter into at puberty: at this stage, children are able to speculate, to hypothesize, to engage in 'combinatorial' thinking. Reality can be manipulated and encoded wholly through mental processes, without pictorial or written aids. Bruner's position differs importantly, perhaps radically, from Piaget's in that he ascribes to language itself, rather than to maturation of the central nervous system, that function which shifts us from one mode of apprehending reality to another, more sophisticated one. He observes, with Piaget, an enactive period in the first two years or so of life when the child cognizes his world through his muscles, and motoric movements and patterns are built up until mental images finally succeed them. Bruner then traces two succeeding cognitive modes. He picks out the years 2 to 7 as years in which the world is handled through an *iconic* mode, and the years 7 upwards as those in which information is primarily processed through a *symbolic* mode. He (Bruner 1966a) tersely distinguishes his stance from that of Piaget's when he says:

We move, perceive, and think in a fashion that depends upon techniques rather than upon wired-in arrangements in our nervous system.

Where representation of the environment is concerned, it too depends upon techniques that are learned and these are precisely the techniques that serve to amplify our motor acts, our perceptions, and our ratiocinative capacities. . . . If we are to benefit from recurrent regularities in the environment, we must represent them in some manner. To dismiss this problem as 'mere memory' is to misunderstand it. For the most important thing about memory is not storage of past experience but rather the retrieval of what is relevant in some usable form. This depends upon how past experience is coded and processed so that it may indeed be relevant and usuable in the present when needed. The end product of such a system of coding and processing is what we may speak of as a representation.

Referring to the three modes of representation as enactive, iconic and symbolic, he continues:

Their appearance in the child is in that order, each depending upon the previous one for its development, yet all of them remaining intact throughout life. . . . By enactive representation, I mean a mode of representing past events through appropriate motor response. We cannot, for example, give an adequate description of familiar sidewalks or floors over which we habitually walk, nor do we have much of an image of what they are like. Yet we get about them without tripping or even looking much. Such segments of our environment —bicycle riding, tying knots, aspects of driving—get represented in our muscles, so to speak. Iconic representation summarizes events by the selective organization of percepts and images, by the spatial, temporal, and qualitative structures of the perceptual field and their transformed images. Images 'stand for' perceptual events in the close but conventionally selective way that a picture stands for the object pictured. Finally, a symbol system represents things by design features that include remoteness and arbitrariness. A word neither points directly to its referent here and now, nor does it resemble it as a picture. The lexeme 'Philadelphia' looks no more like the city so designated than does a nonsense syllable. The other property of language that is crucial is its productiveness in combination, far beyond what can be done with images or acts. 'Philadelphia is a lavender sachet in Grandmother's linen closet,' or $(x + 2)^2 = x^2 + 4x + 4 = x(x + 4) + 4$.

As Bruner points out elsewhere (1966b):

It is the sheer ability to manipulate 'the real world' by the 'powerful productive rules of grammar' that makes symbolic representation such a powerful tool for thinking or problem-saving . . . the range it permits for experimental alteration of the environment without having, so to speak, to raise a finger by way of trial and error or to picture anything in the mind's eye by imagery. 'What if there were never any apples?' a four year old asked upon finishing one with gusto.

Bruner stresses the importance of language for transition from the perceptually-dependent iconic mode to the symbolic mode. If language and symbolic representation are, in an important sense, synonymous, the weight which language must carry in socialization, in encoding the world 'out there', will be critical. Are different language 'codes' going to affect how socialization and subsequent learning-task behaviours will be performed? If this is the case, then we shall have to pay attention to the manner in which socialization proceeds, in sociolinguistic terms. The use of language in differing social contexts compels us in turn to focus on these social contexts to look for underlying concepts which will help organize the welter of family behaviours. Finally, we shall be in a position to look at the way in which affective (i.e. emotional) factors can or should play a part in cognitive growth. It is to the role of language in socialization and subsequent orientation towards learning that we now turn.

A useful framework for the study of subcultural differences in socialization is provided by W. P. Robinson (1972): he concentrates on the mother as the key agent of pre-school socialization. No doubt, of course, Danziger's criticisms of work which assumes socialization to consist of mother-child interaction is justified. Much more work on *family*—and *peergroup*—child interaction is called for, but the number of variables and the difficulty of recording this kind of behaviour make such studies less than easy. By narrowing the focus to mothers and their attitudes towards their children, and then noting how far mothers do in fact practise what they preach, testable hypotheses can be erected and verified. Robinson suggests that the three levels of behaviour which need to be related to social class are mothers' attitudes, mothers' actual and reported behaviour, and children's behaviour. Mothers were asked, in a sample consisting of middle-class and lower working-class mothers, about their views on language and learning. Whereas middle-class mothers saw children as having to be *taught* to speak, lower working-class mothers appeared to hold a passive view of the process of language acquisition, and thought that children learned to speak 'naturally' or 'automatically'. Further, they saw boundaries between home and school as a good thing; teachers were there to teach school material while mothers were responsible for implanting 'role-appropriate' behaviour in the child.

These unexamined assumptions have never really been investigated and Robinson makes a plea for some systematic study of prevailing differential attitudes such as these. Quoting research by Cook, Robinson (1972) observes that the ways in which mothers discipline their offspring can be categorized into three elements: imperative techniques, positional appeals and personal appeals. Cook's findings as to the social class differences in these regulative techniques support the findings of other workers, notably the Newsons, and Hess and Shipman. He found that while no class difficulties were detectable in the use of positional appeals such as 'Do what I say, I'm your mother', middle-class mothers employed more personal appeals and lower working-class mothers more imperative ones. In the lower working class, then, language is used to deliver commands or imperatives and to enjoin compliant behaviour on the child, as becomes his status. The imperative techniques, Robinson suggests, are akin to those electric shock techniques employed in training rats to jump from a 'live' floor-grid to a safe compartment in their cage. In other words, lower working-class children are being exposed to avoidance learning. Middle-class children, be it noted, were equally exposed to positional appeals for role-appropriate behaviour but, in receiving more personal appeals, they were at least assumed to require some sort of *reason* for having to do as they were told. This is the crux of the matter. There is no opportunity for lower working-class children to question their mothers' directives. By contrast, the use of an appeal to middle-class children as persons allows them to ask 'why' without meeting their mother in head-on collision. 'For the lower working class child to contest the validity of a positional appeal or imperative is to challenge the authority of the mother. A middle-class child can question the empirical basis of personal appeals without necessarily evoking such a confrontation' (Robinson 1972 p. 178).

An earlier experiment cited by Robinson sought to discover what answers mothers would make if their child asked them a 'Wh' question. The children were aged five years in this sample. Lower working-class mothers reported that their children might not receive answers: if one was proffered, it would usually be of the 'focus on the proposition' type (e.g. ... always'). Given this response, of course, the lower working-class children's curiosity is being stonewalled. The unspoken message is 'suppress your curiosity.' Lower working-class children were also given less 'referential-type' information (information about the material and social environment) and information was likely, on the face of it, to be less accurate. As Robinson points out, the absence of analogies and other linguistic devices which point outwards serves to reduce the likelihood of knowledge becoming organized. Unlike middle-class mothers, who saw themselves as offering explanations in response to such questions from their children, lower working-class mothers neglected appeals to cause and consequence. The lack of a cogent and coherent 'shape' to lower working-class mothers' replies, implies, as Robinson observes, that what knowledge *is* picked up will be less amenable to structuring. Knowledge cannot easily be 'fixed' in the absence of an interlocking frame of reference, and no frame of reference is being supplied. No doubt this kind of crippling early environment is responsible for the later adverse effects upon school attainment to which J. W. B. Douglas (1964) refers. This 'extreme poverty of environment,' which other research-workers have shown to lead to progressive deterioration in academic ability in North Carolina mill-children and English canal-boat children, is discernible in its effects on children from different social class backgrounds, even if the picture is less extreme. Douglas notes that for all children who are reared in poor homes (in the material sense), middle-class children improve on their 'depressed' test performances between 8 and 11, while working-class children's scores fall off. If then we speculate that lower working-class children, brought up in cramped home surroundings, are fobbed off by their mothers with inadequate explanations and harsh discipline, they still fare worse than their underprivileged middle-class contemporaries. Do lower working-class mothers in straitened circumstances simply have less time for their children than middle-class parents in the same plight? Or is the linguistic environment of the lower working-class gang or street an alternative but equally retarding one? Why does this test-score decline not apply to middle-class children from impoverished homes? In terms of gross exposure to verbal stimuli, some workers have suggested that, compared to the lower working-class, there is much greater richness of verbal interchange between middle-class parent and child: possibly even 'depressed' middle-class families maintain their attitudes and beliefs about the role of the parent in language development, despite downward mobility. The question is unresolved. No doubt subcultural differences, attitudes and folk beliefs towards language and learning are real enough. We should, though, perhaps be on guard against the assumption that deprived children need to be taught *language*. It is the opportunity to exercise linguistic competence, rather than the sheer absence of language, which penalizes the lower working-class or ghetto child. However, Labov's (1969) work on Non-standard Negro English ably testifies, that, given appropriate social settings, linguistic competence is manifestly there in the most deprived ghetto blacks. As Ginsburg (1972) puts it:

> When one considers the fundamentals of cross-cultural language use, it is the similarities, not the differences, that are striking. If this is so, then Labov's work on Negro speech should not be thought to yield results that are surprising. Quite the contrary: it is the conventional wisdom, that of Bereiter and Engelmann, for example, which is hard to explain.

Jules Henry, an American social anthropologist, would no doubt find the lower working-class mothers' covert beliefs about how children learn puzzling. For, as he points out in *Essays on Education* (1971), the universal assumption in preliterate societies is that children do not 'naturally' learn by spontaneous imitation. In this respect, middle-class mothers' attitudes seem to be closer to the universal norm and lower working-class mothers are deviant! Moreover, Henry argues that it is an empirical finding that, for the children in all societies studied by anthropologists, learning of adult techniques has typically been seen by them as the only route to status in their societies. Compelled to rely on more knowledgeable and higher-status persons in order to ascend on the status escalator, or merely to stay in the same place, children have not been expected to look forward to being adult: 'Over and over again, the data shows that children have had to be urged up the status ladder by rewards, punishments and other even more complex devices.... From the standpoint of the child, he must climb the status ladder or suffer the consequences of dependence and deviance.' Such evidence might unwittingly serve as a neat articulation of Western middle-class attitudes towards formal education: namely, that it provides the only secure route to prestigious white-collar and professional employment and lifestyles!

What of deprived communities, subcultures, castes or classes *within* a society? How are they to view learning, given their inferior position in the wider community? Henry points out that in highly elaborated cultures such as our own, the problem has been to transmit the enormous amount which has to be learned to the next generation. Education could be prolonged indefinitely. A solution has been arived at by assigning different activities to different social groups, and ascribing prestige to some but not all these activities. Certain activities, those involving symbolic manipulation of the kind practised by non-manual clerical and professional workers for example, have been awarded higher standing than others. Such employment requires a lengthy formal education—in some cases a third of the lifespan—and status has been conferred by time invested in acquiring education. High or upwardly mobile persons typically have received more education than stationary, low or downwardly mobile ones. Thus, argues Henry, so-called 'social' drives or 'needs' to achieve, to get on, etc, are heavily impregnated with middle-class values. The notions serving to organize middle-class behaviour, like 'achievement' and 'security', are on a bipolar dimension: at the other end of the continuum we find their opposites, 'failure' and 'insecurity'. Adverting to the *phenomenology* of middle-class culture—the hold-all of inert or unexamined ideas and beliefs held by members of the culture—Henry singles out certain salient dimensions. He maintains that middle-class culture holds concepts such as 'hope', 'time' and 'self' as axiomatic or self-evident. Such concepts are by no means universally held, however, and they are likely to be glaringly absent in the case of, say, ghetto blacks in American cities, rural blacks or poor whites elsewhere, and in those families in this country whose incomes fall below the poverty line. Henry illustrates the way in which the very notion of time implies a past and a present from which one can move to a more satisfactory future. These received ideas are closely interlinked, and if they are lacking, all organization of behaviour will be lacking and there will be no conception of organization as such. Henry offers the following example of a temporal dimension: 'Even when we say "Billy no longer wets the bed" we mean that *in the course of time* Billy stopped wetting the bed, although he used to do it. We can therefore imagine that the parent who has no hope has no conception of his child's stopping wetting the bed.'

Henry demonstrates how the concept of 'self' is itself located in a dimension of time. Self implies sub-concepts of past, present and future. To see self as a process (as an upwardly mobile person must) in which change is possible, we need to reflect on our own self as it was, is now and may be made to become. To have such a viewpoint is to see the need to organize our life to bring about the desired future state. If, however, our picture of the world lacks any notion of past, present and future, our behaviour will seem to be disorganized. A 'survival self' will remain, and for this self, only those objects which contribute to our continued functioning will achieve any salience. Other dimensions of experience will drop from our world-view and in this 'flight from death', only percep-

E

tions making directly for survival will register. Other perceptions, other social objects and the way we think about them, will move out of focus. Henry describes a Negro housing project in an American city. Most of the people in the project who are employed have poor, marginal and insecure jobs. In these people, he affirms, the survival self in its flight from death 'becomes preoccupied with activities that give it the most intense sensation of being alive; it is a self that has, at every moment, to feel its life.' He continues:

> Though the Project is almost literally a 'City of Women', for a very large number of husbands are transient or have deserted, we find women talking about husbands as if they existed, and we find unemployed men talking as if they had jobs. In addition, there is the constant effort to build one's self up by inflating one's self, by spending one's money on very expensive clothes and by getting the better of another person.

Thus achievement is delusional also. Locked in a vicious circle of hopelessness by family poverty, skin colour, inadequate or unstable adult models, and the deployment of scarce resources in this 'delusional' manner, black children on the estate lack both any hope of achievement and any fear of failure. The psychological and attendant physical disorganization as it affects a seven-year-old boy on the Project is given in the Readings to this chapter.

In a subculture lacking the prerequisite *order* for middle-class achievement, then, 'learning' will not be a salient percept; if thought about at all, it will be assumed that that is something which happens in 'their' schools and is 'done to' 'our' children. The boundary which lower working-class mothers appear to perceive between school concerns and the different concerns of the mother-at-home lend some support to this speculation. It is not, incidentally, being contended that there is a one-to-one correspondence between black Negro deprivation and the deprivation encountered by Clegg and Megson (1968) in the West Riding, for example. But the disorganization permeating the Project blacks' lifestyles seems a powerful suggestive concept for conceptualizing class attitudes towards socialization and the role the school plays in this process.

Sir Cyril Burt in his classic study *The Backward Child* (1937), remarks: 'If I had to single out one factor in the home which bore the closest relationship to the child's school progress, it would not be the economic or industrial status of the family but the efficiency of the mother.' Wiseman in *Educational Research in Britain* (1968), citing findings from his Manchester surveys of 1951 and 1957, observes:

> The social variables that are strongly associated with educational attainment are certainly economic. . . . But there are stronger associations with such variables as number of NSPCC cases of cruelty and

neglect, number of committals to care, and lack of immunization to whooping cough and diphtheria. . . . Then there is a group of variables, associated with these, but emphasizing dirt rather than the more psychological aspects of maternal care; verminous conditions, scabies, and cleansing notices. These are particularly associated with low percentages of high-scoring children.

Summarizing a subsequent 1963 inquiry, Wiseman notes that factors in the home environment are overwhelmingly more important than those of the neighbourhood or the school. Of these home influences, factors of maternal care and of parental attitude to education, school and books are of far greater significance than social class and occupational level. He points in his discussion to a curious contrast between brightness and backwardness. The factors associated (statistically) with backwardness tend to be those denoting maternal attitude to the *child*, while for brightness the parents' attitude to *education* seems the more important.

Yorkshire teachers (Clegg 1972) working with deprived children in primary schools were able to list over 70 symptoms of deprivation which quite clearly vitiated any learning processes which might be started in the children. The traits ranged from poor, dirty or frayed clothes to behavioural indices such as 'acquisitiveness, unpunctuality, hunger, destructiveness—children at youngest level chew things—stealing, if only to give away.' It is hardly surprising that Douglas's longitudinal survey of children born in the first week of March 1946, based on a national sample, should confirm statistically the raw facts as described by these teachers. Douglas's analyses of test results (verbal-NV intelligence, and attainment tests) reveals a considerable inter-correlation between school success and the influence on teachers of pupils' home backgrounds. Certain home environmental factors such as cleanliness and appearance not only correlate with test scores at 8 and 11, but also with whether teachers place a child in a bright stream or a dull stream. Thus, as we have already seen, lower working-class children from homes in which bed-sharing, or a shared kitchen and bathroom, absence of hot running water, etc were the case, obtained even lower scores at 11 than at 8. Middle-class children from rather similar backgrounds actually made up some of their earlier handicap between first and second testing. Of course 'environmental factors' does not only mean poor homes: the degree of parental encouragement, the stream allocated, the school's 11+ record, all play their part. But we are suggesting that *perceived* inadequacy for schooling on the teacher's part damns even the brightest of lower working-class children. Despite the stated intentions of teachers to stream according to measured ability, Douglas (1964) found that judgments of ability are influenced by the children's home backgrounds. Eleven per cent more middle-class children were found in upper streams, and 26 per cent fewer middle-class in lower streams than would be expected by measured ability at age 8.

The standard of maternal care given to these children during the pre-school years has a greater influence than social class on their chances of being put into the upper streams. Those who during the first six years of their lives were said to be dirty, badly clothed and shod are likely to be found in the lower streams.

Douglas concludes by pointing out that there is an allied tendency to put children from large families into the lower streams.

The larger environment plays a crucial role. 'Good' schools were shown to get 11+ successes even in the absence of parental encouragement, the most salient factor of all. If we remember that middle-class parents get their children into these schools—that is, these schools largely recruit middle-class children—and that, in a 'poor' school, even the cumulatively increasing benefit of parental encouragement loses out, we see the makings of a vicious circle. More middle-class than working-class children attend 'good' schools. As a result, school and home mutually reinforce each other for most middle-class children. For working-class children, however, the opposite effect operates: school and home negatively reinforce each other; the school and the home face different directions. Expectation of success is therefore bright for a middle-class, and gloomy for a working-class child. Indeed, Douglas showed that on the basis of measured ability at age 8, 12 of the children assigned to lower streams ought to have gone on to grammar school but only one in fact did so. Obscure expectations of school, coupled with teacher prejudice—albeit unaware—condemn the lower working-class child to the indifferent school with poor facilities and high staff turnover. Within that school he tends to be further discriminated against, and his abilities heavily underestimated. Cramped home conditions, vigorous socialization based on appeals to status, and injunctions which leave no room for argument, cannot but hinder the best intentions of teachers of working-class children. In view of the enormous wastage of talent, and the *absolutely* greater number of working-class children to middle-class children, we make no apology for dwelling at some length on the inequalities which society, through its selection instrument, the primary school, has compounded. As Henry proposes, disorganization is the salient dimension in the psychological universe of the severely deprived. The consequent inability to provide the security, stability and consistency necessary for anxiety-free intellectual functioning surely needs no further documentation.

SECTION 2

Are children marionettes, then, tugged by the wires of family and social class? After all, don't we often decide to grit our teeth and hang on when the going gets tough? Can we, as individuals, really be so vulnerable to our home and school circumstances? Well, it's possible to answer a cautious yes-and-no to this question. On the one hand, there are the 'sunken' middle-class of Jackson and Marsden's working-class sample described in *Education and the Working Class* (1962), whose 'inner-directedness' enabled them to tolerate the alienation they felt in their grammar school. Or the 'common-man boys' of Kahl's 1953 Boston survey who, although fitted by intelligence for white collar college-graduate posts, only stayed on to make college applications when parental pressure was felt and internalized. In a sense, both Yorkshire and Boston parents had one thing in common: a time and hope perspective. Again, it could be argued that Boston and Yorkshire samples contained only upper working-class parents, lodged precariously between the 'rough' or 'common' working-class and the petty bourgeois above. As such, they held on to a vision which was denied the 'disorganized' mass at the bottom rung of the class-ladder. They had known or had perceived middle-class status and manoeuvrability and had seized on the connection between status and book learning.

I referred above to the need to give a cautious answer to the question of vulnerability. For many, such as the Beal family of Cairine Petrie's (1972) book *Backward and Maladjusted Children in Secondary Schools*, life is a constant struggle which psychologically damages the children. Irregular meals, an absent lorry-driver father, a promiscuous, feckless mother, HP debts, rows with the neighbours, petitions for eviction as a result of drunken disturbances—this was the home background of Sheena Beal. Some children from equally tough but not unloving homes 'make' it. Timothy Winters, the anti-hero of Charles Causley's poem of that name, is one such. For still others such as Christina, a girl cited by Mrs Petrie with an IQ of 127 who had written off secondary school and married young after holding an unskilled factory job, adults are written off. For some, a fantasy world is more exciting than drab reality. For lower working-class coloured (and white) boys in a working-class area of Victorian redbrick terraced houses, originally built to house the local biscuit factory and railway workers, in Reading, football means glamour. Of course, football at playtime is a real hard-knock affair. The glamour is following the idolized players of the big national sides, for the local club is not nationally renowned and is therefore not featured on television. Although many of these boys score two or more years behind their chronological age on reading and attainment tests, they could name and describe the players, colours and recent successes of 'their' team. It is doubtful whether their sisters and girl classmates had any such fantasy outlets. If not recruited to 'bring up' another brother or sister, these girls were given the freedom of the streets. They were the class tomboys. A finding of the National Child Development Study (Davie 1972) spotlighted class differences in attitudes towards adults. Twice as many working-class as middle-class children had 'written off' adults by age seven. Adults had failed as worthwhile models. It was hard not to try to trace other class-related findings back to the home atmosphere: the lack of forthcomingness, 'inconsequentiality', and restlessness, depression and withdrawal were all symptoms teachers over-ascribed to working-class children. Middle-class children were not so depicted. Boys were more vulnerable and displayed more such symptoms than girls.

Have the pre-school 'short' answers and 'shutups' taken their toll? This apathy, or sabotage of what goes on in class, is surely related to what goes on after school. Adults aren't to be trusted with love. It hurts to be rejected. Reaction to disappointment may take the form of introverted nail-biting or extrovert aggression. No positive 'transference' can be made. Teacher is tarred with the brush—all adults are the same.

Boys, who display more emotional disturbance regardless of social class, appear to have a particularly hard time of it in primary school. The National Child Development Study survey 1972 showed that seven-year old boys sought acceptance from other children in a 3:1 ratio against girls. Their sisters were more anxious for adult acceptance. John Wilson (1965) suggests: 'Boys do not want to be like their mothers, though they want their mothers' love; they want to possess their mothers as their fathers possess them.' Wilson argues that girls have the harder developmental task since they must renounce aggression and initiative, confined as they are by family and society. Girls have to be good *girls*: boys can go it alone and become a *person*. They haven't such a constricting role to perform. However, the evidence from longitudinal surveys such as that of Davie *et al* (1972) fails to confirm Wilson's assessment. Evidence of a biological difference in the behaviour of the sexes, manifest even at the nursery school level, is steadily accumulating. Boys are overtly more active and aggressive than girls as a result of biochemical hormonal differences (Hutt 1972). Any oedipal renunciation of mother that a boy has to make would coincide with school entry. Might it not be a plausible explanation of the different orientation boys demonstrate by seven years of age to look at peer-group importance for boys in terms of both a higher activity level and the difficulty of renouncing mother, while attempting to make a positive 'transference' towards a female adult teacher? Boys would, according to this view, experience conflict in renouncing mother while embracing another adult female model; their sheer activity level would predispose them to seek peer approval; while a combination of these constraints would direct them away from the classroom as a rewarding place to be. Girls, as Wilson suggests, are differently motivated. I find his neat summary of the sexes' infantile dilemma extremely suggestive: 'The girl wants to be desired: the boy to get what he desires.' Whether one accepts that this disposition stems from a perception of what the opposite-sex parent is receiving from the spouse is a separate matter. Such a paradigm would go a long way to explaining why girls toe the line in primary school, despite many a fall from grace. Douglas's (1964) cohort survey reveals that women primary school teachers often underestimate the grammar school potential of their 'idle' or 'unruly' boys. Douglas surmises that many women teachers feel scant sympathy for, or understanding of, boy pupils and one would guess that this quickly becomes apparent to the pupils so disvalued. Of course, women teachers could equally be responding to the innately higher mobility in boys. The resultant exasperation or irritation would, of course, have the same outcome.

The work of Bruner, based on Piaget's pioneering Swiss studies, has confirmed the notion of learning as developmental. Whether such cognitive development has to await the ripening of neural structures before it can proceed need not concern us now. A more practical problem for the teacher is to know if learning can be substantially re-thought on lines which will include both emotion and thinking. Work by George Kelly (*The Psychology of Personal Constructs* 1955) and Richard Jones (*Fantasy and Feeling in Education* 1968) promises to provide teachers with a new way of viewing the educational process. One of the advantages, indeed, of Jones's critique of Bruner is that he brings a clinical expertise to Bruner's mainly cognitive exposition.

Jones contrasts the objectives and outcomes of psychotherapy and instruction and arrives at the following model:

$$
\begin{array}{c}
(\text{imagination} + \text{aloneness} + \text{helplessness}) = \text{anxiety} \longleftarrow \text{psychotherapy} \\
\uparrow \qquad\qquad \updownarrow \qquad\quad \updownarrow \qquad\quad \updownarrow \\
\text{instruction} \longrightarrow (\text{imagination} + \text{community} + \text{mastery}) \; = \; \text{creative learning}
\end{array}
$$

As the diagram hints, the roles of teacher and of therapist can only be superficially likened. For if the therapist's job is to reduce anxiety, the teacher's is to arrange or permit learning to take place. Yet the states which therapist and teacher are handling are, in effect, mirror-images of each other. Jones's argument convincingly assures us that we can better clarify instructional objectives and their employment of fantasy and feeling if we contrast teacher-therapist aims and methods.

According to the Jonesian paradigm, the therapist works to reduce aloneness and helplessness which, unchecked, would lead to anxiety. By contrast, the teacher aims to increase continuity and mastery in order to increase the chances for learning to take place. When our feeling of continuity with others is positively expanded, we learn. Mastery of our environment—enactive, iconic and symbolic mastery—is likewise a necessary but not sufficient condition for learning. If *re-learning*, so to speak, is permitted by the psychotherapeutic process, *first-time learning* is facilitated by instruction. By getting their patients to verbalize their images, therapists are laying the ground for cognitive 'looseness' and revaluation to take place. The activity of befriending which the therapist engages in with the client gives the client courage to share, through words and non-verbal communication, the images which have haunted him.

The images are hopefully exorcised in a 'safe', warm, non-judgmental setting.

A teacher, Jones insists, is in business to stir up images. Unlike the therapist, his aim is to manipulate the aroused images for mastery by the child and to make new perspectives available. The therapist invites the client to offer his images so that, in a relationship, they may be safely 'earthed'. Insight is the therapist's putative goal which he attempts to achieve through sharing and even making use of the patient's fantasies. The teacher, however, seeks 'outsight', which Jones defines as the using and possible sharing of one's images. Poetry, art and creative writing, are well-known ways in which outsight operates in practice.

Jones argues persuasively that, in fact, all forms of instruction are set out, intentionally or otherwise, precisely to appeal to pupils' imaginations. Unfamiliarity magnetizes us and we are pulled along like iron filings. McVicker Hunt (1971) refers to this paradigm as the 'problem of the match'. According to this view, increasingly held by developmental psychologists, the teacher should not adopt a passive stance. It is no longer a question of waiting on some supposed 'readiness' which will emerge in its own good time. Rather, as teachers, we need to be vigilant to attend to recognizable cues of interest or surprise.

'On the whole, *I contend that when the child is not interested, when he's bored, then one had better increase the complexity of the circumstances that the child is able to encounter.*' There is a wealth of evidence both from animal psychology and from child development studies that repeated encounters with patterned 'input' induces habituation: recognition provides security ('recognitive familiarity') which novel stimuli incite one to leave, and from which one can explore. 'When one is completely surrounded by the strange and complex, it is as difficult to learn as when one is surrounded by the boringly familiar' (McVicar Hunt 1971). The pre-school life of the deprived child is deprived in that it lacks the opportunities for code-switching from restricted to elaborated which the school takes for granted. Linguistic and therefore cognitive development has been stunted. The demands of a school environment place crippling burdens on the child. It resembles an athletics match for which some of the athletes have had no prior track or field training. We know that, for reasons which are not entirely clear, overcrowding and lack of basic amenities are implicated in a nine month retardation in reading skills at age seven (Davie *et al* 1972). Is such retardation the outcome of a pervasive feeling of helplessness, when confronted by the organized sequencing of learning which a formal curriculum presents? Is the school environment perhaps too complex and strange in its demands —the mismatch too great—to permit coping?

The home allows of no 'mastery' or 'community' amid the material and psychological disorganization referred to earlier. Specifically, the home, for too many lower working-class children, has not offered its pre-school members the opportunity of experiencing sequenced learning. An

American study demonstrated that when mothers were given instructions on how to operate a 'magic pen' which traced horizontal or vertical lines and then instructed their 5-year-old children to execute a drawing, the lower working-class mothers gave fewer, less explicit and more ad hoc instructions to their children than mothers of higher socio-economic status. Middle-class mothers were far superior teachers. How far peers and siblings introduce younger children to useful learning roles is not well documented. Common sense would suggest that a great deal of intensive verbal and motor learning *is* mediated by children at play. Be that as it may, the deprived child will lack a baseline of *recognitive familiarity* on entry to school which will be a severe disqualification. Research into mother-child interaction quoted by Robinson (1972) reveals striking differences in school preparation along subcultural lines. The middle-class child can expect to be told that school will be an interesting place and that any problems or difficulties can be taken to the teacher, who will temporarily take Mummy's place. Not so for the working-class child. From the protocols Robinson cites, the working-class child is simply likely to be told that he is going to school, that he must be good, and must always do what the teacher tells him. No question here of the teacher being seen as a helpful adult: teacher is presented as a disciplinarian figure from whom there is no appeal. Such preambles merely transfer the home's child-rearing schedules, with all their emotional undertones, on to the school. One is reminded of the West Indian father who told his son's primary school teacher: 'You stick 'im, mister!'

Of course, adequate emotional preparation for school is less a matter of class subcultural differences in raising children than it is related to family subcultures. Mothers who have themselves failed to outgrow dependency needs on mothers or grandmothers may use their children as confidants or props. The mother who hovers at the school gate, who insists unnecessarily in accompanying a six-year-old to school, communicates her own anxieties to the child. School is felt, through non-verbal channels of communication, to be a fearful place. All too often, this maternal insecurity filters through to the child. Home is safe: school is dangerous. The dependent child and the future school-phobic child is thus bred.

The intimate relationship between anxiety and learning has been a preoccupation of psychologists for as long as learning has held the centre of the stage in the academic study of psychology in this country and abroad. More effort has been invested in learning and what impedes or facilitates it than any other area. Not surprisingly, the disorientating effects of excessive arousal on learning and behaviour have been investigated both in laboratory animals and in man: two world wars have all too readily provided human 'subjects'. An easily available introduction to the field is provided by D. O. Hebb's article 'Drives and the conceptual nervous system' (1971). Briefly, the matter can be stated as follows: the arousal system located in the brain stem mediates learning: learning cannot take place in the absence of arousal. When the organism is in a state

73

of low arousal (as, for example, upon waking from sleep), responses leading to increased stimulation will generally be repeated until a given arousal-level is reached. As responses are emitted up to this optimal point, the subject will report interest or enjoyment. At the level of optimal arousal, tasks will be performed with zest and efficiency. If, however, the level of arousal is increased by further stimulation, responses will evince increasing disruption and disorganization. The organism will now exhibit random emotional responses, or even freeze into apathy. The severely impaired performance of soldiers in battle conditions, such as blind firing, ignoring orders or flight, lends common sense support to this model of arousal.

A crude measure of arousal in human beings is *emotionality*. This refers to the differential extent of arousal which the autonomic nervous system can muster in preparation for fight-flight. Eysenck (1969) has brought forward evidence that constitutional factors primarily determine the level of one's emotionality. Eysenck's 'emotional extroverts' appear to be more at risk, in terms of the effect their temperament exerts on learning situations, than other groups. Up to 14 or 15 years, stable extrovert children appear to do well at school although this is a personality constellation which favours girls. After early- to mid-adolescence, however, introverted students come into their own, and success at university level appears to be the preserve of the neurotic introvert! However, the matter, especially at the higher education level, is far from resolved. Cluster analysis is currently being employed by Professor Noel Entwistle at Lancaster University, in an effort to utilize data from paper-and-pencil inventories of personality, achievement motivation, study habits and attainment/intelligence.

A clinically-rooted approach to investigating the relationship between personality and learning is suggested by a consideration of Kelly's *The Psychology of Personal Constructs*, published in 1955. Bannister and Fransella, in their appraisal of Kelly's work (1972) describe personal contruct theory as 'an attempt to understand people in terms of the way each experiences the world, and to understand their behaviour in terms of what it is designed to signify for the behaving person.' Sensitive clinicians have always, of course, attempted to get inside their clients' skins by empathy, but the formulation of an orientation to psychology which makes no distinction between an observing scientist-psychologist and an observed patient-subject is relatively new. Since, from the Kellian standpoint, each of us formulates constructs of our world the better to make sense of it, the psychologists' constructs are as open to review and revision as anybody else's. The model of man that Kelly invokes is that of *the scientist*. We each proceed as our own experimenter, testing out our expectations (hypotheses) about our world. These expectations may subsequently be justified (our hypotheses are confirmed) or come to grief (our hypotheses are invalidated). We thus maintain our constructs, or discard them and fabricate new ones.

The distinction in Western philosophical thought between a thinking and a feeling being has hindered psychology's attempts to conceptualize the notions of *cognition* and *affect*. For Kelly, as Bannister and Fransella point out, 'such a dualism is a badly articulated attempt to cope with the fact that man is a process and that at different stages in the process very different modes of experience and activity obtain.'

This novel depiction of man as a process rather than an entity at once betrays the textbook arbitrariness of much of our thinking about human beings. Immediately we are freed from an over-anxious concern to keep emotions out of the classroom. We realize, not unlike M. Jourdain and his prose, that we have known this all our lives. Knowledge was formerly connoted by the word 'wit'. This may also have had the connotation of 'inspiration', as in 'Whit Sunday', the day the gift of tongues was granted to the apostles. 'Wit' in the eighteenth century sense and today conveys aptness and saltiness. Learning has always been associated with an *attitude* towards the world. As 'bright' and 'dull'—favourite epithets of teachers—imply, dullness is emotionally flat, brightness something which dazzles and catches the eye.

Suppose teachers deliberately went out of their way to encourage children *to imagine*: the results would be unpredictable but possibly quite devastating. Of course, a teacher who rules his class with a rod of iron could not expect much of a response if he suddenly bellowed: 'Sandra, tell us your dreams.' Some kind of rapport would be a prerequisite of this kind of work. But it need not, one would have thought, be only the privilege of infants. Certainly, the experimental classes which Bannister *et al* and Jones report on were of an age at which children have not learned to disguise the presentation of self. Moreover, many drama teachers and teachers of English and science—at least those who have thrown out grammar and rote learning of formulae—are already engaging pupils at a personal, inner-life level that is refreshing and offers unforeseen possibilities.

The fantasy play which Mrs Upton, the teacher described by Bannister and Fransella, sponsored, encouraged unpredictable cognitive 'loosening'. Isn't this just what the perceptive drama teacher does in encouraging children to act out a scene from life? Acting, like a fantasy-play, provides an opportunity for trying out other selves—selves we may have been, or prematurely rejected or never dared assume. Fantasy-play, or free association ('What does so-and-so remind you of?') allows children to try out roles, to move beyond self-fixed limits and experiment. Mrs Upton herself took part in the games, suggesting possible new roles for individual children. As when Bruner's four-year-old asked, 'What if there were never any apples?' the fleeting possibility of life being other than it is had been presented. The presentation had been non-threatening and part of a classroom routine. The teacher described by Richard Jones asked her infant class to shut their eyes and describe the passing image aloud and on paper. She also ran a regular 'dreamtime' in which children could air frightening monsters, 'mountain lioneaters', and defuse their nocturnal terrors in the light of day and in good company.

Doubters may object: this sounds like another educational gimmick and indeed, if one could provide no rationale for dream-times, role-playing, drama, dance and the rest, the criticism would stand. Kelly offers an engaging justification. Normally, we make sense of our world by alternating between 'tight' and 'loose' construing. The former involves a few, linked, demarcated and explicit constructs. Our expectations are precise and watertight. The latter implies vague, unrelated and multiple constructs which are inexplicit. Bannister and Fransella cite evidence from group psychotherapy which suggests that prior to revaluing others or ourselves, our constructs are typically loose. We move from firm ground on to the shifting sands of doubt. We admit ambiguity. Dogmatism is displaced by dubiety. As Bannister *et al* (1971) put it, 'we range between "facts" and "dreams". A few brass tacks rescue us from schizophrenia, a fantasy or two from obsessionality.'

This elaboration from tight to loose construing and back again appears to constitute learning. How can we plan for such experiences as will set up the appropriate conditions? Divorce, imprisonment, hospitalization seem rather drastic ways of presenting ourselves with dissonant experience: experience that forces us to elaborate our neat, interrelated constructs into wholly untidy ones. The film footage included in the experimental humanities curriculum project MACOS (Bruner *Man: A Course of Study*) is relevant here. It includes sequences showing Netsilik Eskimoes killing and eating raw caribou meat, seal-hunting and so on. Blood and gore abound. Richard Jones insists that the 'disturbance' evoked by these scenes on the try-out pre-adolescents was a precondition of their learning. If they were to answer the questions 'How is man human, how did he get that way, how can he be made more so?' they must be confronted with 'inhuman' activity. After much discussion, it was decided to have class post-mortem discussions. The teacher posed leading and provocative questions. The children were forced to forge a link between their own circumstances in well-heeled American suburbia and their possible behaviour if forced to live off the wild-life of an Arctic biosphere. The dance teacher, whose lessons following the films had been deluged with requests for dances embodying Death, was reassured. Discussion- and-imagination: a *timetabled* elaboration of tight into loose construing did the trick. Images could be safely 'earthed' in community. Mastery and outsight could be established.

Can teachers get off their pedestals and risk putting their own emotions on display? A headmistress was reported to have told an in-service tutor who counselled small 'human relations' classes in which girls could openly discuss their fears and hopes, 'But that would mean revealing *my* emotions!' It is probably easier for infant and even junior teachers, whose roles may be more flexible and more inclusive, to show how they feel. Nevertheless, a number of secondary teachers are employed—at least in girls' schools—as non-directive 'leaders' of small-group classes.

Secondary schools are increasingly taking on the characteristics of 'total institutions' such as mental hospitals, convents or prisons. They resemble more, perhaps, old-style asylums and gaols, for group psychotherapy on a daily basis is now a feature of many psychiatric hospitals built to accommodate hundreds of patients, as it is of medium-stay prisons like Aylesbury and openly therapeutically-oriented ones like Grendon Underwood. To avoid the wholly destructive possibilities of turning human beings, however mad or bad, into cabbages, prisons and hospitals alike are building face-to-face encounters into their daily regime. Paradoxically, schools which as 'grammar' schools once met in a tiny gallery above the church porch, have swollen into lonely crowds. Children switch teachers and classrooms at the drop of a hat, and although lip-service is paid to form tutors, one suspects that the bad old days of peremptorily taking the register and dinner-money have not altogether passed away. Indeed, primary schools, where a 'primary group' provides security and belonging to children even when it is forty strong, have their problems. Women teachers, one has noted, often affect an unnatural BBC accent when holding a post in a lower middle-class school. As if to say, amid the cramped surroundings in which 'hall' does for gym, prayers, classrooms and midday dinner, 'We are in the school but not of it.'

We must perhaps plan more consciously than in the past for middle- and secondary-schools which permit more face-to-face contact; for teachers who can be assigned a class for three years and move up with it; and for sensitivity and T-group training for teacher trainees as a part of their induction or even 'professional' year. And for counselling skills, at present expensively packaged for a few on a one year course, to be part of the standard repertoire for anyone who enters the teaching profession. Medicine, possibly an even more conservative calling than education, now exposes medical students to psychiatry; in the same way if teacher-training is taught in polytechnic institutions in the future, teachers will doubtless press for the kind of training in social skills deemed necessary only for social workers at present. Gowns, as status symbols in secondary schools, and posh accents, as insulation-markers in primaries, will be museum pieces. Relatedness rather than exclusivity will characterize the middle and secondary school as it has begun to characterize the prison and the asylum.

It may be utopian in 1974 to hope for architectural sub-grouping: cottage schools, so to speak. Yet pioneering psychiatrists such as Maxwell Jones have championed the notion of a social psychiatry in which family groups, family treatment within the home and community clinics, will be the treatment agents. Already, hostels run by a warden have been brought into use for treatment of neurotic patients. These family-type sub-communities provide the privacy yet intimacy in which persons, rather than well-adjusted institutional robots, can function. The de-schooling movement which Illich and Reimer have recently argued for, is implicitly an appeal for face-to-face learning situations. Illich looks to coffee-shops, kiosks, abandoned school-buildings, and traffic-free city centres as learning areas. His suggestion that society can be remade if formal 'schooling'—an institutionalization—is removed, depends significantly on unplanned (in an institutional sense) encounters.

It is tempting to speculate upon a system of 'learning centres' which might bridge the gap—both architecturally and ideologically—between radical reformist thinkers such as Halsey and 'revolutionary' writers such as Reimer and Illich (1971). It is noteworthy, perhaps, that in their articulated planning for 'positive discrimination' for the disadvantaged, Halsey and his team (DES 1972) propose two innovations which would, in fact, deinstitutionalize schooling while maintaining it under another guise. Thus, their suggestion that mothers of pre-nursery children might be used, as they have been in the West Riding, to instruct their children with provided learning materials, is to make parents into teachers. Similarly, their community school sees itself as furthering the Liverpool experiment: mothers were invited in, first for coffee, later for the whole morning. School 'advertisements' were posted in stores and PR outdoor murals proclaimed to Liverpool 8 that the school belonged to the people of the district. The Halsey Report makes a plea for educational visitors who will '[explain] the aims and methods of the schools' and '[encourage] parents to recognize and have confidence in their own capacity to teach.'

So far, so good. It is difficult not to applaud this attack on the offerings hitherto placed before the 'poor' children of our inner city ghettoes, one-industry towns, and dehumanized housing estates. This involvement of parents, social workers and educational home-school visitors appears to stress self-help. Community—whatever that ambiguous word may mean —could take on attributes of sturdy independence, socially responsive agencies. Likewise schools could appear not as missionary outposts in benighted, cultureless wastelands, but as local as the town football team, run by teachers in cooperation with parents who have *themselves* functioned, at least with their toddlers, as educators.

'Promoting partnership on the school premises' may be a way of promoting local interest in the education of 'our' children by 'us'. But parents are not to be let off lightly. 'In Liverpool, the most profitable focus for this participation was found to be the school classroom. . . . These began . . . as "coffee mornings" but widened encouragingly into the afternoon and evening, with parents joining their children working in groups. The success of the evening efforts, when fathers and working mothers had an opportunity to engage themselves, also points to the possibility of weekends as well as evenings as a viable time for schooling.' (Halsey 1972 p. 192)

The heart of the positive discrimination programme is reached on p. 195:

EPA community education, as an element in community development, is about moving on, not standing still. It is about the formation of social personalities with the attributes of constructive discontent. It is about children who are made eager apprentices of community life. . . . [EPA] children, as junior citizens, should be forewarned and forearmed for the struggle. Teachers need to be sensitive to the social and moral climate in which their children are growing up. The application of teaching virtues to a compassionate, tolerant and critical examination of all social, political and moral issues is the highest hurdle along the road to a community oriented curriculum. It could take years and it will require a generous and sympathetic change of heart, not only among educational authorities but in society at large.

This philosophy is old Dewey writ large. Indeed earlier, the Report speaks of having redefined the community school 'as a broad aspect of the community itself. . . . Thus the community school seeks almost to obliterate the boundary between school and community, to turn the community into a school and the school into a community' (p. 189). All this is anathema to those who see the schools as 'processing' consumers and producers of the society which has set them up for this purpose, and we must return to meet their criticisms shortly.

Impressionistic evidence is provided for the ideological position of Illich and Reimer by sensitive classroom teacher-observers such as John Holt (1964). While Holt appears to confuse learning-styles—essentially ways of processing information—with attitudes to learning, his contribution to the debate which Illich and Reimer have entered is salient. It is perhaps, unlikely that the impulsive or unreflective child is necessarily to be characterized as one who cannot tolerate existential uncertainty or feels a lack of trust: reflectivity need not mean that 'the universe can be trusted' even when it *appears* bizarre! But if Holt is confusing a preferred learning style with a personality dimension, he is perceptive in sketching ways in which children actually operate in the classroom. 'Minimaxing', a means of playing for the safe answer: giving the air of understanding when confusion reigns beneath; watching posture, voice and movement for clues to the 'right' answer—every teacher can bear out Holt a thousand times. Why are children aghast at the epithet 'stupid'? Why do they put so much intelligence into devising teacher-deceiving strategies?

Interestingly enough, we can observe 11-year-olds operating in the same way in the secondary classes described by Douglas Barnes (1969). We can read the transcripts of lessons in which the pupils scan the teacher's language (and face, no doubt) for cues to help them give the teacher what he wants. If Barnes's work is confirmed elsewhere, Holt's uncertainty as to where to lay the blame may be answered. While inappropriate learning-styles and fear of being found wrong are important, much of the failure of children to inspect their own thinking may be a habituation-phenomenon.

Teachers, in this view, are too busy extracting the right answer rather than requiring any thinking of pupils. A failure to inspect their own teaching language leads to 'classroomese' and boredom. Values, as Reimer points out, are reversed upon school entry. Whereas before initiative in achievement was praised, now others—the teachers—decide on what shall be learnt, how and when. In short, according to Reimer, what is learned through the pores is how to conform.

May not the apathy, the occasional desperation that Holt records, be explicable in terms of values? The powerfully reinforced drive to conform in an institution that a sociologist would describe as semitotal would seem to meet little discouragement from teachers. Hair length, trouser and skirt-width, or height above knee, are familiar obsessions of teachers —at least when they become headmasters. Perhaps the rush to conform which marks adolescent behaviour inside and outside school derives in some part from the stress which teachers lay upon not doing your own thing.

Perhaps, too, the way in which schools function as selection agencies for society at large rubs off on pupils in a more insidious way than we realized. Access to jobs, social status and power in society, is channelled through the schools. If one gets on the right escalator, so to speak, there's no need to walk up the stairs. And if one misses it, there's little point in doing anything anyhow. Passivity is required of one by the system.

Thus, if the school has become the prime device for distributing values in all countries, one can share the Halsey Report's concern even if dissenting from its proposals for remedying the situation. The final section of this chapter will therefore attempt to examine some of the alternatives which would respond to the demands of social justice. It will also look briefly at such evidence we have for suggesting that learning situations, to be in any way effective, must cater for individual differences and must, wherever possible, be programmed in groups. Groups, however, are envisaged as being smaller, more human and less artificially constituted than the grammar school class: a better model would be the clustering of learners found in go-ahead infant schools.

SECTION 3

Despite the different orientations of the research team that produced *Educational Priority* (DES 1972) and those writers who advocate alternatives in education, there are still surprising and hopeful parallels—even convergences—in their ideas. Ivan Illich (1971), for instance, claims that the school is as relevant to education as the witch doctor is to medicine. Viewing schools as 'dominating institutions' (to quote Reimer) which are rapidly becoming obsolete, Illich and Reimer argue the case for 'opportunity networks' or 'learning webs' of free learners which are championed as the structures of the future. Yet even these de-schooling proposals, like the 'free schools' which have already been set up in some of

80

our big cities, can't help being located in some social context. There must be buildings, equipment and instructors, that is, plant and personnel. Illich for one does not dodge this problem. A radical change in society's use of the environment is a precondition for renewing society through learning.

Kiosks dispensing books and records; viewing screens in city streets; traffic-free pedestrian walkways in which young people and old can work and learn; informal meetings in downtown coffee shops, or even trains: the vision is of a purposeful, self-motivated community, in which continuing education is embedded in society's very fibres by ensuring that teachers of skills can only become masters of their craft *if they share their skills with others*. Personal development is made to depend upon communal action. Mutuality replaces competition. Liberal education, for Illich, is ultimately a dialogue between *equals*. Progression in the acquisition of skills, therefore, is dependent not only on sharing these skills with others but on a benevolently disinterested beaurocracy—a group reminiscent of the Party in Marxist theory—who will administrate and counsel. This infra-structure will arrange for students to be put in touch with instructors, and will manage the clearing house on which interchange of skills and ideas must rest. Masters will thus attract pupils—for wisdom is higher than skill, and the ultimate aim of all learning. The metaphor is grounded in the apprenticeships and scholarly disciples of a Europe in which master-craftsmen in stone, wood, thatching and seamanship attracted apprentices, and famous theologians were responsible for the growth of the centres of learning such as Bologna, Padua and Paris were in the Middle Ages: universities to which scholars flocked from all over Europe to learn and dispute in Latin.

In delineating four goals for the imminent educational revolution, Illich stresses 'liberation': liberation of access to 'things', freedom to share skills, freedom to call and hold meetings by individuals, and freedom to select one's teacher or professional person on the basis of known excellence. He declares (1971, p. 103): 'Inevitably the deschooling of society will blur the distinctions between economics, education and politics on which the stability of the present world and the stability of nations now rest.'

If this statement is read in conjunction with earlier sketches, a clearer picture emerges of the way which the new society will take shape:

If the goals of learning were no longer dominated by schools and school teachers, the market for learners would be much more various and the definition of 'educational artifacts' would be less restrictive. There could be tool shops, libraries, laboratories and gaming rooms. Photo labs and offset presses would allow neighbourhood newspapers to flourish. Some store front learning centres could contain viewing booths for closed circuit television; others could feature office equipment for use and repair. The juke box or the record

F

players would be commonplace.... The professional personnel needed for this network would be more like custodians ... than like teachers. From the corner biology store, they could refer their clients to the shell collection in the museum.... They could furnish guides for pest control, diet, and other kinds of preventive medicine....

Young people would be no more full-time learners than their parents would be full-time workers. Advocating a system in which 8—14 year olds are employed for a couple of hours each day, Illich comments (p. 85):

> We should ... permit a boy of twelve to become a man fully responsible for his participation in the life of the community. Many 'school age' people know more about their neighbourhood than social workers or councilmen [councillors]. Of course, they also ask more embarrassing questions and propose solutions which threaten the bureaucracy. They should be allowed to come of age so that they could put their knowledge and fact-finding ability to work in the service of a popular Government.

Illich's utopia is oddly reminiscent of the educative community advocated by the Halsey Report. Parents are here assigned a role whose revolutionary nature is cloaked by discretion: the NUT has, in this country, always opposed ancillary teachers! Mothers, then, are to structure their child's learning with Piaget-type experiments before nursery school. In the school proper, mothers (and fathers) are welcomed in for coffee, to see how children are progressing, and to use the centre for their own education in the evening. But, reading between the lines, there seems to be no sharp distinction in the authors' minds between parents and teachers. No doubt mothers *will* help out; fathers *will* come along and help with displays. But they will be 'teaching' too. Teaching, in this 'community' environment, in which the curriculum will be 'social' rather than academic, (according to Midwinter), will be the privilege of all. As the Report says (DES 1972, p. 189), 'the community school seeks almost to obliterate the boundary between school and community, to turn the community into a school and the school into a community.' Besides blurring the roles of parent and teacher, the role of teacher and learner are also dissolved into each other (p. 189): 'It [the community school] emphasizes both teaching and learning roles for all social positions so that children may teach and teachers learn as well as *vice versa*, and parents may do both instead of neither.'

The tool subjects, the three Rs, are seen as being 'social' skills in that they will facilitate social reconstruction: for children are to be co-partners in neighbourhood renewal. 'Junior citizens' the Report calls them, and this renewal will demand a quality of dissent within the law—'constructive discontent'—which will be generated and disseminated at the grass-roots of the urban ghetto. As the Report is careful to spell out, all this means is that the teacher will no longer have to stand as scapegoat for social pathology. Drugs and delinquency will be as much 'our' fault as 'theirs'. Indeed, there will be no such distinction between 'in' and 'out' groups.

What emerges from the juxtaposition of Illich and Halsey is that their goals are basically convergent, if not identical: A society made new through 'community'. But whereas Illich sees de-structuring bureaucracy and social institutions as the road to this goal, Halsey looks to *more* schooling, albeit of a radically different kind to what we have now, to achieve this end. The third possibility—a system of independent schools existing outside the present LEA structure—is one which might be canvassed for a number of reasons. These schools, which have already sprung up in Islington, London, central Liverpool, and for a time in Manchester, are able to obtain some local authority funding for the 'evening activities' which they run. The teachers in these so called free schools, however, do not differentiate one part of the school day from another. They have had considerable success in providing learning experiences—a jargon phrase which is necessary here—for lower working-class children who may have dropped out of conventional school for as many as two years. Pottery, astronomy, table-tennis, reading and painting are some of the activities which these schools have, or are trying to, mount. They are springing up at a time when truancy figures for big conurbations like greater London reveal that many children at primary and secondary school are quietly dropping out on a large scale. The discreet visits to such schools of Chief Education Officers, teacher-trainers and the like, suggest that desperate measures require desperate remedies—at least as viewed in conventional terms.

However, the psychological *raison d'être* for such a system of 'alternative schooling' is readily to hand. Theoreticians of such differing persuasions as Eysenck and Hunt have respectively argued for the provision of flexible learning areas in classrooms to cater for personality differences, and for re-thinking our whole attitude to the act of teaching. 'Inasmuch as the optimum rate of intellectual development would mean also self-directing interest and curiosity and genuine pleasure in intellectual activity, promoting intellectual development properly need imply nothing like the grim urgency which has been associated with "pushing" children.' This relaxed attitude to learning (McVicker Hunt 1961, p. 363), could have come from the lips of Illich, Reimer or a Free School organizer, although it was in fact expressed some eleven years before Illich or Halsey were published.

Liam Hudson's (1970) research into learning styles does not in itself imply any modification in institutional procedures. Nevertheless, the varied and preferred ways in which we process information does seem to have important implications for the way in which learning is organized. Hudson's work suggests that schools prefer conformists. His experimental design allocated adolescent subjects into 'high' or 'low' on convergent (IQ-type) or divergent (free-association type) test responses. Moreover there is some evidence that 'democratically' organized schools evoke significantly more divergent thinking—so-called 'creativity' tests— than conventionally organized schools. If one couples this observation with an established trend for divergers to pursue arts and convergers science courses, one can see how institutions may in fact be promoting only one kind of learning: that of the learner who is happy and successful at producing the 'right' responses to a curriculum but finds a novel or unusual response difficult to make. Science courses at school have hitherto placed a premium upon correct recall of formulae rather than upon the acquisition of principles. Today, however, the problem-oriented approach of the Nuffield Science schemes may well be encouraging divergent thinking.

Preliminary experiments show convergers to be more 'syllabus bound' than divergers. 'Sylbs' accept the chore of sticking to the restrictions of a syllabus, whereas syllabus-free pupils, or 'sylfs', actively resent and dislike the constraints imposed. This finding has implications too for the ways in which institutions organize learning. Sylbs have featured in Cambridge University student breakdowns: neurosis was triggered by a syllabus which was frighteningly impossible to cover. At Cambridge, Massachussetts, MIT graduate students resisted attempts to open up discussion 'off' the exam topic. One such attempt by an enthusiastic young professor to introduce Einstein's ideas was followed by a mid-sentence interruption—'Have you marked the quiz?' (Hudson 1970).

The accumulating evidence on the constraints which institutions impose on learning suggests that deschooling in some form would actually *increase* comprehension and serve to maximize cognitive growth. The impressionistic evidence quoted by Ruth Beard (1970) evokes the sense of institutions paying lip service to inquiry but demanding conformity:

... you want to do so much, and you're only given the chance to do so little—for instance attending lectures in the evenings by other societies, reading more widely. I can remember when I first came up, the Vice-Chancellor said that the essence of university was that you should be intellectually excited. But if you are, there is very little chance of fulfilling or satisfying that excitement. (Southampton law student, quoted by Beard).

All sorts of questions are raised here—the alleged knowledge 'explosion', the differing perceptions of institutions held by senior staff and students, the role of the teacher. Ultimately, we have to decide on the kind of society we want and only then can we look at the agencies which handle the transmission of knowledge and attempt to reach agreement on what their functions should be.

Nineteenth century elementary schools taught low-level skills fairly successfully—indeed one might argue that it was *because* society knew what it wanted from its army of literate clerks, factory-workers, shop-keepers and operatives that its schools were relatively sucressful. Yet the three Rs were acquired at the enormous expense of children's feelings, life-experiences, quiddities. None of these were tapped, nor their existence acknowledged. We cannot gauge how much intellectual erosion was created by such a bleak instructional climate.

In a 20th century in which 70% of the jobs that children will do have not yet been invented, learning, its content, and its method, will doubtless require a different ordering.

The old shibboleths of fixed intelligence, and the 11+ as an index of fitness to receive 'academic' education, are slowly disappearing. Syllabuses, both at school and at university, are often written now with the co-operation of junior members of staff. Some higher education establishments even consult their students on curricular matters. The opportunities of CSE Mode Three, an examination which teachers can write to order, are there to be exploited. Institutional staff are gradually learning to speak as professionals whose first responsibility is to their 'clients' rather than to their administrative head.

In such an uncharted world, *learning to learn* may be as important as the tool-skills of the three Rs were for the 19th century. The constraints of social class, sex, specific aptitudes and subculture will doubtless continue to operate, although we are now beginning to grasp to how far these are cultural artifacts, how far they are irremovable biological blocks. We do know something, at however primitive a level, about learning technology although we have yet to formulate a prescriptive *theory of instruction*. What will count as worthwhile knowledge may prove to be the exciting and knotty problem for the rest of the century: for 'knowledge' is socially defined. Are we to move in the direction of applying the basic skills of communication in the service of campaigning for urban renewal? Will there be a stronger tidal pull towards a different kind of face-to-face group—the experience or encounter group—as counselling and guidance specialists move out into middle and secondary schools and carry their gospel with them? Will individualized instruction remould the face of schooling in Britain as it has in the USA so that the teacher is relegated to the role of a technician who handles the videotape or audio-console?

What counts as knowledge is always a heavily culturally-saturated judgment. It is also, as P. W. Musgrave hints, the central question for the sociologist of education.

SECTION 4: READINGS

1 From *The Changing Primary School*
An eighty year old reminisces about his junior school days in a mining village in County Durham.

The teaching staff at the school consisted of the Headmaster—Mr George Askew, who did 90 per cent of the teaching, two teenage male pupil teachers—my brother Tom was one—a female pupil teacher, and two ex PTs of uncertain age. Beck Brown taught Standard 2 and Becky Smiles taught Standard 5. Through all her troubles Becky Smiles tried to maintain a sickly smile, but when aroused by lack of discipline she could box ears and cuff necks in a very determined manner. She carried a small cane, signifying authority, but was not allowed to use it.

Beck Brown had eyes that blinked continually, but were devoid of character. She kept the lesson going in a monotonous way, but made no attempt to maintain her attention. If a pupil became troublesome she sent him out to the schoolmaster's desk for a caning. Mr Askew was a hard worker. For one thing, he did several canings every day—three strokes on each hand and a final flogging over the buttocks at the retreat. He pretended to be upset at these events. I never saw a girl punished in this way. The Headmaster's main job was teaching backward classes, which he did with great energy. Sometimes he would get really roused and literally foamed at the mouth. On these occasions the spray was unpleasant. Mr Askew had a liking for Standard 6. This lesson was supposed to end at noon, but often went on ten or fifteen minutes longer, when the schoolmaster hit on an interesting topic. This aroused resentment with some of the boys. One day about ten of them leaped the school yard wall when the whistle blew for classes at one o'clock. For some reason—or none at all—I was in this group of renegades. We ran up the fields for about two miles. Then we decided we had gone far enough. Enthusiasm having vanished, the question of returning to school was discussed and by common consent we returned to school as fast as we could. As we approached the front door the schoolmaster appeared, cane in hand. He had assembled the whole school in the big room. We were a crestfallen crew. He lined us up, and after a few remarks about wicked boys running away from school, who deserved to be punished, he commenced on No. 1 in the line. That was me. I was the most innocent of the group. With his eyes glaring at me he trimmed the end of his cane with a penknife, and ordered me to hold my hands out. He landed the cane hard and it smarted. Then followed a good flogging. Then he proceeded to the next victim. By the time he reached No. 8 he was short-winded—9 and 10 got off comparatively easily. He ordered us to stay in school at closing-time for more punishment. He kept us waiting while he spent thirty minutes teaching his three pupil teachers.

2 From *And Softly Teach . . .*
Notes from a new teacher's diary. She has been assigned to a class of allegedly unteachable children in a tough north-east school.

November 13th
Gordon Bell quite unreasonable. I tried to discuss his recent behaviour

again with him at playtime, to point out how it hampers us in everything we try to do. He was rather sullen, though not offensively so. After play he came back much more cheerful, quite friendly. He resents correction bitterly, but perhaps this sort of talk does good.

January 13th
In spite of 'improved attitudes' in the last few days Gordon Bell has: climbed into school over the roof after dark (in snow) with his infant brother; stolen two shillings; left the classroom during craft and gone to his father's house for something while I was pre-occupied; gone to the shops and stolen peas, with Jones, during playtime; 'given' all his team house points to get home early; and arranged to stay away from school with David Gray. This afternoon I heard of the plot and sent home for him.

The story of 4C's moods, interests and crises according to my diary is very much the history of Gordon Bell's tempers. He is at the same time the most able, one of the most likeable and one of the hardest to handle boys in the class. Most entries in the diary have a reference to him, both because if anything interesting happens, or anything is well made, he has had a hand in it, and also because he is near the centre of any trouble or ill-feeling. The record of our 'hikes' very largely concerns the way Gordon Bell responded. I have usually tried to include him as often as possible since his need is so great and any progress I make with him immensely benefits the whole class.

Gordon Bell's background is very poor; to survive at all is his achievement. His parents are now divorced. For some time, however, he lived with them while the father's present (second) wife shared the house. Gordon is the eldest of four children, some of them coloured and some belonging to these two wives. Finally the first wife attacked the other woman violently and left the house. The father, according to Gordon's mother, 'turned against Gordon, blaming him for every trouble, even the break-up of the marriage', and she at last took him away to live with her. Most of the Bell children, scattered as they are through the school, are problem children—pilfering and behaving violently. Their father, an unemployed though apparently prosperous man, encourages them to lie and deceive the school about free dinners, etc. Unfortunately for Gordon, the house adjoins the school and he is often sent for by his father, although he always refuses to go. Before I knew his history I used to wonder why he walked by this house stiffly, eyeing it sideways but boasting (as he still does) of his father's car, cine-camera, etc. He now lives with his mother some miles away. When she came to school once after I had realized the situation, I suggested that Gordon should go to the school nearest her new home. She begged that he be allowed to stay where he was. He would soon leave for the secondary school anyway and she might have to give up her home. She seemed a pleasant sympathetic woman and Gordon is very attached to her. He says, though, that she is 'never in of a night'—he gets his own meals. He often brings to school coins, flags, etc, that he gets from the foreign sailors who call for his mother.

The only thing I have not tried is to stop his football since this would be to take away the thing he comes to school for. Last week a more dangerous incident arose through his football. All the boys turned against him when he was unfair in picking a team. This was most unusual since he commands allegiance where he wishes, and I was hopeful he would learn from it. Instead, when another boy provoked him, he attacked with a knife. Luckily it was flat-ended and his stab did no harm. For the next hour and a half I stayed with him and he began to talk more freely about himself. During dinner he shyly told me that 'he'd been sent to hospital because of his temper'. It appears that two years ago, in fury he pushed a child under a car. The child was unhurt, but the driver had stopped and shouted at Gordon, who then threw a stone through the car window. Following this he was sent to a convalescent home for some weeks.

Although he is often so hard to live with there is much to like about Gordon. I believe I am lucky that he has rarely chosen me to quarrel with. While I am constantly protecting others from him, blaming him and seeming to be against him, he sometimes makes deliberate and thought-out overtures to be friendly with me—he asks me to go to the baths, to talk about my family, etc.

3 From *Over the Bridge*

I attribute the miracle to the new spectacles, for it happened only a week or two after that Damascene Saturday night when I walked out of the chemist's shop and saw Lavender Hill, and the sky above it, filled with a Presence of which during my first seven years I had been unaware.

During the succeeding days I never lost for one moment the consciousness of my heightened faculty. I felt it in my fingertips, and in that queer, observing self who had been my companion since I first began to look about me from the cot in my parents' bedroom.

The excitement of this optical stimulation may have put me into a mild fever, for my sleep at night was peopled with great globes of flashing light; and in the daytime I felt my cheeks burning. The second self, the observing self, stepped forward to an even sharper alertness, and I moved under its guidance as though entranced.

Such was my condition one evening after school, when I was sitting at the kitchen table, drawing on a sheet of paper an underground labyrinth, and peopling its corridors and recesses with tiny matchstick figures, a line for the body, four lines for the limbs, and an open dot for the head. This was a pastime to which I had been long addicted but I could now pursue it more minutely.

Tonight, however, I was restless, and I wearied of the game. Bedtime loomed ahead, and I had no inclination to start a new game. Mother or Jack would soon be driving me upstairs. At the moment, they were absent from the kitchen. I looked about me, and saw nothing. I was tired, and not unwilling to go to bed. I looked up at the Swiss clock, in its wooden case on the high shelf over the stove. And I read the time!

At first I could not believe my eyes. The family had wasted hours trying to instruct me in the mystery of the clock face. I was just as dull over this as in the spelling of simple words. The impact on my mind in that instant was so sharp that I have remembered the position of the clock-hands ever since. The time was twenty minutes past six, and the gaslight above the table, over which I leaned and stared, hissed with an occasional impure splutter.

Then, still incredulous, I turned my attention to other objects in the kitchen. On the sewing machine lay Jack's library book, a dirty brown object disguised in a uniform binding with gilt numbers on the back. I picked it up, opened it at the first page, and began to read *The Swiss Family Robinson.*

It is an understatement to say that I began to read. I stepped into another life. I was one of that family on the wrecked ship, passing through the barrier of words, enlarging my small suburban existence by this new dimension. I could not know what was happening, or the scope of this vast inheritance. I heard the sea breaking on the shore of that fortunate island and I shared with Fritz, Ernest, Jack and Franz in establishing ourselves under the palm trees, and in offering up thanksgiving for our safety. I have never lost that island. I have since found Prospero on it, and bewildered princes, learning from them to question destiny and the appearances of the material world. But it remains, and has grown into a larger universe than either intelligence or imagination can comprehend. There have been times when I have confused it with actuality, much to my material detriment, for it is a mistake to come back to this solid earth, still wearing your crown, and making the gestures of a prouder office with which you have invested yourself elsewhere.

At that stage, the enlargement was not literary. The words themselves were not endeared to me. I had merely caught the knack of using them: and how I did it I shall never know, for to say that the subconscious self must have been learning under the dunce's cap does not explain the irrational process.

Mother found me sitting at the table, with the book in front of me, and my breathing body in front of the book. Then Jack followed her, and both of them stood watching for some moments before I jerked my head, saw them, and broke the spell.

'I can read', I said.

4 From *Reuben's Corner*

Our supremely sensitive headmaster had to cope with things other than the physical aspects of poverty. Country children knew about life. As far as we were concerned old Sigmund Freud was not far out when he postulated that experience relating to sex enters into a child's head from infancy. There was not a day when sex did not rear its head, in and out of school. Acute and sustained observation was maintained upon the sex behaviour of animals in the farmers' stockyards. Human refinements were gleaned—mostly on Sunday afternoons—through the absorbing pastime of playing gooseberry on courting couples. There being little incentive or scope for the more usual pastime of train spotting—there were but four trains per weekday upon the single-track line—careful records were mentally made of the sexual prowess of the 'engaged', the 'steadies' and the 'casuals'.

Our classes were always mixed for there was no room for anything else and no point in trying out sex discrimination in village schools. When the girls were engaged in needlework the boys would open their books for silent reading. When the boys had to do a bit of carpentry the girls would have their spell of silent reading. But for them this was a misnomer. They would chatter away, write love letters, ogle the carpentry squad, lift their skirts and do all manner of things to take the boys' mind off tenon saws and chisels. This certainly added to our education.

One day a young Nellie, who sat farthest away from me, sent me a letter.

Dear Ced,
    If you see anything what hangs, pull it.

Love and kisses,
Nellie.

My fly was undone.

But life was going on in other parts of the classroom.

'Come out here, Fred Symonds ... at once. I won't have you eating in class.'

'I ain't eatin', Miss, honest I ain't. I were only chewin' me tongue.'

'Open your mouth!' Mabel looked inside, and sure enough she found nothing but a tongue. 'I don't believe you. You've been eating sweets. Your tongue is stained red. Turn out your pockets!'

Frederick obliged. There was instant confusion. Girls were up on forms, squealing, shrieking, skirts clutched tight to legs. In two seconds flat Mabel Eason joined them. 'Turning out' had produced the following:

One catapult, three snares, one pop-gun, one red handkerchief with white spots, a silver threepenny piece with a hole in it and the havoc maker—as white as snow, with the pinkest of eyes—one albino rat! It had fallen from the slippery desk and run around wildly. The girls remained aloft for some time.

Another day, one of rain and misery, Mabel tried to cheer things up.

'Who would like to come out and recite?'

Not a hand was raised. 'I don't mean a school poem, you can recite one mother has taught you.'

Still not a hand.

90

Then Ethel, the freckled, did her mischief. 'Please, Miss, Ron knows one.'

'Come now, Ronnie. Out the front.'

Blushing, swallowing his spittle, as awkward as a carthorse in a pony-trap, Ronnie lurched out.

'Don't be shy now. Who taught it to you?'

'My Gran, but, er . . .'

'Be a sport. Let's hear it.'

'Roight, then.'

And off he went:

> 'Olly 'ocks an' mistletoe;
> Set the baby on 'is po.
> When 'e's done, wipe 'is bum;
> Show owd Granny what 'e's done.

There were no more invitations to recite poetry that day.

5 From *The Only Child*

The classrooms were dull. They smelt of sand, disinfectant and chalky blackboard dusters. There was a sour chill in the cloakrooms. The walls of some of the classrooms were made of varnished partitions through which you could hear the class next door stodging through the alphabet or the Lord's Prayer or *Thirty Days hath September*. On the walls hung religious pictures, maps of the Empire, photographs from *Child Education*, a large calendar and the alphabet. On the window-sills were bulb vases of dark green glass, and a saucer or two with carrot-tops growing in them. There was nothing of the gaiety and freedom and liveliness of an infant's class today; but I think the class as a whole was a happy one, for we liked our jolly teacher, though I don't believe she taught us very much. I learned to write, painfully gripping the thin ribbed shank of a new school pen, by copying out dozens of times set phrases like 'Virtue is its own Reward.' Those capital Rs were a trial. I remember the funny little exercise books we had to do our writing in, with two very widely-spaced lines to every small page: it was the devil of a job to hold it down, when your steel nib was pressing and pricking the paper. The teacher would walk round, her fat arms comfortably folded over her bust, and tell us to make all our letters slope the same way. This was something I could never do, and it always amazed me, when she extended my down and up strokes with her blue pencil, to see how far from parallel they were. I thought she went out of her way to make my handwriting look worse than it really was.

In class, I was very slow, untidy and silent. I trembled with apprehension nearly all the time. Sums were a mystery to me: I just couldn't add or multiply. The squared paper on which we did sums still makes me unhappy whenever I use it. Reading lessons were a little better, because I didn't mind books. When I first started school, I was able to read fairly well, but there were occasional words that baffled me and held me up. After a few weeks of patient struggling, a dam seemed to burst inside my head: I heard myself reading big words aloud, without much hesitation, and soon I found I could read fluently. The last word to puzzle me was 'laugh.' I remember poring over this odd word in my reader. The sentence ran: 'And so the princess began to laugh and laugh and laugh.' What *could* it be that the princess had begun to do? I was reading aloud, the class listening hard to catch my words, for I had a very soft voice. I came to the first 'laugh,' got my tongue round the 'l,' voiced the 'a,' and—it was like a miracle!—the 'f' sound followed as if instinctively. '*Laugh*!' I said, very slowly. As the other two 'laughs' came with increasing confidence, I really felt like laughing myself, for the first time since I had started school. But I could not imagine why on earth 'augh' should spell 'aff.' I was glad to have mastered the awkward word. Flushed by success, I uttered the first sentence I had ever spontaneously spoken in class:

'Please, miss, doesn't that word *look* as if it's laughing?'

And indeed, those two vowels in the middle of the word looked to me like the open mouth of someone laughing. The other members of the class thought I was 'daft.' The teacher, too, seemed rather taken aback by my question: she was quite a nice woman, but she obviously hadn't looked at the word in that light before.

'Yes, doesn't it?' she replied after a discernible pause, vaguely smiling, narrowing her eyes and putting rather too much 'gush' into her words. I could see she didn't really understand what I meant. Yet I knew I was right, and that she was a booby, and I had one of the few moments of true happiness I ever knew in that school.

Then I asked her why, when the word was written l-a-u-g-h, it was pronounced l-a-f-f.

'Now you little people don't need to worry your heads about that,' she said, and told us to shut our readers.

The USA

6 From *Essays on Education*
David is a five-year-old coloured boy brought up by his great grand-mother, Mrs Thompson, on a low income housing project. James is David's uncle; Sandra is his great aunt. Rachel is a coloured girl of David's age from a stable family. Both families were studied by a 'participant observer' working under Jules Henry.

Observation in David's home
David's home is usually in a state of disarray, while Rachel's is always orderly. The different arrangement of furniture in the two apartments is illustrative. The furniture in David's house is usually covered with an

assortment of articles; outstanding are the persistent piles of clothes that Mrs Thompson is to iron.

The observer [R] asks: 'Whose room is this? Who sleeps here?' Mrs Thompson: 'Room? Whose room? Oh well, I guess it's Josephine's room. I guess she's supposed to sleep here, but you never can tell. The kids just sleep all over. You never know who's going to sleep where. Sometimes I have a hard time finding a place for myself.' R: 'Oh, the kids don't have any special place they have to sleep?' Mrs Thompson: 'No, they just sleep anywhere they want.'

We then watched television and there was very little comment during the programme except for the kids laughing at some of the antics or jokes. When this programme went off, 'Petticoat Junction' came on and we watched it. During this programme, David was sitting over on the bed also. Lila went over to where Mary was and tried to get her to move over so she could sit there too and Mary hit Lila saying, 'Go away, move.' The girls started hitting each other. Mrs Thompson: 'You all stop that. You cut that out. Tillie, give me my switch, give me my belt over there.' Both girls were crying by this time and Tillie looked in a drawer and came out with what seemed to be a plastic-covered extension cord, or a clothes line. It was looped several times over and she gave it to Mrs Thompson who shook it at them saying, 'You all hush up that noise, you just hush up that fuss,' and she sat back down. Lila hit at Mary again. Mrs Thompson: 'I told you about that,' and she got up, and with both hands hit Lila on the ears several times, saying, 'I told you to stop that.' Lila started to cry and Mrs Thompson said, 'Go on in there and clear up them dishes.' On the table, where apparently someone had been eating, were three plates with a lot of bones on them. They looked as if they may have been pig knuckles or pig feet bones. Mrs Thompson: 'Go on in there and start them dishes.' Tillie went also and after a few minutes David went too. R: 'Where is Josephine tonight?' Mrs Thompson: 'Oh, I don't know. I don't know. I'll probably have to send these kids out to her again. I just don't know what I'm going to do with that girl.'

The answer to the question about Josephine is relevant to ghetto life: Josephine is fifteen years old and probably already deep in the ghetto female sexual cycle. Note that Mrs Thompson feels helpless and that she objects to what Josephine is doing, even though she must know that such behaviour is typical. Rejection of the ghetto female sex pattern in judgement, but accepting it eventually as a fact, is characteristic.

The next observation is of James and David. James, arrested because of violence to one of his sisters and for having smashed Mrs Thompson's furniture, has been diagnosed as 'psychopathic personality'. The observation follows.

James entered the room and said to Miss Jones, the researcher, 'You David's teacher? You taking him somewhere?' And [Miss Jones continued] I said, 'No, I'm not a teacher but I'm going to take him out today.' Tillie [a sister] said, 'Granma said he could go. She said he's supposed to go.' James grabbed David, put his arms around him, and all of a sudden slapped him hard on the head. I guess I must have shown some obvious signs of shock because James then rubbed David's head and said, 'He knows I'm not mad at him. He knows the difference between my hitting him when I'm not mad and when I'm mad.' I gave a kind of half-hearted smile, nodded my head, and sat down. When we left, James was careful to pin up David's coat.

In the summer of 1965 David 'took to running away,' says Mrs Thompson, 'with a group of them little bad boys around here.' Sometimes he wouldn't come home until two or three o'clock in the morning. People who knew him would report seeing him all over the place. Once he went all the way down to the river. At her wits' end, Mrs Thompson got somebody to round up David's father, in the hope that he could stop the child from running away. Though David's father shows no interest in him, is not living with David's mother and never appeared in the home, he did come in answer to this summons and, Mrs Thompson said, 'When he brought David back he beat the living daylights out of him. He beat the boy hard for an hour; he just took off his belt and just wore him out.'

When Miss Jones was still getting to know the family, she paid a visit one day, and David, whom she already knew quite well, was called into the room by Mrs Thompson, but was quite shy in responding to Miss Jones:

Mrs Thompson sat down in the armchair by the window and asked me [Miss Jones] if I thought something was wrong with David, if maybe he couldn't learn. She said she tried and tried to get him to speak up and to say something but he just won't. She said she tried to get him in every programme at school and then she corrected herself and said in all the programmes at church. She said that there's going to be an Easter programme and that there was a real good part in it and David was supposed to be in it but he won't say anything. He'll just get up there and mumble and you just can't understand him. She asked me again if I thought there was something wrong with him, that he couldn't learn. I told her I was sure there wasn't. I then asked her what church they attend and she said, 'The People's Church.' She said that 'David just acts so dumb at times.'

Mrs Thompson belittles the other children, and herself. Thus David does not get anything at home which makes him feel intelligent. Observed in kindergarten with his peers at their desks, David is very talkative. When Miss Jones brought him and Rachel to the university to visit me he talked a blue streak, and coherently.

In the next excerpt from Miss Jones' observations we get a good picture of Mrs Thompson's confusion and the lack of respect for her by other adults that come to the house. The reader should recall that Mrs Thompson is illiterate and cannot see well. The Project had been trying to get her to an eye clinic for some time, but in June 1966, we had not yet succeeded, even though we were going to pay the fare and the cost of the glasses.

I [Miss Jones] entered the apartment and sitting on the right-hand side of the table was a white man. On the table was a new portable Singer sewing machine. Mrs Thompson sat down and said that she just wasn't too well, and she had just gotten back from downtown (on a table and chair where the sofa had previously been were a lot of packages) and that that girl (her fifteen-year-old niece) had just talked her out of spending every penny in her pocketbook. She shook her head and said she just didn't know why she had done it, she just didn't know. I asked who she was referring to and she said that she was talking about that big girl that had been there when I was there before. She told me that she had said she wasn't going to buy that girl anything for Easter because she had been disobeying her for about the past three weeks but somehow or other she had talked her downtown and just talked her out of all her money and buying her a new dress, pocketbook, shoes and just everything. She kept repeating that she just didn't know why she had done it. She then asked me if I thought maybe she was losing her mind and I said that these things happen to a lot of people. She shook her head again and repeated that she had said she wasn't going to buy that girl anything. She then said, 'Someone must have sprinkled some gooby dust on her'. . . .

The white man looked in his pocket for something or other and stood up and began talking to Mrs Thompson about this new sewing machine on the table. I think they were continuing the conversation I had interrupted when I arrived. Mrs Thompson told me that she would have to give him the $12 next week and that she guessed he'd take the new machine back and she'd keep her old machine until she had the money and the salesman said it was supposed to be $20, that she had already given him $8 so she could keep the new machine and he'd just pick up the money next week. She said no, she guessed he'd better take the new machine on back until next week because you're supposed to have the $20. The salesman then explained that the $20 had already been paid to the company, that he had taken the $8 she had given him and put the other $12 in from his own pocket and given it to the company; so the $12 she would give him next week would be his, and the company had its money for the machine. . . .

The salesman went and brought in what was apparently Mrs Thompson's old machine. He sat it down and Mrs Thompson said, 'You don't reckon I've got $50 in that, do you?' He said, 'I beg your pardon.' She said, 'You don't reckon I've got $50 in that?' He asked if she meant that the machine wasn't worth $50, and she said, 'I didn't think so but look in the drawer.' She looked in the drawer and started taking some pins out. The salesman said that he had taken everything else out of the drawer and put it on the table back there. (I am unclear myself as to whether Mrs Thompson was wondering if the machine was worth $50 or if she had $50 in the drawer of the machine.) . . .

Almost as soon as he had left the apartment, Mrs Thompson's daughter Sandra, a woman in her middle or early thirties who looked as if she were about seven months pregnant, entered the room. She was wearing a red and white striped maternity top and Jamaica pants. She was wearing a wedding ring. Sandra picked a cloth bag off the table that had the Singer emblem on it and said, 'What this go to? I could sure use this. I could use this.' And Mrs Thompson said, 'Put that down, Sandra, that's to my machine.' The girl said, 'I could sure use this; aw, it's not important.' The salesman then re-entered the apartment and looked around and Mrs Thompson said, 'Sandra, get up and let the man have that seat.' The girl said, 'I'll get up when Sandra's ready to go.' The man said, 'Oh, that's all right,' and he opened his attaché case on the floor and took some papers out of it. While he was doing this, Sandra looked at him and said, 'You don't want this seat, do you?' And he said, 'No.' Mrs Thompson said, 'Give the man the chair'. Sandra said, 'I done ask if he wanted it and he said no.' She was still holding the cloth bag and Mrs Thompson asked the salesman, 'Is that bag mine? Does that bag go to the machine? What's it for?' He said, 'It's to cover the foot pedal with, to hold the foot pedal when you aren't using it.' She said, 'Put that down, Sandra, it's mine.' And Sandra said, 'You don't need this. It'll be on the floor more than anywhere else anyway.'

Mrs Thompson then told the salesman, 'I don't know, maybe I should keep my old machine this week. I made two dresses already but I've got three more Easter dresses to make tonight.' (On a pole lamp by the sofa two new dresses were hung. In all probability these are the dresses Mrs Thompson had already completed.) The salesman said, 'It's easy to use this machine. You'll be able to sew so much better with it.' Mrs Thompson then said, 'But I don't know if I know how to work it and I got these three dresses to make. Maybe I should use my old machine to finish those dresses.' The salesman said, 'Here's the book and do you want me to show you how to use it again? I'll show you.' Mrs Thompson: 'Not right now. I still think I ought to keep my old machine now, even if it is old. I've had it twenty years, let me see ... yeah, been twenty years and I don't know if I can change now. It doesn't act right sometimes and it skips stitches at times but I know how to use it. I'm used to it.' She then asked me. 'Don't you think I'm too old to learn this new machine, these new things now?' And I said, 'Oh, I don't know about that.' And Mrs Thompson said, 'I don't know, I'm too old to be getting into all of this debt. I'm paying $400 for that machine.'

By this time Sandra had gone into the kitchen area and was putting something in a paper bag and she said, 'Hmmp, this one's cracked,' and laid an egg to one side. Mrs Thompson: 'Those are hard-boiled eggs.' Sandra: 'No they ain't. I just took these out of the refrigerator.' Mrs Thompson: 'Oh, how many eggs you taking Sandra? I know you taking a dozen and a half. I know twelve's in a dozen and a half a dozen would be about six more. You ain't fooling me; I know you taking more than a dozen.' Sandra: (who in the meantime keeps putting eggs in the bag) 'Aw mama, you don't know.' Mrs Thompson: 'Sandra, don't take all of my eggs!' Sandra: (looking in the bag) 'Aw, I'm just taking a dozen and one in case one of 'em breaks so I'll have an even dozen. I just took fourteen, maybe sixteen or eighteen.' Then she stops taking eggs and puts the bag to one side. The salesman has left the apartment again, I guess to go back to the car for something. Sandra then goes over to the piano and begins to play something. Mrs Thompson: 'Sandra, don't play the piano, it makes me nervous. I can't take it today.' And Sandra keeps on playing and says, 'Aw it's not long.' Mrs Thompson: 'Sandra, don't play the piano, it's making me nervous I say.' Sandra: (finishes what she was playing) 'I don't know but one number anyway.'

The following points should be stressed in connection with these observations: 1. Mrs Thompson's general confusion and inability to make a decision and stick to it; 2. the ease with which adults, coloured or white, push her around; 3. the chicanery of the white salesman, who insists on selling Mrs Thompson a sewing machine when she obviously will not be able to run it and when she is obviously confused about costs, and about her abilty to pay for it; and 4. the lack of respect for her by members of her own family. Thus David does not have before him models of adults who are honest or solicitous; and the major adult influence in his life, his great-grandmother, does not provide him with any firm basis for making a decision. In sum, David's home environment lacks important dimensions that usually give firmness to life, including perception and cognition.

7 From 'The course of cognitive growth'

I shall take the view in what follows that the development of human intellectual functioning from infancy to such perfection as it may reach is shaped by a series of technological advances in the use of mind. Growth depends upon the mastery of techniques and cannot be understood without reference to such mastery. These techniques are not, in the main, inventions of the individuals who are 'growing up'; they are, rather, skills transmitted with varying efficiency and success by the culture—language being a prime example. Cognitive growth, then, is in a major way from the outside in as well as from the inside out.

Two matters will concern us. The first has to do with the techniques or technologies that aid growing human beings to represent in a manageable way the recurrent features of the complex environments in which they live. It is fruitful, I think, to distinguish three systems of processing information by which human beings construct models of their world: through action, through imagery, and through language. A second concern is with integration, the means whereby acts are organized into higher-order ensembles, making possible the use of larger and larger units of information for the solution of particular problems.

Let me first elucidate these two theoretical matters, and then turn to

G

an examination of the research upon which they are based, much of it from the Center for Cognitive Studies at Harvard.

On the occasion of the One Hundredth Anniversary of the publication of Darwin's *The Origin of Species*, Washburn and Howell (1960) presented a paper at the Chicago Centennial celebration containing the following passage:

> It would now appear . . . that the large size of the brain of certain hominids was a relatively late development and that the brain evolved due to new selection pressures *after* bipedalism and consequent upon the use of tools. The tool-using, ground-living, hunting way of life created the large human brain rather than a large brained man discovering certain new ways of life. [We] believe this conclusion is the most important result of the recent fossil hominid discoveries and is one which carries far-reaching implications for the interpretation of human behaviour and its origins. . . . The important point is the size of brain, insofar as it can be measured by cranial capacity, has increased some threefold subsequent to the use and manufacture of implements. . . . The uniqueness of modern man is seen as the result of a technical-social life which tripled the size of the brain, reduced the face, and modified many other structures of the body.

This implies that the principal change in man over a long period of years—perhaps 500 thousand—has been alloplastic rather than autoplastic. That is to say, he has changed by linking himself with new, external implementation systems rather than by any conspicuous change in morphology—'evolution-by-prosthesis,' as Weston La Barre (1954) puts it. The implement systems seem to have been of three general kinds—*amplifiers of human motor capacities* ranging from the cutting tool through the lever and wheel to the wide variety of modern devices; *amplifiers of sensory capacities* that include primitive devices such as smoke signalling and modern ones such as magnification and radar sensing, but also likely to include such 'software' as those conventionalized perceptual shortcuts that can be applied to the redundant sensory environment; and finally *amplifiers of human ratiocinative capacities* of infinite variety ranging from language systems to myth and theory and explanation. All of these forms of amplification are in major or minor degree conventionalized and transmitted by the culture, the last of them probably the most since ratiocinative amplifiers involve symbol systems governed by rules that must, for effective use, be shared.

Any implement system, to be effective, must produce an appropriate internal counterpart, an appropriate skill necessary for organizing sensorimotor acts, for organizing percepts, and for organizing our thoughts in a way that matches them to the requirements of implement systems. These internal skills, represented genetically as capacities, are slowly selected in evolution. In the deepest sense, then, man can be described as a species that has become specialized by the use of technological implements. His selection and survival have depended upon a morphology and set of capacities that could be linked with the alloplastic devices that have made his later evolution possible. We move, perceive, and think in a fashion that depends upon techniques rather than wired-in arrangements in our nervous system.

Where representation of the environment is concerned, it too depends upon techniques that are learned—and these are precisely the techniques that serve to amplify our motor acts, our perceptions, and our ratiocinative activities. We know and respond to recurrent regularities in our environment by skilled and patterned acts, by conventionalized spatio-qualitative imagery and selective perceptual organization, and through linguistic encoding which, as so many writers have remarked, places a selective lattice between us and the physical environment. In short, the capacities that have been shaped by our evolution as tool users are the ones that we rely upon in the primary task of representation—the nature of which we shall consider in more detail directly.

As for integration, it is a truism that there are very few single or simple adult acts that cannot be performed by a young child. In short, any more highly skilled activity can be decomposed into simpler components, each of which can be carried out by a less skilled operator. What higher skills require is that the component operations be combined. Maturation consists of an orchestration of these components into an integrated sequence. The 'distractability,' so-called, of much early behaviour may reflect each act's lack of imbeddedness in what Miller, Galanter, and Pribram (1960), speak of as 'plans.' These integrated plans, in turn, reflect the routines and subroutines that one learns in the course of mastering the patterned nature of a social environment. So that integration, too, depends upon patterns that come from the outside in—an internalization of what Roger Barker (1963) has called environmental 'behaviour settings.'

Bruner describes the 'three modes of representation' as follows. First, the enactive mode in which reality is represented through the muscles, so to speak. This particularly characterizes the first two years of life. Second, the iconic mode which typifies the years from two to about seven. Whereas enactive representation refers to 'a mode of representing past events through appropriate motor response' (e.g. car driving, skiing or similar adult routines) iconic representation refers to the way our images 'stand for' perceptual events. Children at four or five years encode percepts in a different way from children over ten years: Piaget's classical experiment with the water jars is but one example. Finally, the symbolic mode of representation encodes its referent in an arbitrary and highly abstract way. Chinese ideographs were once iconic—the characters for 'everybody' still resemble two men—but are now as remote from what they signify as the Roman or Arabic numerals.

An example or two of enactive representation underlines its importance in infancy and in disturbed functioning, while illustrating its limitations. Piaget (1954) provides us with an observation from the closing weeks of the first year of life. The child is playing with a rattle in his crib. The rattle drops over the side. The child moves his clenched hand before his face, opens it, looks for the rattle. Not finding it there, he moves his hand, closed again, back to the edge of the crib, shakes it with movements like those he uses in shaking the rattle. Thereupon he moves his closed hand back towards his face, opens it, and looks. Again no rattle; and so he tries again. In several months, the child has benefited from experience to the degree that the rattle and the action become separated. Whereas earlier he would not show signs of missing the rattle when it was removed unless he had begun reaching for it, now he cries and searches when the rattle is presented for a moment and hidden by a cover. He no longer repeats a movement to restore the rattle. In place of representation by action alone—where 'existence' is defined by the compass of present action—it is now defined by an image that persists autonomously.

A second example is provided by the results of injury to the occipital and temporal cortex in man (Hanfmann, Rickers-Ovsiankina, & Goldstein, 1944). A patient is presented with a hard-boiled egg intact in its shell, and asked what it is. Holding it in his hand, he is embarrassed, for he cannot name it. He makes a motion as if to throw it and halts himself. Then he brings it to his mouth as if to bite it and stops before he gets there. He brings it to his ear and shakes it gently. He is puzzled. The experimenter takes the egg from him and cracks it on the table, handing it back. The patient then begins to peel the egg and announces what it is. He cannot identify objects without reference to the action he directs towards them.

The disadvantages of such a system are illustrated by Emerson's (1931) experiment in which children are told to place a ring on a board with seven rows and six columns of pegs, copying the position of a ring put on an identical board by the experimenter. Children ranging from 3 to 12 were examined in this experiment and in an extension of it carried out by Werner (1948). The child's board could be placed in various positions relative to the experimenter's; right next to it, 90 degrees rotated away from it, 180 degrees rotated, placed face to face with it so that the child has to turn full around to make his placement, etc. The older the child, the better his performance. But the younger children could do about as well as the oldest so long as they did not have to change their own position vis-à-vis the experimenter's board in order to make a match on their own board. The more they had to turn, the more difficult the task. They were clearly depending upon their bodily orientation toward the experimenter's board to guide them. When this orientation is disturbed by having to turn, they lose the position on the board. Older children succeed even when they must turn, either by the use of imagery that is invariant across bodily displacements, or later, by specifying column and row of the experimenter's ring and carrying the symbolized self-instruction back to their own board. It is a limited world, the world of enactive representation.

We know little about the conditions necessary for the growth of imagery and iconic representation, or to what extent parental or environmental intervention affects it during the earliest years. In ordinary adult learning a certain amount of motoric skill and practice seems to be a necessary precondition for the development of a simultaneous image to represent the sequence of acts involved. If an adult subject is made to choose a path through a complex bank of toggle switches, he does not form an image of the path, according to Mandler (1962), until he has mastered and overpractised the task by successive manipulation. Then, finally, he reports that an image of the path has developed and that he is now using it rather than groping his way through.

Our main concern in what follows is not with the growth of iconic representation, but with the transition from it to symbolic representation. For it is in the development of symbolic representation that one finds, perhaps, the greatest thicket of psychological problems. The puzzle begins when the child first achieves the use of productive grammar, usually late in the second year of life. Towards the end of the second year, the child is master of the single-word, agrammatical utterance, the so-called holophrase. In the months following, there occurs a profound change in the use of language. Two classes of words appear—a pivot class and an open class—and the child launches forth on his career in combinatorial talking and, perhaps, thinking. Whereas before, lexemes like *allgone* and *mummy* and *sticky* and *bye-bye* were used singly, now, for example, *allgone* becomes a pivot word and is used in combination. Mother washes jam off the child's hands; he says *allgone sticky*. In the next days, if his speech is carefully followed (Braine, 1963), it will be apparent that he is trying out the limits of the pivot combinations, and one will even find constructions that have an extraordinary capacity for representing complex sequences—like *allgone bye-bye* after a vistor has departed. A recent and ingenious observation by Weir (1962) on her $2\frac{1}{2}$-year-old son, recording his speech musings after he was in bed with lights out, indicates that at this stage there is a great deal of metalinguistic combinatorial play with words in which the child is exploring the limits of grammatical productiveness.

SECTION 5: QUESTIONS FOR DISCUSSION

1 Describe your first experience of 'insight' as a child at school. It needn't have been an academic discovery at all, but might have come about by hearing a particular story, making something by yourself, singing or acting in a school play or concert.

2 Gordon Bell, the boy who 'ran' 4C, (see Reading 2), was clearly trying to establish some sort of positive relationship with his new teacher,

although in some danger of alienating her sympathies. Why did he apparently avoid openly quarrelling with her? What might his 'deliberate' and 'thought-out overtures' towards her conceal? (Before answering this question, read John Bowlby's *Child Care and the Growth of Love*) Afterwards: What do you consider the significance of Gordon's temper?

3 De-schoolers such as Ivan Illich argue that we learn (or fail to learn) crucial skills at home rather than at school. As skill-centres, present day schools are prodigal of time and money. Indeed, a Puerto Rican study found that as much as 80% of class time was spent on administrative routine and 'behaviour control', 20% on learning.

Do you consider that this statistic fairly applies to schools you are familiar with? Count Registration, dinner money collection, announcements etc as administration, classroom prayers, 'lining up', praise and rebukes, threats and expulsions from the classroom as behaviour control.

Do you think the school should involve itself with the home and invite parents to come into the classroom, as the Halsey Report suggests? Or could schools be replaced by cheaper, neighbourhood-based learning networks of an informal kind (See Ivan Illich's *Deschooling Society* for details of possible networks.)

4 Richard Church and James Kirkup appear to have learned certain reading skills unaided.

Is this impression correct? What role might in fact have been played in their achievement either by a perceptive mother or a competent infant teacher? Do you feel such a supportive role was indeed present but has gone unacknowledged?

5 Jules Henry suggests that learning is impossible for most deprived children coming as they often do from homes in which breakfast is not provided, in which rows echo into the night, in which overcrowding makes sleep difficult. He pleads for teachers, students and others who work in such schools to eat breakfast with the children as an act of fellow-feeling: a calming ritual to begin the day with.

What immediate steps do you think one could take in rundown slum schools (EPA schools) which would *make* them more caring?

REFERENCES

BANNISTER, D. and FRANSELLA, F. (1971) *Inquiring Man: The Theory of Personal Constructs* Harmondsworth: Penguin

BARNES, D. (1969) *Language, the Learner and the School* Harmondsworth: Penguin

BEARD, R. (1970) *Teaching and Learning in Higher Education* Harmondsworth: Penguin

BROWN, R. (1965) *Social Psychology* New York: Collier Macmillan

BRUNER, J. S. (1966a) 'The course of cognitive growth' in R. M. Jones (ed) *Contemporary Educational Psychology* New York: Harper and Row

BRUNER, J. S. (1966b) *Studies in Cognitive Growth* New York: Wiley

BURT, C. (1937) *The Backward Child* London: University of London Press

CLEGG, A. (1972) *The Changing Primary School* London: Chatto

CLEGG, A. and MEGSON, B. (1968) *Children in Distress* Harmondsworth: Penguin

DAVIE, R., BUTLER, N. and GOLDSTEIN, H. (1972) *From Birth to Seven* London: Longman

DES (1972) *Educational Priority Volume 1* (Halsey Report) London: HMSO

DOUGLAS, J. W. B. (1964) *The Home and the School* London: MacGibbon and Kee

EYSENCK, H. J. (1969) Personality in primary school children *British Journal of Educational Psychology* 39, June, 109–30

GINSBURG, H. (1972) *The Myth of the Deprived Child* New Jersey: Prentice-Hall

HEBB, D. O. (1971) 'Drives and the conceptual nervous system' in *Personality, Growth and Learning* London: Longman

HENRY, J. (1971) *Essays on Education* Harmondsworth: Penguin

HOLT, J. (1969) *How Children Fail* Harmondsworth: Penguin

HUDSON, L. (1970) *Frames of Mind* Harmondsworth: Penguin

HUTT, C. (1972) *Male and Female* Harmondsworth: Penguin

ILLICH, I. (1971) *Deschooling Society* London: Calder and Boyars

JACKSON, B. and MARSDEN, D. (1962) *Education and the Working Class* Harmondsworth: Penguin

JONES, R. (1968) *Fantasy and Feeling in Education* Harmondsworth: Penguin

KAHL, J. A. (1953) ' "Common man" boys' in A. H. Halsey, J. Floud and C. A. Anderson (eds) (1961) *Education, Economy and Society* New York: Free Press, Collier Macmillan

KELLY, G. (1955) 'The psychology of personal constructs' in D. Bannister and F. Fransella (eds) (1971) *Inquiring Man: The Theory of Personal Construits* Harmondsworth: Penguin

LABOV, W. (1969) *The Logic of Nonstandard English* Georgetown Monographs in Language and Linguistics 22

MCVICKER HUNT, J. (1961) *Intelligence and Experience* Oxford: Ronald Press

MCVICKER HUNT, J. (1971) Using intrinsic motivation to teach young children *Journal of Educational Technology* 2, 78–80

PETRIE, C. (1972) *Backward and Maladjusted Children in Secondary Schools* London: Ward Lock Educational

ROBINSON, W. P. (1972) in A. Cashdan and P. Grugeon (eds) *Language in Education* London: Routledge and Kegan Paul

THORNDIKE, E. L. (1921) *Educational Psychology* New York: Columbia University Press

WILSON, J. (1965) *Logic and Sexual Morality* Harmondsworth: Penguin

Winnicott, D. W. (1964) *The Child, the Family and the Outside World* Harmondsworth: Penguin

Wiseman, S. (1968) 'Social deprivation and education' in H. J. Butcher and H. B. Pont (eds) *Educational Research in Britain 1* London: University of London Press

READINGS

1 Clegg, A. (1972) *The Changing Primary School* London: Chatto
2 Newcastle upon Tyne Institute and Faculty of Education Research Committee (1967) *And Softly Teach* ... Achievements and Teaching 3 Newcastle: School of Education
3 Church, R. (1966) *Over the Bridge* London: Heinemann
4 Mays, S. (1969) *Reuben's Corner* London: Eyre and Spottiswoode
5 Kirkup, J. (1970) *The Only Child* London: Pergamon
6 Henry, J. (1971) *Essays on Education* Harmondsworth: Penguin
7 Bruner, J. S. (1966) 'The course of cognitive growth' in R. M. Jones (ed) *Contemporary Educational Psychology* New York: Harper and Row

Chapter 3: Adolescence

We are used to thinking of adolescents almost as a separate breed. They lounge in groups on the street corners; they gather in their own cafes and bars; they have their own shops. We, and the popular press, know about their clothes and hair styles, their music and their festivals. And teachers know them—the fourth formers, the school leavers. Teachers and parents almost dote on the adolescent who shows few of the symptoms, who passes through these years still neat and tidy, still working, still aiming at a worthwhile job or career.

The difficulties and the problems of adolescence clearly exist. They are problems of personality growth and social adjustment that confront secondary schools every day of the school year. There are a number of obvious features of our own society that provide, at any rate, something of an explanation.

Our teenager problem, if that is what it is, may be related to the length of time young people have to spend in this limbo between childhood and adulthood. Popular versions of the work of social anthropologists have shown us other races in non-industrial societies where there are 'rites of passage'. In our society, there is no defined moment when the child becomes a man or a woman and is clearly accepted as such by the community. The twenty-first birthday party no longer has a great deal of significance.

The transitional period, too, is lengthened in our society by a number of other factors. Throughout this century, as standards of community health have improved and diet has changed, so the age of maturation has dropped. Puberty can now start at primary school age.

At the same time, or so it is alleged, family patterns are changing. Young people grow up more frequently in the 'nuclear' family situation. They do not have the benefit and the support of grandparents close-by or of other relatives. Increased independence has meant increased isolation and increased uncertainty about many of the norms. In our society, too, there is the institution of education. An important part of the socialization process is no longer a family responsibility. And this is a more recent development than we sometimes think. Mass education has a short history. It was less than 200 years ago that the radical William Cobbett was protesting at the notion of schools and demonstrating in his own family the values of an education that is part of family life.

We are aware, too, that young people in an industrial society are also a 'market'. There are commercial pressures upon them that have quite clearly strengthened since the Second World War.

As a result of these and other factors, young people are thrown much more into the company of their peers than used to be the case. Of course, peer groups are to be found in many different societies. In our society, children and young people find themselves throughout their school lives in the company of their own age groups. The whole notion of a 'teenage market' continues this assumption so that the mixed age group can seem to many less 'natural' than the peer group.

This quick sketch of some of the surface phenomena of modern adolescence in an industrial society leaves most of the questions unanswered. We turn now to look at some of the results of research by social scientists. By and large, the psychologists have been most deeply concerned with problems of personality development and learning. Because of the apparent nature of the phenomena, it has often been the sociologist or, at any rate, the social psychologist, who has been most interested in the period of adolescence.

There are some obvious points of entry. Is there any factual basis, for example, to many of the popular conceptions of adolescence? In 1959, Mark Abrams was able to show the commercial significance of adolescence clearly enough; young people had money to spend and were spending it on clothes, music and entertainment at a considerable rate. Teenage expenditure amounted to £830 million in 1959 and may have more than doubled by now. But what of the other popular beliefs? Schofield (1968) showed that promiscuity was far from widespread—contrary to the mythology of the popular press—though there is some evidence of changed expectations about boy/girl relationships among young people themselves.

Schofield's figures, in fact, showed that by the age of eighteen one boy in three and one girl in six had experienced full sexual intercourse. It is very doubtful if this is much of a change on the past except that contraception, when understood and used, has made pregnancy a good deal less likely. The evidence also suggests that much of the intercourse that does occur is between boys and girls who subsequently marry each other. Older attitudes are still strong in spite of the daily references to and stimulation of sex in the mass media. It is not altogether surprising that some young people find middle aged attitudes to sex hypocritical. What does need stressing is that young people are placed by our society in a difficult situation. The adolescent has to find his own morality, his own way to a lasting human relationship.

There has been, however, an increase in the crime statistics relating to young people. Convictions among young people aged between 14 and 30 have been increasing at an annual rate of a little over 10%. The trend as shown by Home Office figures has been towards crimes against property and crimes of violence. Female offences, too, have increased, but by far the greatest number of people found guilty of indictable offences are male. In 1969, for example, 57,121 males between the ages of 17 and 21 were found guilty of indictable offences compared with 6,259 females.

Are young people marrying earlier? Is there a teenage vote that can be identified? How serious is the drug problem? There is now some kind of statistical information relevant to all these popular issues. It can be found in the statistics regularly issued by the Registrar General, for example, that there has been a tendency for earlier marriages. There are perhaps two and a half times as many 'teenage brides' as there were in 1938, just before the war. The increase has been most marked in the working-class—the class with the highest proportion of young workers and the lowest proportion of those in higher education.

Abrams and Little (1965) have found that young voters reflect the attitude of their elders. They are just as involved or indifferent. Middle-class young people vote Conservative in much the same proportions as their elders, for example. Class is more important than age.

Evidence on drugs is hard to come by. But what statistics there are suggest that the problem remains very much a minority one. As of old, the young man on a night out is more likely to be high on beer than cannabis.

There are changes but clearly they are not very dramatic ones—at least on the criteria popularly advanced. However, we should probably bear social pressures in mind as we consider now what is known about the behaviour of the adolescent in the peer group and in schools or colleges.

As we have noted earlier in this book, whenever we begin to study any section of the British people as a section or a group, we are likely to find that social class considerations are relevant. Elizabeth Bott in her import-ant study *Family and Social Network* (1971) notes social class differences in family network patterns. The working-class pattern is that of the close-knit family group with relations, especially grandparents, close at hand and clearly defined role-relationships within the family. Because of the distinction between male and female roles, boys and girls themselves experience sexual segregation on the part of their parents. Bott notes that a further consequence of this type of family organization is a greater generation gap. The children of such families grow up in single sex peer groups and, whatever the cultural difficulties in the school, school organ-zation, in this respect, tends to reinforce the pattern. In a new final chapter in the 1971 second edition, Bott continues:

> When boys go to work they do not have to change their place of residence, so the friendships of adolescence can be continued into adulthood to form an adult peer group; it consists of friends, most of

whom are neighbours, some of whom are kin, and some of whom may be workmates. It is balanced by close-knit female networks of kin and sometimes friends. . . .

Children who are brought up in families with very loose-knit networks which are likely to be middle class, experience at home at least the ideology if not also the behaviour of a joint conjugal relationship. Social distance between parents and children is less than in the case of families in close-knit networks, and parents usually know about their children's friends and their activities together. Peer groups exist but are not so cut off from the family.

Readers will notice that this analysis supports the sociological argument developed by Bernstein as to the constraints upon language, or rather speech, imposed by class cultures. Elizabeth Bott's argument, read in full, can also be taken in conjunction with White's account (reprinted later p. 118) of 'skinhead' mobs in Birmingham. As Bernstein himself has commented (1970):

The class structure influences work and educational roles and brings families into a special relationship with each other and deeply penetrates the structure of life experiences within the family. The class system has deeply marked the distribution of knowledge within society.

Indeed, the findings of *Enquiry 1* (Schools Council 1968) that young school leavers and their parents took a far more strongly vocational and instrumental view of the role of education than did teachers, fits well the more general sociological concept of social class as a pervasive agent limiting and restricting almost all aspects of life for the working class. J. W. B. Douglas (1968) has also drawn attention to the difference between potential and expectations among working class young men and women. His studies produced the forecast that the next generation of manual workers would include 18% in the top third of measured ability.

Basic studies such as these have led sociology in a number of directions. In particular, there have been a number of research projects that have looked at the value conflicts between home and school. *Social Relations in a Secondary School* by David Hargreaves (1968) is a classic study already. It looks in particular at the development within the school of an 'anti-culture', a consequence of conflicting social class value systems. Hargreaves studied the problems in a secondary modern school. Colin Lacey (1970), as part of the same research project, did an equivalent study of a grammar school. He was concerned, among other things, with the problems of the working-class boy in adjusting, or not adjusting, to the middle-class academic ethos. The able working-class boy has to face a sharp conflict of values. King, one of Colin Lacey's subjects, reports:

When it became known I had passed [the 11 +] all day my friends parents' attitudes towards me changed to repulsion. I was treated as a 'puff' and was a 'brainy soft-arsed mardy'.... The school is alright apart from homework. Outside temptations are distracting. Because of this homework I sometimes feel like giving it all up. I want to live on an island and be self-sufficient.

Lacey comments:

... the clash between the school culture and the peer and neighbourhood cultures to which he [King] was deeply committed led to ambivalence in his attitude to the school. It is this ambivalence that predisposes working class boys towards the anti-group culture within the school.

Dissonances of this kind are always very disturbing, and the human being, at any age is likely to search consciously or unconsciously for a resolution to the conflict opposing value systems have generated internally. Balance Theory, to use the psychologist's term, provides one possible account of this process. Heider (1958) argued that beliefs, attitudes, feelings and behaviour will always adjust to reduce tension and achieve balance. If, for example, two adolescents are friends but one of them dislikes school, then the other will either drop his friend or change his attitude to school and begin to dislike it. Diagrammatically, it can be shown like this:

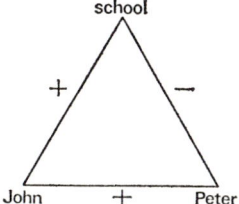

More generally, from the point of view of the school, there is a conflict between the social background of the youngster and the school:

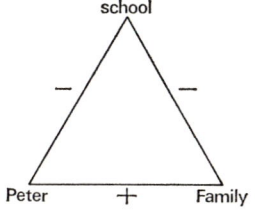

We have already noted this particular conflict. It tends to be more acute during the early years of adolescence for reasons which will be discussed later. In any case, a boy or girl from a working-class background is likely to be less at ease with the rule-structure of a school than the middle-class boy or girl. As D. F. Swift (1966) puts it:

> . . . a working-class point of view on education (most social classes feel that education is A GOOD THING) will tend to be imposed upon the child together with other external rules. There is a greater likelihood that the child will rebel against this as against other arbitrarily imposed rules. There is then a further factor that even where the working-class child internalizes the value it will mean something different to him. Horizons will be lower and understanding of the situation and its requirements less efficient.

The evidence adduced in Chapter 1, Section 2 about language development and social class differences is relevant. If it is true, and the sociological and linguistic evidence to date seems to suggest that it is, that modes of socialization in lower working-class families and, in particular, the limitation of speech to restricted codes, have the effect of blocking access to knowledge, then we have a much more sharply defined explanation of much adolescent hostility to school. Lawton (1968) found clear differences in both spoken and written English between his working-class and middle-class groups of young adolescent boys. When elaborated code was demanded, the working-class group tended to have marked difficulties and there was often the tendency for sentences to break down. Certainly, the present author's part replication of Lawton's experiment confirms Lawton's findings, at least in part. There can be little argument now about the kinds of difficulty that the language of the school can present to children. Faced with the somewhat artificial task of writing from cold on an essay topic or of constructing complex sentences, working-class boys tended to suffer linguistic breakdown. Writing oscillated between the incoherent and the colloquial.

It is important, however, to stress the precise limitations of this kind of research. It does *not* suggest that speakers of restricted code are never able to shift to an elaborated code. In discussion, both Lawton's and the present author's subjects were able to talk vigorously and cope, if required, with a modest level of generalization. As the work of Labov also demonstrates, there is no reason whatever to believe that the language of working-class boys and girls (and adults) is not fit for all normal human purposes—including discussion of life and morals. The problem lies in the formulation of knowledge in our society. Bernstein has always stressed that his educational aim is one, not of change, but of helping people to secure access to the knowledge that is the basis of control. The very boys and girls who stumble over some school tasks will write taut and imaginative verse and find ways through language in which to express and understand personal experience.

In any case, there is today a very much greater exposure at all class levels to elaborated codes. Radio, television and the mass media partly operate, it is true, to keep readers at a low level of the personal, concrete and trivial. Nevertheless, it is impossible to escape a great deal of exposure to standard English forms.

The difficulties still remain. It seems likely that many boys and girls from lower working-class backgrounds go through their school days without ever really understanding most of what the school has attempted to teach. What Bernstein and his colleagues have shown is that we are dealing with a *teaching* problem. Provided there is understanding of the nature of such a problem it is open to solution. Meanwhile, the evidence of the failure, in general, of schools to help these young people continues to pile up. Does our society, indeed, want to open up to all an education that has hitherto been limited to a comparative elite? The solution is rather more than a different approach in the classroom to the Newsom child.

Michael Carter (1966) showed how low the job aspirations of many young people really are:

> They 'do not mind much' what jobs they get, are not particularly bothered. This means that for the majority of leavers the transition to work does not involve disappointment or dissatisfaction with the type of job attained.

Why this should be so, especially in a society that depends on advanced technology and will have increasingly little use for the unskilled, deserves some explanation. Career ambition is not often part of the texture of working-class life. A skill or a good wage may be important and the virtues of solidarity perhaps even more so. Apprenticeships are not what they once were and, in spite of prognostications about the uncertain future for youngsters devoid of skill, Britain, a low wage-cost country, still provides a great deal of employment for the unskilled and semi-skilled.

As Michael Carter puts it: ' "The main thing" parents feel, "is for the kids to be happy"—but the hope that a child will find work in which he will be happy does not extend to making an analysis of the ingredients of work, or of the sort of attributes that their children have which might suit them for particular sorts of jobs. Still less does it extend to taking active steps to ensure that a good job is found. On the contrary, the parents tend to take the view that once the child leaves school he is very much in the hands of fate—"If they've got it in them, they'll do well, if they haven't there's nothing you can do about it." ' How unlike most teachers!

Margaret Mead (1943) in her discussion of socialization in Samoa comments on the way Samoan children differ from American in their preparation for work:

> So our children make a false set of categories, work, play and school; work for adults, play for children's pleasure, and school as an inexplicable nuisance with some compensations. These false distinctions are likely to produce all sorts of strange attitudes, an apathetic treatment of a school which bears no known relation to life, a false dichotomy between work and play, which may result either in a dread of work as implying irksome responsibility or in a later contempt for play as childish.
>
> The Samoan child's dichotomy is different. Work consists of those necessary tasks which keep the social life going: planting and harvesting and preparation of food, fishing, house-building, mat-making, care of children, collecting of property to validate marriages and births and succession to titles and to entertain strangers, these are the necessary activities of life, activities in which every member of the community, down to the smallest child, has a part.

To wish a return in Britain to such a society would be futile romanticism. But to mistake the diagnosis is to find no cure or the wrong one.

The wholly different socialization of the Samoan boy or girl does serve to stress the unusual quality of our own civilization. The human norm is socialization within the family or the kin. We have a society where the stress is exactly the opposite—upon individuality and competition. As Edmund Leach (1973) put it:

> Cultural comparison shows us that it is a norm of human society that the adult world should consist in kinship groups, but because we have rejected this standard pattern we have had to create a special set of formal institutions (schools, polytechnics, universities and the like), which will tear young people away from their normal environment and give them the illusion that it is the true nature of man to engage in a Hobbesian war of all against all.

What we are seeing in some working-class difficulties (and perhaps the rebellion of some middle-class young people) is the ongoing clash between industrial society and older norms. It is not just school. Work is outside the kinship group.

Even with the raising of the school leaving age to 16, boys and girls will leave school for the sharply different experience of work at many different levels of maturity. Carter comments on the ordeal work can be for the less mature. Those who have developed apathetic or hostile attitudes to school will be very anxious to leave; they may have developed preconceptions about the freedom attached to money and employment that reality then destroys. Those that are left pursuing higher education have their difficulties, too. Brian Jackson (1962) in *Education and the Working Class* quotes a working-class grammar school girl:

> All they were interested in was growing up as fast as they could and getting out. Going out with boys and wearing make-up and high-heeled shoes. They wanted to leave school. They always seemed much older than I did. I felt immature with them, I always felt as though I was one step behind. . . .

Frank Musgrove reported in 1966 on a study of adolescents in a Yorkshire industrial area. He was concerned with what they felt to be their needs and whether these needs were met or not. Musgrove, as a tool for analysis, made use of a distinction noted by the great American sociologist, Talcott Parsons. Parsons suggested that *expressive* needs are those emotional needs that demand immediate satisfaction. *Instrumental* needs, on the other hand, are those needs that we feel when we think in terms of goal: what must I do or learn to achieve the goal? Clearly, school largely serves instrumental needs. Home, clubs, peer groups largely serve expressive needs. Like school, work meets instrumental needs; there is not much fun on the production line, let alone 'job satisfaction', but the pay packet will buy important satisfactions.

The trouble is that human beings have expressive and instrumental needs simultaneously. An activity that meets only one kind of need is likely to be either dissatisfying in the long run or productive of frustration. The failure of some schools to meet expressive needs is one of the factors causing the troubles variously reported with adolescents. Musgrove notes particular problems with his grammar school pupils. Their comments are much in line with those of the girl quoted by Jackson (1962). In particular, they show signs of a depressingly negative self-concept. These sixth formers are much troubled by doubt about themselves. They feel guilty about their attitudes and uncertain of their aims and abilities. Musgrove concludes that these doubts are partly the consequence of the failure of school to meet expressive needs at the right moment.

J. W. Getzels and P. W. Jackson (1962) have studied the highly intelligent and the highly creative adolescent. Their work is quoted in *Creativity* edited by P. E. Vernon (1970). Their starting point is the difference of approach to problems of the high-IQ subject and the high-creative subject, perhaps more familiar as the converger/diverger distinction. The authors comment on their findings:

> It seems to us that the essence of the performance of our creative adolescents lay in their ability to produce new forms, to risk conjoining elements that are customarily thought of as independent and dissimilar, 'to go off in new direction'. The creative adolescent seemed to possess the ability to free himself from the usual, to

H

'diverge' from the customary. He seemed to enjoy the risk and uncertainty of the unknown. In contrast, the high-IQ adolescent seemed to possess to a high degree the ability and the need to focus on the usual, to be 'channelled and controlled' in the direction of the right answer—the customary. He appeared to shy away from the risk and the uncertainty of the unknown and to seek out the safety and security of the known.

Getzels and Jackson point out some of the social implications of psychologists' findings on creativity. It is likely that schools—particularly schools with a strong academic bias—favour the convergent thinker and stress the desirability of right answers. They conclude:

It is, we believe, unfortunate that in American education at all levels we fail to distinguish between our convergent and divergent talents —or, even worse, that we try to convert our divergent students into convergent students. Divergent fantasy is often called 'rebellious' rather than 'germinal'; unconventional career choice is often labelled 'unrealistic' rather than 'courageous'.

This last study dealt with very able adolescents. Clearly there is a relation between the convergent/divergent continuum and human needs for expressive and instrumental gratifications. Certainly, if schools are inclined to favour the convergent thinker, then the naturally divergent will not find much satisfaction of his expressive needs.

We turn now to the problems of less able boys and girls. One of the more important pieces of research conducted in this country over the last twenty-five years or so has been the longitudinal study by J. W. B. Douglas of 5,000 boys and girls. In *All Our Future* (1968) Douglas and his colleagues Ross and Simpson report on their work with these children between the ages of 11 and 15. In one section, they look at school progress in terms of emotional adjustment. Their teachers were asked to produce assessments of behaviour; available also were mothers' reports of difficulties or symptoms of distubance; at the age of 13 the children were asked to complete a self-inventory. This last consisted of 15 items describing attitudes and actions typical of neurotic children together with a further 15 items relating to introversion and extroversion. The children were asked to mark those statements that seemed to be true for them.

What the work showed was a correlation between adverse teacher assessment and those children whose self-inventory was biased towards neuroticism. The pupils 'who chose a large number of neurotic statements made lower scores than those who chose few.' Douglas concludes:

The conclusion to be drawn from this study of the relation between behaviour and school performance is that it is not only the grossly disturbed children that are affected, there is a continuous gradient in performance running from those who have few adverse teachers' comments, no symptoms reported by the mothers, and low neuroticism scores to those who are picked out by all three measures. The more adverse items reported, the lower is the performance in school.

It is only in the most extreme group that there is evidence of relative deterioration in performance during the years at school. For the majority with some or many symptoms, or signs, of disturbed behaviour, test performance is equally poor at each age. This suggests that the basis of their educational difficulties lies in the pre-school years.

Such a conclusion is cold comfort, though it is clear how Douglas's findings tie up with the research reported earlier in this book on both social class and socialization.

Douglas also studied his large group of children in terms of their sexual maturation. In any group of young people there will be variation in the age of onset of puberty. Because of the tremendous general improvement in dietary standards, there is no longer, in Britain, any relationship between the age of onset and social class. There is, however, a relationship between age of onset and family size. There is a tendency for children in small families to reach puberty earlier. Douglas also shows that there is a relationship between educational attainment and puberty. Children who became early developers, were found to have been already showing, at the age of eight, signs of being ahead of those who subsequently became late developers. Nor do the tests give any support to the idea that the late maturers catch up.

A number of Douglas's conclusions are of interest. He notes again the relationship with family size. He notes too that the early maturers tend to achieve better 'O' Level results and, consequently, to stay on longer at school:

In the selective schools, though not in the group as a whole, an unexpectedly high proportion of the mature girls leave at the end of the fifth year; a further division by social class shows that these leavers come mainly from manual working-class families and that mature manual working-class boys also tend to leave grammar school immediately after taking their 'O' Levels. ... In the secondary modern schools the more mature boys and girls from each social class stay on longer than less mature. ... And this view is supported by the finding that in mixed but not girls' only grammar schools, it is the early maturing girls who stay on longest.

The conclusion about secondary modern school leavers may be thought to be some further justification for the raising of the school leaving age to 16.

We have looked at the adolescent in terms of educational attainment, life chances, attitudes to school and work. During this complicated period of growth, he or she is, more importantly, learning to be a person. Learning to be a person means learning to take a satisfying place in a society. It may be thought perhaps that schools and other institutions nurturing the young may neglect this in some measure, but one major task that faces our adolescent is the development of social skills. The development of an ability to interact successfully with others in itself depends upon the development by the adolescent of a clear sense of identity. As Richard Jones puts it (1972):

> The social skill to be learned during this period, and it is very much a *social* skill, is to be one's self, to stand for and against things consistently and expressly, in ways that make one recognizedly one's own man, in private and in public. To the extent the young man or woman succeeds in tempering his renewed concern with his body and sex with the ability to think and dream on grand scales, and to recognize and make recognizable that he has put the stamp of individuality on his particular blending of these, he comes to invest life with expectations of its being distinctive. We say he develops a sense of ego identity. To the extent he is unable to subordinate his capacities for the reproduction of life to his capacities for the reproduction of mind, or cannot make social graces of his essential loneliness, he comes to invest life with expectations of its being something one can get lost in. We say he develops a sense of ego diffusion. It is as ill-advised here to think of identity versus diffusion as it is to engage in either-or thinking in respect to the other growth crises. The word is still 'and'. What a poor thing would intimacy be, for example, to one who could not feel lost without his love.

The words of Richard Jones bear pondering and then discussing. They bring us to the work of those psychologists who have been concerned with the problem of self-image. There have been earlier references to this but it seems to be generally agreed that adolescence is a crucial time in the development of the self-concept. There is common sense in the notion. On the threshold of maturity, there must be a conscious awareness of the self. Without such an awareness, there can be no settling into any of the possible roles of the adult man or woman. This conscious awareness of the self can take many forms. It is culturally determined, in any case. Who we are and what we are depends on who and what people think we are.

Again, as we have seen earlier, the young adolescent learns about himself from others—how they talk about and to him, how they react to what he does and says. The cues are internalized; new impressions modify memory and gradually perception of the Self take form. Concepts of the Self develop. J. W. Staines (1958) puts it this way:

> One method of analysis of this complex Self-structure is to see the Self in three levels or phases, each level having a number of sectors or categories. The first level is the Cognized or Known Self which comprises all those characteristics of the individual that he recognizes as part of the 'Me'. Whether or not these correspond to objective reality or to what others think about him does not matter. The Cognized Self is what the individual perceives and conceives himself to be. The second level of the Self, called the Other Self, is what the person believes others think of him: 'The teacher thinks I'm no good at English.' The third level is the Ideal Self, part wish, part 'ought', the standard to be reached: 'I ought to be more careful of detail.' These elements of the Self are of supreme importance for behaviour since many of the individual's actions are ordered by his constant efforts to maintain and enhance these various aspects of the Self-picture.

Self-concept, then, is the product of many forces. There is the biological urge to self-maintenance. There is the inherent capacity of the individual, within his social constraints, to accept or rebel against the cultural influences to which he is subject. Very few, in fact, do rebel. There is still much plasticity in adolescence. It is common for young people to try on many roles. Some of the oddities of their behaviour apparent to adults stem from just this. Until we have tried a number of roles, and judged the reaction of others, how can we know our true part? The young adolescent male plays rough and boastingly to try out his own manhood. The young adolescent girl teases and flirts to test her own femininity. Both can see themselves in many different occupational roles. Both boys and girls live, during this time, a fantasy life often of rich Walter Mitty proportions. The quarrels with parents are part of this process. Occasionally, the quarrels can be bitter and precipitate action that both sides come to regret. Usually, it is a kind of punctuation to the passing days of youth. Douvan and Adelson (1966) in America have suggested that the quarrels, however awful they may feel at the time or even in retrospect, are often about trivia. They are not about fundamental norms. There is a kind of agreement to disagree, a pseudo-rebellion. For the scope of rebellion, in any case, is socially limited for the vast majority. We can never escape the image of ourselves that the environment has printed. But it may be that we can in some measure control and modify internally an otherwise wholly social being.

The process of arriving at an identity is not easy. Adolescents must, in a society which gives so much time to the process and which values individual differences so highly, try out roles and possibilities. As Erikson (1965) puts it:

Young people, depending on where they live will try out a number of gangs, or cliques or organizations or movements. It is very hard for their parents to understand what makes them change from, say, a pacifist to an extreme militarist organization. The necessity to total-ize one's outlook and one's associations at any given time is an adolescent trend.... Adolescence is at an end when one's sexual maturation is completed *and* one's psychosexual role defined and accepted.

SECTION 2: READINGS

There are three categories of reading in this section. In the first place there are reports from 'field' work among adolescents. David White, for example, reports on his personal investigation among near-delinquent teenage gangs in Birmingham. Mary Morse quotes from workers involved with young people who have, in a sense, opted out of current society. Brian Jackson analyses an adolescent or young activity which, in Huddersfield and undoubtedly in many other towns, helps young people to cope with pressures.

In the second category, we find the somewhat more speculative com-ments of David Hargreaves. He is a social psychologist deeply involved in education and with young people. From a personal point of view he analyses something of the nature of what is now commonly called 'youth culture'. This is not to say that his observations are not based upon a great deal of experience and research work. Hargreave's (1968) own *Social Relations in a Secondary School* is already something of a classic study of the development of apathy and hostility among adolescents in a secondary modern situation.

Thirdly, we have one example (Harrison) of a research project into adolescent attitudes. The tentative nature of the findings and the short-age of other work can only reinforce Peter McPhail's own work and his comment upon the lack of serious studies of this age group.

1 From *Brum's Mobs*

Anyone looking for these Birmingham 'mobs' will find them a few yards from New Street station. Their names are sprayed in paint on the blank walls of brave new Brum: Quinton, Ladywood, Smethwick and North-field, to name the largest. Except Smethwick, these areas are the suburbs of semi's and tower blocks in which the city has solved its housing problem. The mobs' names are cut into the back of bus seats and daubed on pub walls: '*Smethwick Boot Boys' Territory—Keep Out.*'

But what is there behind the names? In the official view, the magis-trates' view, the mobs are barely organized bands of young hooligans who fight in packs because they're afraid to fight on their own; who fight with knives, razors and hammers because they're too weak and too small to fight with their fists.

The mobs see themselves (and everyone else) differently. To them, a mob is a group of mates, 'brilliant mates,' who look after one another, who obey 'mob law' as opposed to 'society law,' and who unwittingly follow ancient codes of revenge, loyalty to a leader, and the defence of territorial rights.

These two views collide when an act of extreme violence is committed. As it was on Thursday, 10 December, last year. In a scuffle near a Selly Oak discotheque, a 17-year-old boy stabbed a 16-year-old boy in the back. The boy later died in hospital, and his attacker was charged with murder. It probably meant little to the shocked Birmingham citizen that this killing was the climax of three years of escalating mob warfare.

Two mobs were involved in the incident that led up to the killing—the Quinton Mob and the Northfield Mob. In the mobs' estimation, Quinton was then a developed, probably overdeveloped gang, while the North-field was just emerging. The two mobs had been on reasonably good terms up till then. The killing changed all that. 'The day after that boy was stabbed, every mob in the city suburbs was looking for Quinton,' a Townies mobster told me. 'No one set eyes on them for three months. Now they just talk, they don't do anything.'

The Quinton Mob is now a slightly punch-drunk prizefighter, reminiscing endlessly and too-easy game for young mobsters who want to prove themselves. I spent most of a week talking to them, and was fortunate enough to be able to test some of their claims in the company of other mobs.

Quinton is a sevenpenny bus ride from the city centre. Its uniform, red-brick housing, punctuated by tower blocks rising out of scrubby meadows, gives it some of the charm of the Kingston by-pass. It boasts two pubs—one for the old, quiet men and one for the lorry-drivers and ex-pubfighters—and little else. Here, in the pub for old, quiet men, I meet Bob. At 18, Bob is a lieutenant in the Quinton Mob and the leader's heir-apparent. He explains quickly the five years' history of the Quinton Mob, and extraordinarily involved saga of alliances, misalliances, 'bundles' and gang-bangs. He talks quietly and proudly, with the kind of reverence for mob activities a man would reserve for his hobby. He has an exceptional knack of seeing mobs as a network of territorial groupings as valid as Greater Birmingham's boroughs, or the city's five police divisions.

He estimates that there are 20 main mobs in greater Birmingham. Added to this are the smaller 'satellite' mobs. These may be 'stars,' the 13-15-year-old junior mobs, or the sub-groups. The 'stars' took their designation from the Quinton Star, Bob is quick to point out.

The sub-groups are tied down to more specific areas than the main mobs. For example, at Northfield, there is also the Ley Hill Mob, the Egg Hill Mob and the Dimsdale Boot Boys, the latter drawn from just one street. Bob estimates that, all told, there must be 4,000 kids involved in some mob or other.

The dominant activity, however, is fighting. And the fighting concerns 'territories.'

A pub may be mob territory. In its time, the Quinton Mob has laid claim to the Punch Bowl in Wolverhampton Road South, the Duke of York in Harborne, both in or near Quinton; and the Hole in the Wall, the Costermonger and the Gilded Cage, in the city centre. 'It's a dare to walk into an enemy pub and not be recognized. Even if you're recognized and get cut up a bit, you can go back to your mates and show them what you got for invading.' Raids into enemy territory are carefully worked out, Bob claims: 'In the old days you'd find out where they were, get tooled up and ask "What's to bus route?" Now mobs have got cars, Ford Transit vans, so they can get in, splatter them, and get away quick.'

Territories can also be definite geographical areas. For over two years, Quinton has been 'at war' with the Smethwick Mob to the north. Now an alliance—engineered by Bob—holds them uneasily together. But the demarcation lines are still fresh in the memory. From the Old House at Home, outside Harborne, to the King's Head on the Hagley Road, was no-man's land. The Hagley Road was the line drawn between Smethwick and Quinton. A mass of paint-spraying and a long record of fights bears witness to the strategic importance of the disputed King's Head bierkeller. It is now closed down.

Now another line has been drawn—through the open valley that divides Quinton from Bartley Green and from the Northfield Mobs in the south.

The strangest part of Bob's theory of mob practice concerns the mob ethic. 'Mob law says if one stands, all must stand with him and fight, even if its just a wild young lad. Mob law says ten kids don't go for one. That's a wanker's trick. [Besides its normal meaning, 'wanker' denotes any vicious cowardly fighter, anyone too weak or puny to fight, or simply a harmless outsider.] Society law says you're guilty because you've beaten someone up or killed them. But mob law says if this happens in a fair fight, you've done no wrong. Mob law says you don't grass on your mates, even it it will get you off a charge. Mob law says you *look after* your mates.' This self-protection is perhaps the most impressive feature of 'mob theory.' But how much is pure theory?

The killing—the stabbing made enemies of Northfield and Quinton—introduces the most puzzling feature into the mob scene. According to a detached youth worker who spent the best part of a year working with the mob, the killing sobered up the Quinton mob and encouraged its fragmentation.

Undoubtedy, the mob is over the hill. Bricker is watching his step; Billy, who, according to another core member, 'goes really wild when he's pissed off, screaming and charging,' now has a regular missus. But, even so, the mob will still fight. Two months ago, Quinton heard that the greasers were after them. They decided to give them what they wanted, and beckoned them out of the Tow Rope cafe, west of the city centre, to

120

an expensive brawl. They no longer carry the expensive weapons of two years back—table legs wrapped in barbed wire—but are still shrewdly 'armed.' One evades the 'offensive weapon' risk with a sharpened screwdriver. 'I need it for work.'

As far as the mob are concerned the killing hasn't bust them up. They admit it cooled them down. But somehow they *still* fit it into the way of mobs. 'It was unnecessary. It was so pointless that we knew it couldn't have been a core member,' says Bricker. 'It was a "fringe" kid, a parttimer who likes to belong,' says another. 'Because if you belong to a mob, particularly Quinton, people respect you. You can get a girl easy. And it was a "fringe" kid who grassed.' 'I'm sorry, really sorry, for his parents, but it happens. A kid gets wild,' says Bricker.

Not much open remorse. Perhaps through bravado, or perhaps because of the ruthless application of mob law. And yet the mob never convinced me that they stuck rigidly to the standards they applied. For example, their core contained acknowledged 'wankers.' 'Why do we put up with them?' answers Bricker, 'because they're our mates.' 'They're a laugh. You can't hate them.' 'Milko's a wanker. Really vicious. He'll never fight clean. But he's a mate.'

By this time, I am curious to know how other, related mobs, measure up to Quinton. For it seems that the theoretically universal 'mob law' is two-edged. It can make sense of inarticulate comradeship or it can falsely rationalize hooliganism and thuggery.

Are mobs different from simple hooligans? If we take their labels seriously, yes. For they represent self-supporting units which have a real social value. When *Birmingham Evening Mail* looked at the mobs in its series, 'The Outsiders,' last year, it began an attempt to find premises for the organized gangs, which ideally they would run themselves. The detached youth worker at the same time began to work towards the idea of encouraging indigenous leadership of a club formed from the Quinton Star. This was to have been run by Bob. Sadly, very little has come of it, mainly because the education departments who could have helped took so long to act and when they did, bound the idea tightly with red tape. 'The Star are going to be a lot worse than we were,' Bob now predicts.

But youth centres, mob premises or what have you, may not be the answer at all. At Northfield there is a fine £12,000 youth centre at Shenley Green, but even so a good many of the Northfield Mob aren't interested. Perhaps the answer lies right outside youth centres. Perhaps the self-protecting units of the mobs should be allowed to evolve, but harshly discouraged from a violence that often they are more afraid of than anyone else. Could they exist without the dangers of violence?

In Quinton there is the story of Porky. Porky is now getting on, but when he was younger he made his name in the neighbourhood by cornering a 'sex maniac' who had been pestering Quinton people, offering either to turn him over to the police or to knock hell out of him. The 'maniac' decided he didn't want to be taken to the police, and ever since then Porky has lived pretty well on a reputation gained in a single act of violence. Will the young mobsters still have to identify themselves in this rather sad way?

2 From *Working Class Community*
What is the Jazz Club?

The Jazz Club has lasted thirteen years so far. Its oldest members are in their thirties, and they joined 'the crowd' as schoolboys and schoolgirls. It began with one of the post-war generations of teenagers. Its class and educational basis appears clear enough. New members are recruited to the central group, fairly slowly—so its age range has been steadily broadening: 15 to 29, 15 to 30, 15 to 31 . . . Marriage doesn't take the older ones away, only new jobs or personal disaster does that. It's obvious what the Jazz Club is *not*. It's not a club needing the permanence of buildings and officers. It doesn't want organizing, as the bus driver's failure suggested. It likes to keep together, yet keep on the move. It isn't a soft drink and coffee club. There must be beer. This cuts it off from the large audiences of grammar school girls who sometimes 'take up' a folk club or student club. As a society the Jazz Club meets as a group of drinkers most nights of the week, and always has done.

Is it a *jazz* club? It is for Tony or Tommy. With both of them jazz is involved with very private realities. Yet very few others listen to the music with much attention, even among the musicians themselves. And certainly the taste for jazz doesn't become more discriminating. All look down on rock 'n roll, skiffle, beat, pop, folk, or the latest style that sweeps the top twenty. But within jazz itself, interest drifts rather than sharpens. For most of the group, jazz—even if they like it a lot—is the occasion, the setting, for their society, and not its *raison d'être*. 'But I mean, how many people come down to hear good jazz. If they want to hear really good jazz, they wouldn't come out at all. You'd stop at home and play Morton records, wouldn't you? But that's the last thing I go to the Jazz Club for. There I like it as background to all that's going on.'

But what is going on? I think that what happened originally was that a group of working-class boys at grammar school found themselves at odds with the social and academic demands of their school. 'I hated the etiquette, the sugar tongs part of it.' Yet at the same time they were excited and enthusiastic, and the colour and music of jazz and the jazz myth satisfied them in a way that the GCE demands of the schoolroom never could. They fell in love with the literature of jazz too—the prostitution, violence, drugs of New Orleans went along with its music, vitality, imagination. If the life of New Orleans was an exaggerated image of working-class life, the stimulating generalized emotions of jazz were a hazy image of what the world of art could offer. The school avoided the first and didn't particularly lead to the second. The Jazz Club has ever since slowly recruited from this type of grammar school pupil. Eight years later, for example, two new members—girl and boy—discussed the school dance at the girls' grammar school.

'It's like a lot of sixth formers trying to do a Billy Butlin. There are different kinds, like—there are a few couples who've come to dance, and they do. Then there are the others who're just going round the floor to see if they can knock into old so-and-so. And then there are the ones standing around. It's the band that tries to be like Butlin's too. This time there was this band leader, for example, who said "Next it'll be the Lancers, and those who aren't going to dance, should go up into the balcony and they'll see a *lovely* sight!" Well that kind of thing—it makes me sick!'

'Yes, and you can't be comfortable. You feel the mistresses are watching you. You feel you're under their eyes.'

'And no wonder some of them are "misses"? Their dresses were shocking! Perhaps they find teaching's a greater call—but what taste! Really shocking!'

'It isn't right for all the girls either. There's that lot who usually go dancing to the Masonic, and they feel it's all a bit below them. And then there's the ones who go to Chinnie's, and it's all a bit too high for them.'

'What about refreshments too. When you go to a dance, you get to wanting your refreshments and things around about nine o'clock. Or most guys do anyway. But what happened? The staff and their guests and so on had theirs then, and the room was closed to everyone. We had to stay outside until they were finished, before we could have anything.'

'Yes, I know. It was given out in Assembly before. There were special times for the Lower Sixth and for the. . . .'

'Special times! It makes you sick.'

'Oh yes, and Miss Scotland has got the Astronomer Royal to come along from a lecture he was giving earlier that evening. That was given out in Assembly too. We hadn't got to all stare and stop talking when he came in. When we got there, some of the fourth formers asked Peter if he were the Astronomer Royal.'

'I was very tempted to say yes, too!'

But the link with education seems to go rather further than this. Many of the Jazz Clubb members, like Steve or Patrick, had a great deal of trouble in reaching and lasting through higher education. It could take them ten years or more between leaving school and obtaining a further qualification. Taken one by one, the club's members present an astonishing variety of 'broken' educations. The club also offered securities to those on the borderlands of mental illness or suffering from other anxieties. There was always for example, an amount of only half-recognized homosexual worry. One player was always quarrelling with his mates' girl friends and at almost any moment over a ten-year period you could hear the latest girl friend of his latest mate, irritated, angry or puzzled with him say 'Why are you so hostile tonight? You always seem hostile to me.' It took him a decade to realize himself that he was homosexual, and before that very few indeed of 'the crowd' had perceived his problem. Most—despite the education and including some in a similar plight—would probably have been rather shocked.

Difficulties of this kind clustered round the jazz club but were not its centre. That remained in the entanglements of the working-class boy, having passed through grammar school, running into all manner of emotional checks from sixteen onwards. Other people were involved, but these were the centre—just as old men remain central even in a bowls club with many young or women members. The Jazz Club was a community with a fairly subtle structure. Unlike the working men's clubs it wasn't in any sense 'local'; it was inconceivable that it should have premises or a constitution, or that the instruments should be owned by the club, not the individual. Yet it was nevertheless a community, and not like the grammar school itself, simply an élite in training. It had points of resemblance to the clubs—from its informal but effective style of leadership which was quite different from the public school prefect manner, to a rather delightful insistence on the 'difficulty' of jazz which much resembled the similarly false 'difficulty' from which brass bandsmen often sought to create their mystery. But to dress in uniform, like a brass band or a top twenty beat group, was inconceivable—that was altogether too close to the ethos of grammar school.

As the Jazz Club shifted around Huddersfield for thirteen years it carried on a kind of long flirtation with the older working-class groups. There were cricket matches against mill teams—with the Jazz Club team eccentrically dressed. There were months when a very drab working-class pub was in favour because it had a pianist who played popular songs of the twenties and thirties ('Jack Dempsey')—with which 'the crowd' characteristically, were more word-perfect than the labourers who used the pub. There was a long adoption of an outlying pub where the choir gathered round the bar after evening service and part-sang spirited Methodist hymns ('Crown Him') in between pints. 'The crowd' all knew the 'Huddersfield Anthem'—'Pretty Flowers'—a lovely Napoleonic broadside, of which the rest of Huddersfield knows only the first line and a vague patch of its soaring melody. And there were several attempts at setting up comic Edwardian song acts on the working men's club circuits. It was a love affair. The Jazz Club—despite the New Orleans myth and the educational background—was very much a Huddersfield club. It didn't lead to social promotion or to high art—there was no 'transfer' at all from jazz to classical music. Its function was to hold together and sustain a steady stream of post-1944 Act pupils. As a floating community, it became admirably and intricately designed for that purpose—and the feeling of how to do *this*, was the real inheritance from working-class Huddersfield.

3 From *The Unattached*

This book is a report of a project sponsored by the National Association of Youth Clubs into the problem of those young people for whom no youth organization seems to have value. It made use of young social workers whose task it was, incognito, to make effective personal contact with the unattached. It is an interesting and moving example of 'field work'.

The first extract summarizes the problem and the approach. In the second, one of the workers reports on a discussion with the father of one of the boys.

It is useful to narrow the term 'unattached' to those who do not belong to a youth organization and who are also unhappy and/or delinquent, and unless otherwise stated it will be used in this rather specialized sense. It must not, however, be assumed that young people in this narrowed category shared identical attitudes, problems, or emotional characteristics. Differences will be seen in age (eleven to twenty-five years), social class (professional-middle to lower working-class), social value and aspirations, family background, vocational capabilities, and delinquent tendencies. These wide variations make it difficult to generalize about all the youth in all the areas. For example, in each locality it was necessary to discover the social norms for groups and individuals, and then assess deviant behaviour patterns and attitudes in the light of these.

But there were some similarities. After all the information about the unattached had been collated, it could be seen that their inability to join a youth organization was no more than one expression of a much wider pattern of unstable behaviour. Other expressions of it were to be found in their attitudes towards work, school, leisure, home and family, money values, the opposite sex, and adult authority in general. Much of the unstable pattern seems to be due to frustrations of various origins, which could usually be traced back to a single or a combination of factors. These were emotionally poor home backgrounds; a lack of or poorly developed physical, intellectual, or social skills; some sort of emotional maladjustment. In some cases failure to achieve unrealistic or unattainable goals they had set for themselves or had had set for them caused frustrations or boredom. Good examples of these were the aspirations of the Seagate group to become famous writers, artists, and photographers without accepting the need to work gradually towards these goals. In other cases part of the cause for frustration and boredom was the abject social and cultural poverty of the environment. In all cases there was very little ability on the part of any of the unattached to accept responsibility for what was happening to them. They saw themselves as unfortunate victims of circumstance. This, coupled with other factors such as insecurity and ignorance of the possibilities, helped to induce feelings of impotence and a general belief that little could be done to change their lot.

Another characteristic in all areas was a general inability to postpone immediate pleasure for the sake of future gain. It came out in attitudes towards money (saving and spending) and in an inability to undertake training for vocational advancement. With some young people, on the surface at least, 'bumming' had become a recognized, accepted, and valued way of life. But shame and discontent still crept through and there was considerable evidence that this way of life was yet another cover-up for insecurity and fear.

A hand-to-mouth philosophy governed the lives of these youths; leisure-time interests were short-spanned, constantly changing, and interspersed liberally with periods of boredom and apathy; friendships suffered because they were incapable of sustaining any effective feelings of obligation or consideration for others. Small close friendship groups were undoubtedly a necessity; they provided a measure of the support, security, and recognition that they all needed, but the existence of such groups was brief in duration because of this inability to sustain friendships. Another marked characteristic was a craving for adventure: youth clubs were usually rejected as being too tame, and excitement was often sought through delinquency: avoiding payment of rail fares, petty thieving, entering cinemas and dance halls without payment, violation of property, drinking, and experimentation with drugs. Sexual promiscuity may also be included here, but there was evidence that this was as much an attempt to resolve conflicts over personal relationships and sexual roles as it was to satisfy any craving for adventure. A less extreme example of the craving for adventure was a reluctance to spend even a single evening a week at home, or the frantic search for parties. The spontaneity which accompanied all this was an outstanding feature. With the exception of some older coffee-bar youths in Northtown there was very little premeditated delinquency or any planning behind the various escapades.

Finally, the unattached showed pronounced hostility towards adults. This was directed particularly towards adults in authority: parents, teachers, employers, and the police. As a result adult discipline, including parental discipline, was often quite ineffective. There was also the feeling that adults did not understand them. All adults in authority were classed as 'them'—those who were opposed to and against 'us'. The coffee bar's freedom from adult demands and control explained much of its popularity. Conversely, the reluctance to enter a youth club was often a revolt against being organized and being told what to do by someone who was perceived as being a patronizing, interfering, or hostile adult.

This is a generalized picture. Seldom did one individual show all these characteristics. Nevertheless much of the description holds true for a large number, particularly among the older groups in Seagate and North-town. Age was an important factor affecting the extent to which the attitudes and problems had become crystallized. Many of the symptoms were already visible with the younger groups, but the problems really began to express themselves by about the age of sixteen or seventeen when the novelty of the first job had worn off, work was becoming boring, and the question of adult authority had become particularly acute. Many of the attitudes and feelings voiced by older groups in Northtown and Seagate could be described as cynical or even embittered and it became painfully clear that attempts to attach this type of young person to any of the usual youth clubs would be unlikely to meet with much success.

Making contact
When the project was originally conceived none of this information about the unattached had been established. Nor could valid information be gained about them or help of any real or lasting kind be given them unless the workers could find a way to approach them, gain their confidence and trust, and ultimately be accepted by them.

Opportunities for contacting young people within the terms of reference, it was reasoned, could be found at a number of points, classifiable generally into situations of work, school, and leisure. In the work setting contact might be possible either in working alongside the unattached, or in occupying some sympathetic position such as that of a personnel, welfare, or sports officer. In the school setting the only possibility seemed to be the direct approach offered by the teaching role. In the leisure setting the possibilities were as variable as the young person's capacity to devise ways of spending it. Coffee bars, dance halls, cafés, public houses, parks, recreations grounds, and street corners were just a few venues which suggested themselves. In view of the exploratory nature of the project the Central Advisory Committee felt it valuable to investigate as widely as possible all three approaches—work, school, and leisure—to enable an assessment of the relative merits and demerits of each as a practical means of making contact. The test of whether a given means of contact had been successful or not was to lie in the nature and quality of the relationship which developed out of it. A 'successful means of contact' was one which permitted the development of a strong relationship with unattached groups or individuals. A 'strong' relationship in turn was defined as one which was basically characterized by warmth and by holding the trust and confidence of the unattached, in contrast to a 'casual relationship' which permitted no more than a superficial expression of pleasantries or hostility....

Brian and his father
I met Brian R's father by chance one evening. He recognized me from the play and seemed anxious to talk about Brian. Things had come to a head at home and Brian had decided to leave and live in a flat. Mr and Mrs R. were surprised, concerned, and upset about this and Mr R. wanted to know from me what to do about it.

The impression of Mr R. that I had formed from Brian was that he was a reactionary, physically brutish individual.... The impression derived from meeting Mr R. was quite different, although it became clear why there existed such a strong disapproval from Brian. Mr R. started in real poverty and has achieved materialistic success by hard work and perseverance. His standards are staunchly conventional and he naturally fails to understand how any other set of values can be worth while. In particular, he cannot comprehend the arts-college world, 'what it is for' and 'where it will get anybody'.

Mr R. has seen Brian's growth as simply bewildering and has accordingy attempted during the past four or five years to clamp down on it; he has forcibly tried to check Brian and does not deny instances of brutality. The result, however, has been unsuccessful. Mr R. is now aware of this but not clear what to do instead. Added to this lack of understanding is a strong element of irrational stubbornness, shared inherently by father and son, which has served to perpetuate the gap between them.

Brian had now presented a showdown by intending to leave home. Mr R. wanted a happy family and was prepared 'to rethink'. Because of this, he talked to me for about an hour. He considered me as a person who knew his son well and yet who was also approachable in the sense of being responsible and adult.

Briefly, I suggested that there was an immediate need for someone to relinquish his pride and break the deadlock. It was improbable that Brian would give way, and I attempted to show that his behaviour could be explained in terms of adolescent rebellion—which was not as abnormal as Mr R. seemed to think. I suggested that instead of being aggressive and cynical towards Brian's interest in art, it might well be helpful, if possible, for his father to show more sympathy towards what he was doing.... I then tried to put the case for the art student so that Mr R. would see that it is not entirely a wasteful way of spending time.

Mr R. seemed to accept much of what I said. Whatever the influence of this meeting, it was pleasing to hear a few days later that Brian no longer intended to leave home. Howard asked 'Why the change?' and Brian replied briefly that his father had altered his attitude.

4 From 'Relationship between home background, school success and adolescent attitudes'

We know that the majority of the students experiencing success in school come from home backgrounds that can be characterized as advantaged with respect to the expectations which are held by the school. We know also that the vast majority of the students not experiencing success in school are from disadvantaged home backgrounds, again with respect to school expectations. However, there are some students, though they are few in number, whose school performances and home backgrounds are not consistent with the reality just described. Inconsistent with the successful school performance which is associated with advantaged home conditions, there are students from advantaged, or, if preferred, middle-class backgrounds who are not experiencing success in school, and there are also students from disadvantaged lower-class home backgrounds who are successful in school.

The presence of these inconsistent students, as they might be termed, can be detected in the research which has dealt with the nature of the relationship between home background and performance in school. Bloom *et al* (1965), after an extensive survey of the research literature, stated that the majority of the studies concerned with this relationship resulted in significant (positive) correlations on the order of 0.30 to 0.50 between sociological indices of home background and assorted measures of school achievement. One explanation for the variance which remained unexplained is the presence of the inconsistent students.

Though these students emerged as an aberrant phenomenon in such research, a review of the literature revealed that virtually no effort has been expended to try to understand the phenomenon. The research reported here represented such an attempt. Selected for study were the attitudes and views of these students.

First, for advantaged students who are successful in school, the expectations of the school and the internalized motives of these students, their attitudes, will tend to be congruent. Furthermore, the attitudes of these students and the values in their advantaged culture will also tend to be congruent. These conditions can, and most often do, provide for preferred behaviour, and this preferred behaviour can, and most often does, result in a successful school performance.

Secondly, for the disadvantaged students who are not experiencing success in school, the expectations of the school and their internalized attitudes will tend to be incongruent. But, the values of the disadvantaged culture and the attitudes of the students will tend to be congruent. The situation for the disadvantaged students, then, is such that the values available during socialization are not the same as those which are in evidence in the dominant advantaged culture, and, consequently, these values are not the same as those which serve as the context for the expectations of the school. These conditions are such that the disadvantaged student does not, and most often cannot, experience success in school.

Using these propositions, others were derived to make explicit hypothetical interrelationships among cultural values, student motives, and school expectations for the two inconsistent student types.

First, for the advantaged students who are not experiencing success in school, the expectations of the school and the attitudes of the students will tend to be incongruent, and, furthmore, their attitudes and the values of their advantaged culture will also tend to be incongruent. Their lack of success is reflected in the incongruency between their attitudes and the expectations of the school. Because, as previously noted, the values of the advantaged culture are congruent with the expectations of the school, we can expect the attitudes of these students to differ from those attitudes found in the advantaged culture.

I

Secondly, for the disadvantaged students who are experiencing success in school, their attitudes and the expectations of the school will tend to be congruent, but their attitudes and the values of their disadvantaged culture will tend to be incongruent. Their success in school is mirrored in the congruency between their attitudes and the expectations of the school. Because the values of the disadvantaged are not, for the most part, congruent with the expectations of the school, we can expect to find that the attitudes of these students do differ from the attitudes found in the disadvantaged culture.

To conclude this discussion of the theoretical framework, the proposition basic to the inconsistent student types is given further emphasis. This proposition was, in fact, the major hypothesis of this study. It was hypothesized that the attitudes of the inconsistent students would be incongruent with those of their associated majority group who, for the advantaged-non-successful students, were the advantaged-successful students, and, for the disadvantaged-successful students, were the disadvantaged-non-successful students. . . .

Discussion

The thesis of the study was confirmed. The attitudes of the inconsistent students were found to be incongruent with those of their associated majority groups. The attitudes of all four groups, though, tended towards the 'preferred' direction. Moreover, it can be said that, for the most part, the attitudes of the disadvantaged-successful students were like those of the advantaged-successful students and the attitudes of the advantaged-non-successful students were like those of the disadvantaged-non-successful students. These findings were true for the view of the environment, where the disadvantaged-successful students expressed the most optimistic view of the future, and for the attitude towards school groups, and for the peer group attitude towards education, where the preferred attitudes were agreed to most strongly by the advantaged-successful students followed by the disadvantaged-successful students.

A notable exception to these results was the attitude towards education. In this instance, the attitudes towards education of all four groups were congruent and tended towards the 'preferred' direction, a finding which did not support the hypothesis nor the results of previous research (Hieronymus, 1951; Charters, 1953; Evans, 1965; Lavin, 1965). The conclusion which is suggested by the finding of this study is that the attitude towards education does not distinguish advantaged students from disadvantaged students, nor successful students from non-successful students.

Though the successful students differed from the non-successful students with respect to the attitudes of their peer groups towards education, these attitudes also distinguished the advantaged students from the disadvantaged students, suggesting that this attitude is related to performance in school as well as to home background. This conclusion, it seems, is somewhat incompatible with the conclusion reached as a result of the analysis of the student's own attitude towards education. If we can assume, however, that the students had internalized their own attitudes towards education, then one plausible explanation for the seeming inconsistency is that the student's attitude towards education is not the direct result of the influence of his peers but rather the result of some other, yet undisclosed source.

The major hypothesis of this study was developed as a logical extension of the model of social behaviour of Getzels (1966), and, when this hypothesis was confirmed, the conceptual model was supported. Also, the model was extended to encompass such problems as the one posed in this study and other studies which stem from this one.

In generalizing from the results of this study, there are cautions to be acknowledged. Only four attitudes were studied, suggesting a need to replicate this study but to sample other attitudinal dimensions from the affective domain. Consideration should be given while contemplating such a study to estimating home background by means other than socio-economic characteristics as Bloom *et al* (1965) have suggested. Socio-economic status characteristics are, at best, omnibus estimates of home culture.

5 From *Interpersonal Relations and Education*

We have come to accept adolescence as a difficult time. This is hardly a new phenomenon. As the shepherd remarks in *The Winter's Tale*:

> I would there were no age between ten and three-and-
> twenty, or that youth would sleep out the rest: for there is
> nothing (in the between) but getting wenches with child,
> wronging the ancientry, stealing, fighting . . .

Recently we have come to speak of a *youth culture*. It is one of those sociological terms which has passed through the Sunday colour supplements into common parlance. It is a conception we shall have to examine carefully. The background is relatively well known. In contrast to life in earlier ages, the young are now all compelled to attend school for a minimum of ten years, a growing minority of older adolescents continuing for between one and ten years more in further or higher education. One of the main effects of schooling is the segregation of the adolescent from parents and small children for several hours each day. Since schools are age-graded, adolescents spend a tremendous amount of time in school with persons of their own age, and this spills over into out-of-school associations. In addition, the adolescent has in the post-war era become an important consumer. He has money to spend and a whole economic market has grown up around him to cater for his needs—or in some cases to promote needs which can then be catered for.

It may help to clarify some of the issues if we introduce the concept of *reference group.* The term was first introduced by Hyman (1942) and has subsequently been developed by social psychologists (notably Newcomb, 1950; Sherif, 1953; Shibutani, 1955) and sociologists (notably Merton, 1957). Traditionally, a reference group is a group in which a person seeks to attain or maintain membership or in whose terms he evaluates himself. Kelley (1952) has suggested two main functions of reference groups. The first function is *normative* and is specified in the definition just given. Here the person wishes to become a member of the group or to maintain his membership in it. To do this, he conforms to the group's norms, adopt its values and evaluates himself in these terms. The members of the group become his significant others. With respect to the normative function a reference group can be negative. A negative reference group is a group of which a person would like to cease being a member or of which he would have definite antipathy to becoming a member; he would not evaluate himself in the group's terms. The second function of reference groups is *comparative.* In this case a person uses the reference group as a standard of comparison with which to estimate his own position. For example, as a university teacher I might use school-teachers as a comparative reference group when they are given a pay rise. I may have no interest in them normatively, i.e. I do not want to become a schoolteacher or to conform to their norms, but I may take their pay rise as a basis for estimating my own financial position. By comparing my position with theirs, I might feel economically deprived. Thus groups, whether or not one is a member, can be used as reference groups with one or both functions.

To make the concept clear, we can consider the data of the Lumley study (Hargreaves, 1967) described earlier. The low stream pupils used the high streams as a comparative reference group. They complained that the high stream pupils were given privileges denied to them. They felt deprived relative to the upper streams. Yet at the same time they used the upper streams as a negative reference group with respect to the normative function. The norms and values of the upper streams were the inverse of their own; they did not want to be transferred into the higher streams and intentionally under-achieved in order to avoid transfer.

The adolescent is not, by definition, a member of the adult group. He is a member of the adolescent group as a whole and he is a member of one or more particular friendship groups within the totality of his age-mates. All these groups can form reference groups, both normative and comparative, to the adolescent.

Comparative reference groups
The adolescent resents the fact that he legally cannot drink alcohol until he is eighteen.

The adolescent complains to his parents that he is not receiving enough pocket money. He argues that nowadays all adolescents get more than 15p a week to spend.

The adolescent feels badly treated because all his friends are allowed to come home late on Friday and Saturday evenings.

In these three examples the adolescent is using adults, all adolescents and his particular friendship group respectively as comparative reference groups.

Normative reference groups

(*a*) *Positive.* An adolescent grows his hair long because all the members of his friendship group do so and he wishes to conform to this norm in order to be accepted.

An adolescent refuses to grow his hair long because he knows that his parents and other adults disapprove of the style and he wishes to be accepted by them.

(*b*) *Negative.* An adolescent grows his hair long because he knows that his parents and other adults disapprove. He does not wish to be an adult or to acquire their norms and values which he despises.

The adolescent grows his hair short because he wishes to dissociate himself from his adolescent friendship group where long hair is the norm.

Thus an adolescent may determine his hair style in response to various social influences. The concept of reference group helps to clarify this social influence. Hair style can be determined in relation to adult or adolescent reference groups, positive or negative. It may represent conformity to a positive reference group, adult or adolescent, or a reaction against a negative reference group, adult or adolescent. It may of course, be a combination. For example, he may grow his hair long in order to gain acceptance in his peer group (adolescent positive reference group) *and* in order to reject the values of adults (adult negative reference group). A third possibility is that the adolescent may be caught between two positive reference groups. He may be pressured by his friends to grow his hair long and by his parents to keep it short. Presumably the final length of his hair will indicate which is the stronger of the two positive reference groups.

We can now set up three basic reference group situations.

Type A   Peers form a positive reference group.
Adults form a negative reference group.
Type B   Peers form a negative reference group.
Adults form a positive reference group.
Type C   Peers form a positive reference group.
Adults form a positive reference group.

The proponents of youth culture seem to be arguing that the adolescent is basically in a Type A situation. The argument of the first part of this chapter will be that this is an erroneous view, based on a superficial interpretation of the facts and an inadequate conception of social influence during adolescence. The argument maintains that Type B and C situations are very common for most adolescents and that very careful research is needed before we can explain an adolescent's actual behaviour as belonging to a particular Type. As the illustration of length of hair indicates, it is very easy to mistake a Type A situation for a Type C situation.

If the majority of adolescents are basically in a Type A situation, if they possess values and norms which conflict with those of adults, then we should expect relationships with parents and other adults to be generally poor. Much of our present evidence seems to suggest that in general adolescents have favourable attitudes to parents and to adults.

It seems reasonable to suggest that adults interpret adolescent behaviour as deviating from accepted social values and standards much more radically than is really the case. It would be an excellent rationalization of their hostility. The generation gap would then be perceived as much students, Niles (1968), following the pioneering work of Brittain (1963) more pervasive and fundamental than it really is. Certainly the evidence does not point to such a pervasive disjunction in values. One of my own in the United States, put adolescent girls in a situation where they had to choose to accept the influence of parents or peers in the solution of certain problems. In matters of taste or personal appearance, peer influence was preferred to that of parents. For instance, 65 per cent of the fifteen year olds would change their hair styles to please friends rather than parents and 76 per cent would adopt a dress colour approved by friends rather than parents. But in more important matters, especially those involving moral questions or long-term decisions, parental influence tended to be accepted. For example, when faced with the problem of which of two boys she liked equally well she should date, only one-third accepted the recommendation of friends rather than parents. When reassured by friends to stay late at an exciting party at the cost of worrying her mother, less than one-third actually stayed.

One form of adult resentment against the young may spring from the fact that adolescents express some social values more openly, with less guilt, shame or ambivalence. One of the dominant values in our society is hedonism—having a good time. In my view this is not, as some have argued, a value confined to youth. We all seem to be scrambling to make money, and more money, in order to worship the gods of entertainment, food and drink, holidays abroad and the rest of the pantheon. Bingo and football pools enjoy an unprecedented boom among adults. It is known that whenever there is a very large win on the pools, large numbers of irregular punters fill in their coupons with renewed vigour and hope. Indeed, the points system for the Treble Chance was changed in order to increase the chances of a single person scooping the pool.

Not surprisingly many young people come to worship at the same or similar shrines. The difference is that the young do not have the responsibilities or the restrictions of adults and can thus indulge themselves rather more thoroughly. The adult stresses the so-called 'balanced view'. He says, 'I'm not against your having a good time, but remember ...' and the 'but' is always restrictive. But the adults would probably follow the same path, if only they could. Indeed, much of the entertainment provided by television, films and books or magazines seems to be aimed at giving adults vicarious pleasure by recounting the experiences of real or imaginary persons who can.

The other difference is that adults are caught in the midst of a changing and progressively more affluent society. With more wealth, leisure and opportunity many adults are beginning to shed the Protestant and puritanical ethic of the middle classes (and perhaps the working classes) of the past. As a result they tend to be genuinely ambivalent in their values and attitudes. They espouse the current hedonism but try to articulate it with the more traditional values of hard work and deferred gratification, and a traditional sexual morality. As a result they have one foot in the past and one foot in the present and are not sure whether to move forwards or backwards. They tend to be inconsistent and at times hypocritical. The woman who has nothing but contempt for the young but spends a fortune on making herself look as young as possible represents a whole generation of confused adults who expect young people to do as the adults say, not as adults do. . . .

One of the most striking social changes in this century has been the change in parent-adolescent relationships. The central aspect of this change is the shift in power between the two. The adolescent has made marked gains in power, increasing his rights and reducing his obligations *vis-à-vis* his parents. It is not long since we were being harangued by public figures about 'the distressing abdication of parental authority'; currently we seem to take it more for granted. We do not expect, for example, our adolescent children to seek our permission in areas where it would have been normative to do so fifty years ago. Adolescents no longer need our consent about the way they spend their money or their leisure time, or about the friends they wish to go around with. The parent who does try to intervene in such matters is quite often told that it is none of his business. In the interest of good relationships parents concede their former rights and powers, though often after fighting a brief losing battle that precedes the reluctant retreat.

The remarkable aspect of this change is its impact on the school. All teachers accept that relations between teachers and pupils have become much more informal and friendly in recent years, even in the very traditional grammar schools. Yet—and this is the point—this has not been accompanied by a marked power shift. Pupils today have hardly any more rights than they had half a century ago, nor do the teachers want to concede such rights. In this respect the school has lagged behind the family. Not unnaturally, adolescents often—but by no means as a general rule—expect an increase in rights to match the growth of informality and the power shift that has taken place at home. As a result teachers tend to

135

be ambivalent in their feelings and behaviour towards pupils. They approve of the informality, within limits, but when the pupils take things 'too far', when they ask for or demand rights that are not traditionally theirs, the teachers tend to swing back to the old authoritarianism. The school is normally much more restrictive and autocratic in structure than is the home, despite the general air of informality and friendliness that prevails in so many secondary schools. The difference between reality and appearance becomes obvious when new rights are desired by some pupils. Heads are content with school councils, as long as the function is advisory only, subject to the veto of the staff or head. Once the council wants power in areas which the staff regard as of more than peripheral importance, the proposals are rejected as unthinkable. More traditional headteachers try to preserve their conception of school in spite of the social changes elsewhere in society. Pupils who do not accept their assigned role, who fail to obey the school rules, even on such relatively minor matters as the styles of clothing and length of hair or jewellery, are punished or even expelled where this is possible. 'Pupil power' is a frightening word to many teachers and headteachers; they try to eliminate such dissenting groups as militant products of a permissive society who are potential sources of conflict and contamination within the school. (This remarkable over-reaction becomes evident when one reads the documents of the Schools' Action Union, which are very moderate in their demands and reveal a deep and idealistic concern with education. It is no less than tragic that the schools cannot tap this idealism rather that attempting to reject or suppress it.) The teaching profession has failed to learn a lesson from the universities, for it is not realized that in effect the school is setting itself up as one of the few remaining authorities against which the adolescent can rebel. Curiously, too, many teachers do not seem to recognize that much of their behaviour seems hypocritical to the pupils. The teachers preach democracy and talk about education for independence and creativity. What they mean is their own style of democracy which excludes the school itself. Independence and creativity must operate within the teachers' assumptions. If the pupils develop an independence or creativity which actually questions or rejects the teachers' assumptions, they are ruled out of court. It is easy for the teachers to explain things away in terms of a minority of troublemakers or 'outside influences' or 'militant anarchists'. It is much harder to recognize the deeper and more general social changes that are taking place in society and in the school and to accept that today's difficult minorities have a curious habit of becoming tomorrow's moderates.

Let us now examine in further detail some of the growing problems and conflicts between teachers and pupils. Smoking is a traditional school problem with boys, though recently the problem has grown more acute. In 1970 a report by the Tobacco Research Council showed that in the seven-year period since 1961 fifteen-year-old boys increased their average weekly consumption of cigarettes from 13.4 to 19.2, and girls from

4.1 to 7.8. There is evidence now that pupils are beginning to smoke at an earlier age—7 per cent of boys beginning to smoke at the age of six or under. Young people can now afford to buy more cigarettes and are now frequently smoking with parental consent. Yet very few schools allow their pupils to smoke in school. This is obviously a very difficult issue, but we cannot escape the fact that the school is in this area being more restrictive than the home, forcing the pupils to do their smoking illicitly in lavatories and other such places.

Drink is a relatively new problem, partly affected by the adolescent's ability to afford the cost of alcoholic drinks and partly by the greater social acceptability of drinking in the older adolescent. In some areas it is now customary for young people, not always over the age of eighteen, to meet socially in pubs rather than coffee bars. Teachers are having to face the problems of pupils arriving at school functions 'under the influence', and to police the pupils to prevent illicit drinking at school dances. I know of one school which has abandoned its annual dance for this very reason. In this school the teachers dare not go into the pub near the school after a school function since they know it will be full of their own senior pupils.

Drugs present quite a new problem for schools, especially when we remember that almost all adults have neither current not past experience of them, unlike the case with cigarettes and alcohol. Because drug-taking is not socially acceptable among adults, teachers tend to regard it as a much more serious 'crime' than smoking or drinking. Yet this is a problem which is likely to grow during the next decade, with respect both to the smoking of cannabis and to the taking of amphetamines, barbiturates and opiates. There is a widespread fear and ignorance of drugs among teachers as among adults in general. The reaction of many headteachers to finding one or more cannabis-smokers or drug-takers among the pupils does not suggest that they will be able to deal with such cases rationally or sympathetically, or in a way that will inhibit the spread of drug-taking and the development of a drug 'underground' among senior pupils either on or off the school premises (McAlhone, 1970).

Sexual problems, too, are making a greater impact on the life of the school. Conscious of being to some degree *in loco parentis*, and fearing that sexual relationships between pupils may take place when they are in the school's care, teachers feel a need to supervise pupils very closely in this respect on school holidays and at other school functions. Teachers know that if the pupils commit what most adults would regard as sexual misdemeanours when they are in the school's charge, then the school will be harshly judged by parents and public. It is an unenviable position for teachers. When sexual scandals or pregnancies do arise, the offending pupil(s) is expelled or quietly extracted from the school. There remains a latter day form of being sent to the far reaches of the Empire. In effect, schools are reluctant to face sexual problems, even though they are aware of their existence among the older pupils. They are unwilling to encourage an open discussion of these problems and do not take the initiative in encouraging a dialogue between pupils, teachers and parents. They prefer not to see, taking action only when a crisis situation affords no alternative, such action dealing with the symptoms rather than the root of the problem.

Most important of all, the social life of the adolescent in school has, from the teenager's perspective, a definite old-fashioned air. The school offers activities of an intellectual quality (debating and scientific societies), sport, and the sort of activities traditionally associated with the church youth club (table-tennis, country dancing). Most teenagers do want these activities, but increasingly some also want the sort of activities provided by commercial enterprises but for which the school is generally unwilling to cater. Even the school parties traditionally provided by teachers for the younger pupils are often regarded by these pupils as 'square' or insufficiently sophisticated.

All these factors suggest to me that the school is likely to play a less important part in the social life of the pupils. The teachers are unwilling to adapt to the changing needs and expectations, in this field as in others. Many adolescents will continue to accept the school's facilities—leading teachers to believe that all is well—but they will also demand activities that are provided, or will be provided, elsewhere, either by commercial undertakings or by the pupils themselves. More and more the gap between the school's extracurricular social life and the other leisure activities of many adolescents will widen. In turning to commercial enterprises for leisure activities or in creating their own, such adolescents are in a vulnerable position with respect to commercial exploitation and are likely to reduce the amount of informal contact with responsible and caring adults.

Tragically, it is the pupils who are in most need of adult help and care who will most readily turn away from the school's extracurricular social life. The pupils most affected will be those from working-class homes, those who are less committed to traditional middle-class values and to the intellectual life of the school, those with the lowest intellectual attainments and behaviour ratings, as the research of Sugarman (1967) shows. Sugarman himself believes that it is the pupils who are alienated from school who turn to teenage culture—listening to pop records, going to dances and coffee bars, following adolescent fashion in clothing and hair styles, smoking and dating—as an *alternative* to the pupil role. (This is clearly an argument that is similar to Coleman's.) Whether it is more a question of such pupils doing badly at school because of their home background and/or because of their commitment to pop culture, or vice versa, there is undoubtedly a major problem posed for the school, a problem which defies easy answers but which must be tackled if we are not to be overtaken by events. Certainly matters are not helped by the inclination of many teachers to deride pop culture openly, rather than recognizing it as a useful basis for the education of discrimination and artistic appreciation. How few music teachers, for example, know anything about contemporary pop music, which is so familiar to and so enjoyed by most adolescents. If their own musical taste is ridiculed or despised or treated with condescension by the teachers, is it so surprising that these attitudes are reciprocated to the teachers' musical preferences, effectively blunting the pupils' musical sensibilities and interests for many years to come? In ways such as this the teachers often enlarge the generation gap and reinforce the adolescent's commitment to pop culture. The teacher's avowed intention to educate often boils down to a demand that the pupils unilaterally and unconditionally accept the teacher's valuations. Any movement on the teacher's part (in our musical example, permitting the pupils to play pop records on the last day of term) takes the form of a half-hearted concession to valuations of a lower order.

6 From *The Age of Social Experiment*

The hypothesis which I wish to suggest is that adolescence, meaning that period in the individual's life between the onset of puberty and the time when he is able to cope with adult problems and responsibilities to the extent that he is accepted as an adult by adults, is the period during which the number of 'social experiments' which he makes rises to a peak and then falls again. Social experiment remains a feature of adult life and shows a marked increase at specific times, for example when an individual marries or attends a social skills course, but adolescence is the principal period of 'social experiment'.

I believe that this hypothesis is useful in at least two ways: (1) it provides a means of relating a number of existing theories of adolescence, and (2) it suggests a new approach to work with adolescents in social psychology.

Definition of a 'social experiment'

By a 'social experiment' I mean any situation when an individual exhibits a trial attitude or takes a trial course of action which effects and calls forth a reaction from any other individual or group of individuals, whether the attitude is adopted or action taken with a view to testing reaction, or with no conscious aim.

The pattern of social experiments

The only point which I would like to emphasize is that the social experiment is a learning situation for the vast majority of adolescents.

Evidence which suggested this hypothesis

1 When I used the critical incident technique with 690 English schoolchildren between the ages of thirteen and eighteen, asking them to cite examples of incidents when adults behaved badly towards them or handled a situation involving them badly, I found:

1st   that the most common classes of incidents—adult restriction, demands, punishment, hostility (meaning superiority, ignoring, or not listening to the adolescent), and criticism were generally reactions to experimental behaviour on the part of the adolescent. (This was true both when adolescents had supporting and positive parents and teachers and cited two good incidents to three bad, and also where they had hostile and negative parents and teachers and cited only one good incident to three bad).

2nd   that between 60 and 70 per cent of all the incidents cited had been initiated by the adolescent.

3rd   that, when they were interviewed about why they had behaved in a certain way, about 40 per cent of adolescents would use such a verbal form as 'I had to find out what happened if I tried (or did) X.'

4th   Eighteen-year-old grammar school boys questioned about why they had cited fewer bad critical incidents involving adults than fifteen, sixteen, and seventeen-year-olds mostly commented either that they had discovered ways of handling adults or had found out about adult ways of doing things.

2 The Literature

(a)   The literature on adolescence contains a number of references to the experimental nature of adolescence, without, as far as I know, any systematic study being attempted.

(b)   Gesell found that adolescents, particularly between the ages of fourteen and fifteen, admired and identified themselves with actors and actresses.

(c)   Eduard Sprangers argues in *Psychologie des Jugendalters* that the need for the adolescent to establish ego-unity leads him to experiment with different aspects of his own ego.

(d)   The application of the hypothesis to E. Erikson's theory of ego-identity.

(e)   There are a number of documented pieces of work in the form of papers and articles, but which lend support to the notion that adolescence is an experimental period. Some of the most interesting evidence is concerned with delinquency and pathological development related to the subject's inability to interpret feedback or to give the cues which will ensure that he receives feedback.

The function of social experiments (a rationale)

A development of the argument is that the most fundamental kind of human learning is experimental or trial and error learning (even where this inability involves imitation). The contention is that a sense of identity only follows the ability to predict the effects of one's actions and to modify one's environment. The effect of puberty on the child's 'good adjustment', the need to abandon a dependent relationship for an adult relationship with adults on terms of equality means that social experiment is most important during adolescence.

What are the specific questions to which adolescents obtain answers through social experiment?
(The interest here lies in the special 'moves' which adolescents make.)
The general question 'Who am I?' leads the adolescent to ask further:

1   What can I cope with? (The use of motor cycles and the behaviour of the lone rock climber indicate that feedback is still important in these situations.)
2   Is my self-concept accepted by others? (Examples: boasting, 'telling the tale'.)
3   Is my social approach effective in terms of establishing the relationship which I want? (Example: 'chatting up girl'.)

In more detail:
(a)   Can I control other people's emotions and if so, how? (Examples: Telling father he is a ******! Making love.)
(b)   Can I influence other people's opinions and if so, how? (Example: arguments about pop stars.)
(c)   Can I control others' behaviour and if so, how? (Example: baiting a schoolmaster.)
(d)   How can I earn peer-group approval? (Sartre—imitation.) (Example: acting hard towards outsiders.)
(e)   How can I establish my independence of adults' rules for adolescents? (Example: attack on school rules.)
(f)   How far can I go without destroying a relationship? In other words —to what extent will people allow me to be myself? (Examples: arguing with parents and forcing a compromise. Brinkmanship.)
(g)   Are people's actions predictable? Using same approach at different times with same person, with different people. (Example: teasing.)

4   What does X want of me and is it consistent with my self-concept? (Examples: inviting demands from others. Seeking associations with the heterodox to see. . . . !)
5   What are the social norms in this group? (Example: 'trial' behaviour, e.g. drinking.)
General conclusion from first piece of work—adolescents who feel recognized, who receive positive feedback, are least aggressive and most sensitive to others' interests—in other words they mature most rapidly.

Note: Work is going on by McPhail and others to test these hypotheses and others. The whole area is in need of further research. There is also a need for informed discussion partly among young people themselves and certainly among all those concerned with young people.

7 From *Exit from Childhood*
To begin with many of the girls described the difficult emotional flux of

adolescence. They wrote about how, along with the new excitement, had come malaise and depression—moods in which Huddersfield seemed a shabby backcloth to their forlorn identity.

'I begin to wonder what was the point of it all, why were people living on this earth? Why was I who I am? At these times Huddersfield seems to be an extremely dirty town and very miserable. Especially with the rain and the fog, the dull monotony of the daily routine, the miserable feeling of being alone—life in Huddersfield then feels hardly bearable. At one time I was even getting to the point of hating school, but now I seem to be emerging from that slough.'

They know what has to be expected from adolescence, but against this has to be placed the seeming fickleness of adults:

'They treat us like children, and expect us to behave in a mature, adult fashion. Parents say that 'moods', especially of elation quickly followed by depression, are all part of growing up. What they do not seem to realize is that they cause these moods especially when we feel depressed and miserable by their constant nattering and criticism.'

At home the turbulent angers at being treated now as a child, now as adult, can burst into open, but equally perplexing argument:

Obviously the main problems of my growing up is the relationship between myself and my parents. These fluctuate considerably between being told 'You don't know what you're talking about', and that I am 'careless beyond all measure', to being complimented on my logic by my father when I have got the better of a discussion with my mother.

But this varied from girl to girl, and some felt that in general they lived as adults on Saturday and Sunday, but as children at Silveredge on the other five days:

Home life is not punctuated with noisy rows and deadly silences. There, at least, one is accepted as a more adult person and treated as such. At school, however, this is not so. During the week one is treated as a child, as one in a crowd, with no personality or feelings. The mere thought of wearing a beret because three hundred other girls do, fills me with something more than annoyance. This appears to be a major problem, the difficulty of changing back into a schoolgirl after two days of being 'grown up'—and having to return to school uniform again.

On the other hand, few—especially from middle-class backgrounds— felt differently and were satisfied by the tokens of coming maturity they received at school:

I think my main problem has been trying to catch up with the girls that have grown up before me, and who do not approve of my too childish behaviour and hairstyle. They keep telling me that 'everyone is clamping down on us' at schools, that we need more freedom, more responsibility, and that we should not be treated like children. Personally, apart from righteous anger at the occasional stupidities and unfair judgments of the staff (not always concerning myself), I find in school as much freedom and happiness as I wish. I enjoy being in the sixth form for the childish reason that I can use the front door, wear a skirt, and answer the telephone.

But what didn't vary much from girl to girl was the sense that either parents or teachers might at any time knock them back into childhood by snatching away the adult respects and responsibilities that the girls felt they needed:

At one time I am told to remember that I am now nearly seventeen, and that is the time I realized that I was growing up; and then soon after I am told that I must do this, do that, conform to this regulation and abide by that law. Naturally it is very pleasing when people tell us we are growing up, and give responsibility, but the next moment when you are treated like a child, it is most upsetting.

From these pressures the girls often turn aside into inner worlds of fantasy: 'I often allow myself to lapse into dreams' says one girl. 'I am normally very active' continues another,

But sometimes I am just in the mood to think, and I have to sort myself out. Sometimes, when I am just thinking, my mother or someone else tells me I am just wasting time and ask what it can be that needs so much thought. I think that because older people have already taken their place, and presumably accepted it, they tend to take it for granted and cannot understand that we have yet to do this.

Many girls mentioned private thinking into religion, and though here and there this seemed no more than a polite recognition of an 'expected' subject, there were some for whom it seemed a very real part of these adolescent turmoils. Pauline Duce brings to her religion fears and doubts that are hardly tamed by rational enquiry:

As a child I often had nightmares about the existence of the world, going on and on and on—until I had to stop thinking about it. The grammar school gave me a new approach to these problems, especially the broadcasts in the sixth form. I began to think more profoundly at my being at all, and thought up reasonable answers for my own questions. Some of my problems concerning death were solved for me

143

by the books the minister lent after discussions with him, but still I have problems about the ultimate end of the world—whether it will come by nuclear war, or by Act of God.

Other girls, almost with a sense of surprise at the sceptical thrust of their own intelligence, find their childhood securities suddenly displaced:

I begin to wonder why on earth God should send his son to a tiny speck of dust such as us. I suppose this is trying to fit in scientific fact with religion and sometimes unfortunately I cannot. I begin to question whether Jesus was God's son, or whether he was merely a man with greater than average powers who thought he was the son of God. And then I wonder why, if Moslems and Buddhists think theirs is a true religion, why should ours be the only true one. Sometimes I even wonder if there really is a God at all.

And others like Brenda Drysdale know very clearly what is personal and what, for them, merely belongs to formal school training:

Religion has its problems and at the moment I am in the throes of deciding whether I am agnostic or atheist. Of course, practically everyone who has been through the mill of the sixth form knows all the arguments on the subject, and they are not worth repeating here. I am too unfeeling and inquisitive to be religious.

SECTION 3: QUESTIONS FOR DISCUSSION

1   For many students, adolescence is a comparatively recent experience. Older users of this book may now find objectivity about the experience a little easier. Write an impression of your own adolescence. It should not be a record of events or even feelings recollected, but an effort to assess. There are a number of possible ways of tackling such a task, certainly including poetry. But, either as part of the piece of writing or as an addendum, make a note of any insights into your own past that you have gained from this section.

2   A number of issues arise from the material in this chapter:

   1   What are the consequences of social class differences in socialization by adolescence? Is it too late to do anything?

   2   David Hargreaves, in particular, takes what might be described as a 'permissive' view of youth; certainly, the implications of what he says run counter both to traditional classroom wisdom and to the views of other thinkers on education such as Jacques Barzun and Granville Bantock. How might the case against Hargreaves be argued? What evidence is there? Discuss fully his view of youth and the implied changes in education.

   3   How does a man or woman, do you think, arrive at a concept of the Self? To what extent is the Self-concept culturally determined?

Consider evidence from other cultures and from sub-cultures within our own society.

3 How can a secondary school most effectively provide for differing adolescent needs and learning styles?

4 What are the factors that cause the development of 'anti-school sub-cultures'? What do you think is the best way to cope with the problem?

5 During such a period as school practice make a study of an adolescent boy or girl. You will need to develop personal relations and talk to your subject, so tact will be needed to ensure that your subject talks freely though aware that a study is being made.

6 How can schools best prepare their young people for the working world? Should education, as desired by many parents and their young, be more vocational? If schools are not good at meeting 'expressive needs' why does Enquiry 1 suggest that young school leavers do not value the attempts of the school to meet such needs?

7 Discuss the sources and consequences of the various myths about teenagers—including those held by teenagers themselves.

8 Make a study of adolescent peer groups. When and how does a peer group become a gang?

9 How can conflict arise between the Ideal Self and the Other Self? How do adolescents resolve conflicts over self-image? Are there any immediate practical considerations for the classroom teacher?

10 Many adolescents in our schools seem indifferent to what the school offers, lacking in curiosity, and unable to express themselves or their thoughts effectively. Consider these commonplace observations in the light of the research associated with Bernstein and his colleagues. Is it too late to do anything at this stage? The American linguist, William Labov, as a consequence of profound studies of New York urban social dialects argues that in fact urban speech among the working class is not 'deprived'. It is as capable of abstract thinking and concept-handling as any other language. Read Labov's attack on interventionist educational policies (reprinted in Cashdan and Grugeon 1972). What do you feel about this issue?

REFERENCES

ABRAMS, P. and LITTLE, A. (1965) The young activist in British politics *British Journal of Sociology* 16, 2

ABRAMS, M. (1959) *Teenage Consumer Spending* London: London Press Exchange

BERNSTEIN, B. (1970) Education cannot compensate for society *New Society* 26th February, 344–7

BOTT, E. (1971) *Family and Social Network* London: Tavistock

CARTER, M. (1966) *Into Work* Harmondsworth: Penguin

CASHDAN, A. and GRUGEON, P. (1972) *Language in Education* London: Routledge and Kegan Paul

K

Douglas, J. W. B. (1968) *All Our Future* London: Peter Davies

Douvan, E. and Adelson, J. (1966) *The Adolescent Experience* New York: Wiley

Erikson, E. (1965) *Childhood and Society* Harmondsworth: Penguin

Getzels, J. W. and Jackson, P. W. (1962) *Creativity and Intelligence: Explorations with Gifted Students* New York: Wiley

Hargreaves, D. (1968) *Social Relations in a Secondary School* London: Routledge and Kegan Paul

Heider, G. (1958) *The Psychology of Interpersonal Relations* New York: Wiley

Jackson, B. (1962) *Education and the Working Class* London: Routledge and Kegan Paul

Jones, R. (1972) *Fantasy and Feeling in Education* Harmondsworth: Penguin

Lacey, C. (1970) *Hightown Grammar School* Manchester: Manchester University Press

Lawton, D. (1968) *Social Class, Language and Education* London: Routledge and Kegan Paul

Leach, E. (1973) *Times Educational Supplement* 2nd February

Mead, M. (1943) *Coming of Age in Samoa* Harmondsworth: Penguin

Musgrove, F. (1966) *Family Education and Society* London: Routledge and Kegan Paul

Schofield, M. (1968) *The Sexual Behaviour of Young People* Harmondsworth: Penguin

Schools Council (1968) *Enquiry 1: Young School Leavers* London: HMSO

Staines, J. W. (1958) Symposium: The development of children's values III The self picture as a factor in the classroom *British Journal of Educational Psychology* 28, 3, 97–111

Swift, D. F. (1966) Social class and achievement motivation *Educational Research* 8, 2, 83–95

Vernon, P. F. (1970) *Creativity* Harmondsworth: Penguin

READINGS

1 White, D. (1971) Brum's mobs *New Society* 21st October

2 and 7 Jackson, B. (1968) *Working Class Community* London: Routledge and Kegan Paul

3 Morse, M. (1965) *The Unattached* Harmondsworth: Penguin

4 Harrison, F. I. (1968) 'Relationship between home background, school success and adolescent attitudes' *Merrill Palmer Quarterly* 14

5 Hargreaves, D. (1972) *Interpersonal Relations and Education* London: Routledge and Kegan Paul

6 McPhail, P. (1971) 'The age of social experiment' in *Personality, Growth and Learning* London: Longman

Chapter 4: Us and them

The smokers' union line up outside Mr Gryce's room:

> 'I'm sick of you boys, you'll be the death of me. Not a day goes by without me having to deal with a line of boys. I can't remember a day, not one day, in all the years I've been in this school, and how long's that? ... ten years, and the school's no better now than it was on the day it opened. I can't understand it. I can't understand it at all.'
>
> The boys couldn't understand it either, and they dropped their eyes as he searched for an answer in their faces.

Barry Hines in *A Kestrel for a Knave* paints the picture of the 'traditional' working-class school—the concealed warfare between staff and inmates. But literature is full of school horrors. The Dr Arnold of *Tom Brown's Schooldays* is a rare bird in fiction. There is conflict between boys and masters in most of them. And the joke is anything but dead as a glance at comics or TV can show.

The stereotype of the teacher dies hard. Think also of the innumerable literary caricatures of village schoolmistresses—even in autobiography, seen through the mists of time. Though every citizen of Great Britain has had some experience of teachers, there often seems to be little knowledge or understanding of what manner of human beings these 400,000 teachers are.

In this chapter, we look at some of the work that has been done on teachers themselves. Who are they and what are their problems? What do we know about the relationships between teachers and pupils? What are the pressures of the job? What actually happens in classrooms?

Until quite recently there had not been a great deal of work done by sociologists and psychologists on the teaching profession, but the volume is now growing fast. In particular, as we shall see, there is now much interest in analysis of actual classroom behaviour—the interaction between teacher and children.

147

First of all, who are the people who join the profession? Fifty years ago, elementary school teaching was certainly a means of escape from the working-class. For a bright working-class boy or girl who had got one of the few scholarships to the local grammar school, it could be virtually the only way to a higher education and the middle-class. In 1955, Floud and Scott found that about half of all teachers came from lower middle-class families. There is some evidence to suggest that the old pattern has changed. Perhaps because of general improvements in working-class conditions and the pull of many other careers, there are now proportionately more middle-class entrants to the profession. Floud and Scott in 1955 looked at the social background of their teachers in terms of the type of school in which they were teaching. The higher the prestige of the school the higher the proportion of teachers with a wholly middle-class background. This, of course, merely reflected the social composition of the university population. Since 1955, however, it seems clear that college of education entrants have become more rather than less middle class.

Yet Jackson and Marsden found in their 1962 study of working-class children in a northern grammar school that over half of the 88 young people ended up as teachers. Sixteen girls and 38 boys went to university; 1 boy and 20 girls went to colleges of education. Out of this group, no less than 46 became teachers. The authors comment:

> It is very hard to do justice to this large number of teachers. Manifestly there were some for whom teaching was an inevitable and natural activity, an overflowing of the self in an unforced desire to share delight and knowledge with the young. But the major emphasis did not fall here. Far more frequent was the man or woman who had drifted from certificate to certificate, and then, lacking any decisive urge to strike out in a chosen career, had let the automatic nature of the educational process take the decision for them: they had stayed on as long as they could, adding a teacher's certificate to their other certificates, until they found themselves back in the classroom. It was as if education had never nourished in them any other capacities except those needed to score high marks in academic examinations. . . . What kind of teachers will they become, shaping other working-class children?

Nevertheless, of course, teachers have been fairly successful pupils at school. Prior to the development of comprehensive education on any scale, entrants to the profession came from mainly selective schools. Today, in any case, they will have experienced sixth form work in comprehensive school.

There is some research on the motivation of the would-be teacher. In 1967, Ashley, Cohen and Slater attempted an analysis of the reasons for entering teaching among students in a Scottish College of Education. They varied according to social background and to the type of school in which the student proposed to teach. Students of working-class background and would-be primary school teachers tended more to emphasize an interest in the job of teaching itself. Overall, there were more mentions of the conditions of work than anything else. Other categories of response included: the satisfaction of personal needs, the value of education to society, and such negative responses as the inability to think of anything else.

Scottish evidence can only be suggestive as far as England and Wales are concerned because of the differences in the educational system. In the same year Altman (1967) looked at the motivation of mature students. Few mature students enter teaching for the money—there is just as much to be earned outside. This group stressed the 'opportunity to be helpful to others' and the satisfaction they anticipated would grow out of really using their abilities and of being creative.

It is a pity, however, that we know so little about ourselves. As early as 1911, Coffman, an American, was pointing out how much easier it would be for society to create the educational system it needed if more was known about the background and motivation of the profession. Post-World War II and in the Sputnik era, Americans became distinctly worried about their teachers. In 1956 Liebermann commented acidly:

> The majority of teachers are coming from homes which are culturally unpromising if not impoverished. They are coming from homes in which light popular books and magazines or none at all are the rule.... The families from which teachers come are generally inactive both politically and in community affairs. Their social activities are likely to be confined to fraternal orders and lodges.... Families in the upper lower and lower middle classes usually have rather limited experience in the fine arts such as music or painting. Attending movies, playing cards, listening to radio and watching television, and visiting the neighbours are the most popular recreational outlets for these classes.

Just like the pupils, in other words.

What is really interesting about such an outburst, whether or not it has relevance for Britain, is the implicit assumptions about the role of the teacher. In 1951 the anthropologist, Margaret Mead, described what she felt to be three major ways in which teachers see their tasks:

1 *The grandparent role* Education is the passing on of the accumulated wisdom of the folk—the heritage, the cultural tradition. There seems to be something of this approach lurking behind the strictures of Liebermann. Teaching dominated by such values is intensely conservative.

2 *The child-nurse role* The teacher strives to inhabit the world of the child and values the ways and fantasies of the child. Self-expression beomes a goal and the here and now is all-important.

3 *The parent role* We live in a time of rapid change. As the past rapidly

becomes remote, so it becomes harder to prepare for the future. The teacher is thus vitally needed for the task of helping children to take control of a world unknown and not yet born.

There have been many attempts since then to list or describe the roles of the teacher. They tend to be either variants on Mead or classifications of the tasks that teachers are expected to perform. What all lists have in common is an acceptance of the role of the teacher as *instructor* and as *disciplinarian*. It is not possible to think of a teacher who does not in some way concern himself with the promotion of learning and a control of the learning situation. This is not really to say very much. In this sense both A. S. Neill and Mr Gryce are instructors and disciplinarians. We need to look rather more closely at the way teachers conceive their role in the classroom.

For example, every college of education student learns sooner or later, perhaps on his or her first teaching practice, that there can be a gap between what the college preaches and the school practices. Sometimes this is no more than the inevitable gap between theory and the same theory modified by immediate practicalities. But often there is more of an edge to it than that. In 1967 Finlayson and Cohen looked at the educational concepts of a group of students and compared them with those of a group of head teachers. They differed, of course:

> The direction of these differences show that the head teachers' conception of the teacher's role is generally in a contrary direction to the changes noted in the first two years of the students' training. In fact, the head teachers' conceptions go beyond the mean responses of the student-teachers' conceptions towards a relatively organizationally oriented, child-dominating, and conformity-desiring point of view.

Further, the survey showed an interesting movement of opinion among the students. The period of maximum liberality of educational thought was the second year of the course. As in the third year, the time of actual teaching loomed, so there was a tendency to revert to older ways of thinking and edge closer to the headteachers' conceptions. Finlayson and Cohen ascribe this movement to the detachment of college staff from schools and the impact of periods of school practice. W. K. Hoy's work in America tends to support this hypothesis. What a college of education is doing is socializing its students. They are learning the role of a teacher with all the values and norms that cluster round the role. But this is only a first phase. The socialization of the teacher is only completed in the schools themselves. As Hoy (1968) puts it:

> During socialization, both before and after entrance into the profession, each teacher forms his own version of the necessary orientations for effective pupil control. It appears likely that as the new,

idealistic teacher comes to his first position, he will be confronted with a conflicting set of norms and values concerning the control of students. During the initial phase of the socialization of the prospective teacher, professors of education stress the desirability of permissive pupil control, while 'discipline' as it is actually practised in the public schools emphasizes the need for more authoritarian controls. More experienced teachers tend to oppose permissiveness and embrace a more custodial pupil control ideology than do inexperienced teachers. In fact, in some schools, the ability to control is often equated with the ability to teach.

Perhaps one of the troubles is our own uncertainty about the 'training' a teacher needs. Colleges are not clear whether they are offering higher or vocational education—an uncertainty unlikely to be removed wholly by current reforms. Allied to this is the general suspicion of the intellectual, for anti-intellectualism is almost as rife in education as it is among 'practical' people:

Intellect is pitted against feeling, on the ground that it is somehow inconsistent with warm emotion. It is pitted against character, because it is widely believed that intellect stands for more cleverness, which transmutes easily into the sly or the diabolical. It is pitted against practicality, since theory is held to be opposed to practice, and the 'purely' theoretical mind is so much disesteemed. It is pitted against democracy, since intellect is thought to be a form of distinction that defies egalitarianism. (Hofstadter 1964)

We look now at the staffroom and the school hierarchy and at the ways in which teachers see their job and their pupils. We shall find ourselves using the theatrical metaphor of the role a great deal. Classroom life is only part of the experience of the human being who is a teacher. The pupil only sees him in this context and the teacher, by and large, only sees the pupil in his role as pupil. The part of teacher is, however, played throughout the school day—with the head, with colleagues and in encounters with the caretaker or with parents. Indeed, some teachers find it difficult to switch roles when they get home!

Much of the interesting work described below has been done, unfortunately, in secondary schools. David Hargreaves (1968), in his study of Lumley Secondary Modern School, and Colin Lacey (1970), in his study of Hightown Grammar School (both part of the same Manchester University project), looked carefully at the staff and their attitudes and problems. There is a serious need for similar 'in depth' studies of junior schools. It is likely that there are parallels—certainly in the larger urban junior schools—with many of the attitudes and behaviours reported in these two pieces of research. We shall, however, be able to look at some American research in kindergarten classes and in elementary school.

British schools are organized hierarchically. This generalization does not wholly apply, however, to the small junior school with its teaching head. But as soon as administration takes the head out of the classroom for a significant part of the day and the Burnham scale allows for responsibility payments, then we find something of a formal organization with each teacher in his place in the structure of authority. It is not easy, in fact, for a head in Britain to be wholly democratic, that is, a chairman of the staff seen as a committee or an adviser to a pupil democracy. Law and custom place responsibility and authority on his shoulders. Nor, of course, is there any consensus about school democracy. It is unlikely that there ever will be—in a democratic society, anyway.

As we have said, the pay structure recognizes differentials between graduates and non-graduates and with a first class of 'good honours' graduates. There is an elaborate superstructure of responsibility payments. It is quite possible for an ambitious young teacher to achieve Head of Department status early. So the average staffroom reflects a curious status blend. Age and experience has to be weighed in the scales with salary and official status. All kinds of things in a school reflect status and power. In the old-fashioned primary school, the more experienced teacher took the 'A' stream, the scholarship class, or, later, the class most likely to do well at the 11+. In many secondary schools, seniority still decides the timetable allocation of the 'plum' teaching jobs. In Lacey's grammar school, for example, heads of department almost monopolized sixth form teaching and work with the 'express' streams. However, it is worth noting from the experience of the author, that this unequal division of labour may reflect realities. In a small comprehensive school, the head of department may be the only one qualified and willing to teach at 'A' Level.

The staff commonroom, too, reveals hierarchical differences. Older members sit in the best chairs in the best corner, usually well away from the door! Young teachers and students inhabit the fringes. Cliques meet in corners of the school—laboratories are always well equipped for 'brewing-up'. As Hargreaves points out, groups within the staff form through shared interests—cards, crosswords, politics, religion, and subject or academic interests. There is many a commonroom, in colleges of education as well as schools, with specific areas which are the territory of particular subject groups.

Another important marker of status is extra-curricular responsibility. In a secondary school, for example, status may attach to the master in charge of a particular game. Someone, usually senior, in the English Department is editor of the school magazine. Running an activity is a well-known method of securing status and, in due course, of achieving promotion. And yet every school staff has one or more members whose extra-curricular activity is born of love for the activity and for the children and has nothing whatever to do with status. Such a teacher is, in the end, respected and even envied.

Reputation among colleagues also decides status. The apparently incompetent 'can't keep order' have little. The tough are respected, however reluctantly. In some schools, there will even be 'in' and 'out' groups. An 'arty' English teacher may become the nucleus for a group of 'progressive' near-rebels.

But in the main, as with so many occupational human groups, common experience tends to push everyone in the direction of consensus norms. As David Hargreaves (1972) puts it:

> Within most staffrooms there is a mediocrity norm, which like the mediocrity norm among the pupils seems to prohibit too great an enthusiasm and too great an effort. Teachers should not arrive too early at school; they should not spend all their lunch time marking books or preparing lessons; they should not supervise too many extra-curricular activities. Such behaviour prevents a teacher from being 'one of the boys'. When teachers do contravene this norm they find themselves teased by their colleagues and are laughingly accused of seeking promotion from the head. Sometimes teachers seem very anxious to deny the existence of this norm, but it exists in most staffrooms in some form. Its presence is betrayed by the fact that most teachers prefer the teacher who is constantly late and who cunningly manages to escape various duties (so long as they do not then have to be undertaken by another teacher) to the teacher who is so keen and efficient that he makes all the other teachers feel a degree of incompetence or guilt.
>
> An associated norm is the norm of cynicism. Teachers are not expected by their colleagues to be enthralled by the job of teaching or rapturous about the pupils. ... Combined with this cynicism is a degree of anti-intellectualism. Teachers are not expected by their colleagues to be talking about educational issues unless it is of a narrow curricular focus or concerned with the latest policies of the head, the Local Authority or the Minister of Education. ...
>
> Perhaps the most favourite topic for staffroom discussion is the pupils. They provide an endless source of amusement and outrage. Such informal conversations have two important effects. First, they pressure teachers into reaching a consensus about the 'goodness' or 'badness' of particular pupils or classes. ... Second, teachers who have not met a particular class or pupil before cannot help but be influenced by these established reputations. One of the main functions of teachers' staffroom gossip is to create preconceptions and expectations in the new teacher's mind prior to an actual teacher interaction.

There are schools, of course, where mediocrity is overcome, where professional discussion is accepted and where the idealism and enthusiasms of the young teacher are matched by the experience and enthusiasm of the old. What we need to know, and this includes appointing committees, are the conditions that, once established, can give a school purpose and momentum.

Certainly, one of the factors is organization. In most schools, we still work by the class and its attendant timetable. In secondary schools, we work by subjects. L. C. Taylor (1971) observes:

> Because we have to group boys in classes of roughly equal size and assign masters to them, we are forced at present into constructing a timetable in which everyone changes classes at defined moments. The bell is king. It demands that we learn in episodes of rigid, equal length. It cuts short our dimmest and our brightest moments indifferently. The timetable becomes a sort of solemn Mad Hatter's tea party. No matter what—how—where, when the bell goes we must all move round and face in any old order, one dish or another on the table before us. It may be necessary; it is certainly bizarre. Which of us would choose to study this way? ... Learning in fixed instalments is calculated to nip in the bud the more delicate inducements to learning. It cuts across tentative understanding, cumulative absorption, growing excitement, half-informed invention and simple pleasure. Bell's gone—move on—and wake the Dormouse up.

Interestingly, the remedial class (if there is one) is usually kept free from this compulsion. And freedom from the bell may not be the least of the freedoms of the junior school. The effect is as bad on staff as it is on pupils. To shift gear from 3C to the sixth form is not easy. Staff enthusiasms suffers as much as student.

So, in the secondary school a fair proportion of a teaching day is spent in the mechanics of lesson change. Teachers, in any case, have to spend quite a proportion of their time on tasks that are not, strictly speaking, teaching. Part of the time the task is simply supervision. But quite a proportion is taken up with administration or housekeeping—completing records, collecting money, playground duty, clearing up materials, issuing and collecting materials, dealing with raffle tickets, maintaining AV equipment, coping with accidents, cloakroom and toilet supervision etc. J. H. Duthie in 1970 published a survey commissioned by the Scottish Education Department into the time spent by teachers on non-teaching duties of a kind that could reasonably be performed by auxiliaries. The results varied a great deal from school to school—depending, no doubt, on help already available and the role of the head. Most teachers in the survey were spending between 2 and 3 hours a day on this kind of work. The information supported the suggestion that there should be an auxiliary to every two teachers.

Duthie found it very difficult to analyse what activities could properly be classified as teaching, rather than, for example, supervision or comforting. There were no acceptable tools for analysis. In America,

154

J. S. Kounin (1967) looked at the problems of class control. The terminology he developed to analyse discipline, class management and pupil response has an irreverent brightness. He used the term 'withitness' for a skill requiring an eye at the back of the teachers' head and a sense of the significant bad behaviour. He also talks of 'overlappingness', or coping successfully with two issues simultaneously. He then suggests that it is useful to analyse movement and change in the classroom in terms of smoothness or jerkiness:

> A smoothness-jerkiness dimension correlates highly with managerial success. This score is based upon the percentage of a teacher's transitions from one activity to another that contain:
> 1 *Dangles*—initiating an activity without immediate follow-through;
> 2 *Flip-flops*—stopping an old activity and initiating a new one and then engaging in an action such as asking a question about the old one; and
> 3 *Thrusts*—busting in with the initiation of a new activity without engaging in any action to ascertain the target group's readiness to receive the induction.
>   Still another dimension of teacher style has to do with techniques of inducing activity-flow and movement. Movement slow-downs and drags consist of such teacher initiated actions as:
> 1 *Target fragmentation*—having individual members of a group move when the group as a whole is to move;
> 2 *Prop and actone over-emphasis*—stressing papers, pencils, books, or sitting straight when 'doing arithmetic problems' is the molar task; and
> 3 *Sheer overtalk.*
>   These techniques may be said to produce friction in the activity flow and correlate negatively with managerial success.

The language demonstrates the lack of study of teachers in action. For one thing, teachers often are suspicious (with some cause) of observers. There is a tradition of the classroom as a fortress cut off from prying eyes.

Then, again, there is a lack of symmetry in classroom relationships. The pupils form a group of thirty or so; the teacher is an individual. This is probably why it is unusual for teachers and pupils to be seen together in private conversation outside a lesson. Most talking by a teacher to a pupil takes place in the context of a public event—the lesson. And usually it is the teacher who occupies the position of power. He controls the direction of the lesson, the nature and form of interaction. The organization itself gives him the power to exercise this control.

At this point, the language of social psychologists shifts rather from the fairly simple metaphor of roles. Some almost seem to be describing hostile forces. Certainly, it is a fact of some classrooms that there is conflict—conflict sometimes won by the teacher and sometimes by the pupils. In other classrooms, there is concord—that is, teacher and pupils are indeed *role partners*; they collaborate fully on mutually understood goals. Yet in very many classrooms there is what social pyschologists sometimes call *pseudo-concord*. By this is meant a state of partial agreement. Disagreement is limited and there are some working arrangements. It is, of course, inevitable that there should be some dissatisfaction in a class. No teacher can please everyone all of the time. There must always be pupils who feel left out at a given moment, who make less impact than others, who cannot get all the attention they need because there simply is not time. Every pupil has some experience in a classroom, for example, of delay—waiting for a turn to speak, to ask a question, to have work 'marked'.

These comments are perhaps all rather obvious, though not all teachers seem to appreciate the constraints on both teacher and pupils in a given classroom situation. The distinctions we have been making are preliminary to looking more closely at the dynamics of teaching.

Colin Lacey (1970) uses this diagram to illustrate some of the factors involved when a teacher makes an 'on the spot' decision:

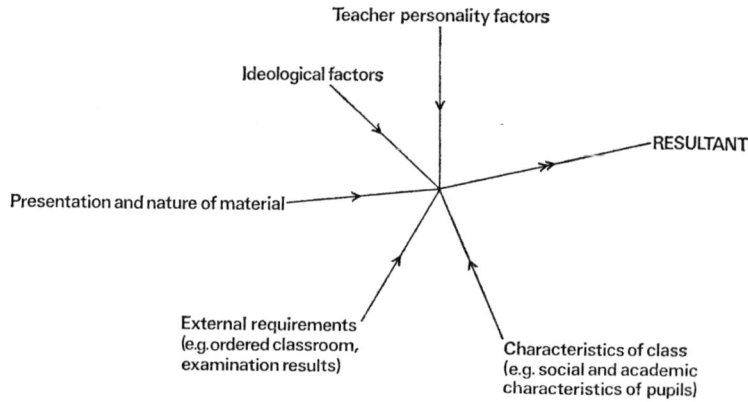

Although a decision is reached without the conscious consideration of all these factors, they are there to influence the decision that is made. The consequence of the teacher's assessment of the various factors is revealed in his performance. Each 'on the spot' decision is a response to the immediate. It is equally part of a personal performance which is the product of the various forces operating in the classroom.

It is a very complex business and virtually defies full analysis. Indeed, though some of the analyses of classroom behaviour that have been offered by psychologists seem complicated enough, they are all inadequate in one way or another. What can help is to isolate aspects of teacher-pupil interaction in an attempt to discover their contribution to the whole. There is now a deal of such work in progress at varying levels of interest and significance.

First of all, the process of achieving any kind of satisfactory classroom performance is not easy. Any teaching practice makes this clear. So will the first session with any new class or group of children. The role of teacher has to be learnt and this takes time and experience. It is partly a matter of acquiring techniques—exhausting enough—and partly of acquiring a *persona*. Most people have come across the unhappy teacher who seems to increase the noise level as he enters the room. He is the butt of the pupils—sometimes outside the classroom as well as in.

Fortunately, though such a teacher never manages to develop a satisfactory persona, most teachers do. As Lacey (1970) puts it:

> The essential elements in this development are:
> 1 The establishment of *role distance* between teacher and taught; the establishment of a more formal atmosphere, where the teacher does not become personally and emotionally involved. He manipulates or manages from a distance.
> 2 The teacher develops a presence which is associated in the minds of the pupils with a set of appropriate behaviour patterns.
> The secret of the successful teacher is that he is rarely challenged.

This is not an idea that always appeals to college of education students. Put baldly, the adoption of a persona seems contrived or artificial, and indeed, we probably all know teachers who do wear a pedagogic mask. But even in the most informal teaching situation, the teacher occupies the role of teacher and must employ the behaviour that is consonant with his goals.

Colin Lacey's first criterion of role distance immediately raises another problem. Consider the acting metaphor a little more. Of course, an actor must be involved in his part. Feeling is deeply necessary. But he must also be in conscious control of his performance. So with a teacher. He must be involved with the children and care for them. But if he is to be any use he must be in control of himself and then of the situation.

There is a great deal of argument at the moment among some teachers as to the limits of the teachers' responsibility. Is the infant school teacher a mother-substitute? This may be demanded of her—but how can she fulfil this role for, say, a deprived child, one of 30 others, in a few hours a day for 40 weeks a year? Yet, faced with countless children in distress, let alone the pressures of urban life upon the young, many teachers have come to feel that they must take on something of a therapeutic role. Teaching must minister to the whole person. The argument is notably strong among teachers of English who feel, justly, that in literature we can meet people facing all the joys and ills to which flesh is heir. There is no doubt that an understanding teacher can help, though usually only partially.

On the other hand, can this degree of involvement in the problems of a child not sometimes be dangerous? Professor Bantock (1967) argues that the teacher must assume that he is dealing with the normal. The teacher has no right to assume that 'oddities' of behaviour and feeling are symptoms of some deeper problem which he must penetrate. It is only when the strange and the disturbed impinge upon the general consciousness of the classroom that the teacher must act. If this happens, Professor Bantock argues, then there is a need for proper specialist assistance.

> Now there are a variety of reasons why it is undesirable for one person to operate in the two different roles with the same child. . . . The relationships between child and therapist and child and teacher are of quite a different order. Teachers and therapists are concerned about different things: the teacher seeks to work with the child's interest in the real world, interpreted as either the external phenomena of sense experience or the internal one of conscious wishes and desires provided these betray neither unusual nor pathological symptoms. The therapist concerns himself only when the external or internal worlds appear under pathological aspects when the aim is the understanding of what lies behind the symptoms, not the conscious manipulation of the external world in the name of curiosity or creativity. (Bantock 1967)

Sir Alec Clegg in *Children in Distress* (1968) quotes a retired Scottish headmaster, Sir James Robertson:

> As teachers, we can only meet the educational needs of this tragic time by accepting a relationship of almost unlimited self-committal as in friendship itself, with the just added element of tenderness that answers to the dependence of the child. You may see in the young, either immature samples of a species which has evolved in an environment too difficult for itself to cope with, or you may see in them the half-grown of a race divine in its nature but sadly flawed in its present state. Either way your success in dealing with them will be a function of a deep and abiding respect for them as persons, possessed of all the intrinsic elements of human dignity and worth, but denied meantime by their own immaturity and a largely hostile social milieu, the assurance and understanding which the years somehow bring to us all. That mockery and sarcasm are unthinkable in relation to youngsters must be taken for granted, but that is not enough—in their insecurity they need from us an unsentimental gentleness and a quiet courtesy.

Are the terms too grand or the demands too vaguely large for the unpleasant, uncouth and disturbed children making the lesson impossible? Or is Sir James uncomfortably right?

Problem children raise very acutely all the arguments among educationalists about the role of the teacher. We all, inevitably and perhaps usefully, feel the gap between ideals and practice. The organization of many schools reveals the gap:

> 'They're not interested in us. It's all 4A and 4B. 'Cos they never take us out do they? I admit there's a few that's scruffy in our class and you can't take them all out but if they just picked the ones that aren't so scruffy it would be different.'

> 'It's dead cushy at this school. You don't do owt. You're supposed to do writing but they don't check the books so you don't have to do it.'

> 'The Head calls you, don't he? He calls you rotten and gives you a lecture. He tells you you're a layabout and all that and tells you to get your hair cut. And if you don't you won't get a reference. But I don't want a reference.'

These boys at Lumley Secondary Modern School (quoted by David Hargreaves 1967) remind us yet again that the determinants of learning include ourselves and the way we organize the experience of education. If, as at Lumley, we not only stream the children but ensure that the less able are taught by the more inexperienced or less confident members of the staff, then we should not be surprised at the consequences.

Because of the raising of the school leaving age and the pressure of public concern about delinquency and semi-illiteracy, there has been some concentration of research into the problems of working class boys and girls. We have looked at some of the fruits of this work:

> During one Art lesson the teacher picked up a painting done by Derek and took it to the front of the class. When he called the form to attention and said, 'Boys, look what Derek's done,' Derek immediately began to laugh delightedly. But the teacher continued, 'This is a very good picture,' Derek was overwhelmed with confusion and embarrassment. He had assumed that the teacher was using his picture as an illustration of *bad* work.

> It is important to stress that if this effect of categorization is real, it is entirely unintended by the teachers. They do not wish to make low streams more difficult than they are! But it does imply that the teacher needs consciously to adapt away from these effects if he does not wish to reinforce the negative self-conceptions of lower stream boys. To treat 'bad' pupils as 'good' pupils may appear to be unrealistic, but it may be a form of manipulation which is essential

to the teacher if he is to change the values and attitudes of those pupils who turn against the system of the school. (Hargreaves 1967)

The relationship between teachers and pupils is an odd one, as teachers themselves know. It is neither parent-child not employer-employee but it sometimes feels like an uneasy mixture of both:

> The masters saw boys as being morbidly interested in their free time activities and conversations. Two boys acted as waiters to the staff at each of the house dinners. When I asked some of the teachers why they thought the boys volunteered and so missed some play time, one of the reasons suggested was that they liked to hear snippets of conversation and retail them to their mates.
>
> On the other hand, whereas pupils rarely observed the staff as a group, staff commonly observed pupils interacting in a group—in the classroom, in games, out-of-school activities, in play etc. In all these activities there was ample opportunity to observe them interacting and to assess not only their academic but also their social characteristics. However the transparency of the situation is to an important extent illusory.

Lacey goes on to point out that this failure on the part of the staff to understand the nature of the boys' interest and concern with them is only partly a consequence of the age difference. More significantly, it is a question of the difference in *function*: how can staff possibly know in any depth the informal life of pupils in a school?

Few teachers, for example, *actively* discriminate against a child because of his race or class. The race issue, though seemingly simpler than that of class, is almost as complex. It is very difficult to assess when racial discrimination in a classroom starts. Lacey comments on a boy who claimed, obviously unreasonably, that he hated all teachers!

> What we forgot was that the boy's experience of us *as teachers* did not contain anything like this variability. Just as *he* was viewed by most of the teachers as rather lazy, poorly behaved and lacking in strength of character, so he felt that *all* teachers disliked him, were unfair to him, and made his life miserable.
>
> ... Differentiation is affected by social class simply because class-linked handicaps are taken into the classroom situation by the working-class child much more frequently than by middle-class children (the child has not done homework, is upset by differences in accents, by teachers' attitudes, and therefore lacks enthusiasm and ambition over long periods). .... Working-class children percolate downwards in the differentiating process because they are harder to teach and more difficult to control within the classroom situation. (Lacey 1970)

It is, of course, a truism in theory if not always in practice, that teachers' prophesies are usually self-fulfilling. It is thus no surprise to learn that research shows that teachers tend to like and call 'good' the child who conforms to expectations of hard work. Indeed, there is clearly often some confusion between ability on the one hand and achievement with effort on the other. There is a kind of halo effect. Teachers like those who display a range of likeable and amenable qualities. It is not surprising that such pupils work hard and do well. They are not necessarily the most able. Many researchers (Jackson 1964, Douglas 1964, Barker Lunn 1970) have shown the tendency of schools to discriminate between working-class and middle-class children. This is especially noticeable in streamed schools, both primary and secondary. It is not just a matter of intelligence or attainment. In many schools, the stream in which a pupil is placed depends largely on the recommendation of the teachers. What the evidence shows is that there is a tendency for a working-class child of the same measured ability as a middle-class child to find himself in a lower stream than the middle-class child.

Nell Keddie (1971) in her article 'Classroom knowledge' discusses the attitude of teachers taking a course with a group of A stream academic pupils, 'well-motivated' pupils, as one of the teachers describes them. A head of department talked about his aims in terms of 'rationality', 'educating people to be aware of what's involved in making political decisions'. Such work, he hoped, would assist young people to become 'more autonomous and rational beings'. Nell Keddie comments that this kind of enquiry-based course already makes certain assumptions about the pupils. If pupils work at their own speed, then the more academic will move ahead of the rest. The organization of the project work, with individual work cards etc, stresses an individual and competitive approach. Teachers were overheard to claim that this kind of independent work would help the A stream pupils in sixth forms and universities. Such a course implicitly fits the vocational aims of the more successful pupils but seems not to fit, in the pupils' eyes, the vocational needs of the less able.

The picture is perhaps becoming a little gloomy. It is easy to fall into a kind of educational determinism that feels that little can be done short of the revolution or de-schooling. Schools, such pessimists assert, are inescapably class-biased institutions to be accepted or wholly changed. And yet there are many schools where children of very mixed backgrounds and abilities work together happily and purposefully—as do the teachers! We now turn to look at some of the conditions in which learning takes place. But, first, to complete the preliminary picture, how do teachers look to pupils?

There are two main sources of evidence in this country, both rather disturbing. First of all, there is *Enquiry 1 Young School Leavers* produced for the Schools Council by the Government Social Survey in 1968. Secondly there is the work of F. Musgrove and P. H. Taylor

161

L

(1969) reported in their *Society and the Teacher's Role*. There is fascinating and worrying material in *Enquiry 1* on job-getting and the inadequacies of the guidance currently available. The young people in the survey are refreshingly frank about the degree of usefulness and interest they found in the subjects taught in school. There also emerges a remarkable lack of concord about the aims of education between the young school leavers and their parents on the one hand, and their teachers on the other. Teachers are inclined to describe the aims of education in terms of character building, in developing personal independence, in acquiring self-confidence, in knowing the difference between right and wrong. Teachers were very much less inclined to rate as important the more mundane vocational objectives—preparing children for jobs and teaching them 'things of direct use in jobs'.

The children and their parents thought quite otherwise. They put the vocational aims of education first and, it is interesting to note, cultural aims virtually nowhere. There was little support for drama, for cultural visits or for sex education. Certainly, one possible conclusion to be drawn from the evidence is that there is a hidden conflict about roles between home and school. Do parents feel that schools are usurping their role? Do teachers feel that they must make up for what seems to them the deficiencies of the home? This particular conflict seems, judging by evidence from comparative education, to be peculiarly British in this form.

Musgrove and Taylor (1969) confirm the findings of *Enquiry 1*. 'Pupils,' they say, 'expect teachers to teach. They value lucid exposition, the clear statement of problems and guidance in their solution. Personal qualities of kindness, sympathy and patience are secondary, appreciated by pupils if they make the teacher more effective in carrying out his primary intellectual task. At least in our day schools, there appears to be little demand by pupils that teachers shall be friends or temporary mothers or fathers. They are expected to assume an essentially intellectual and instrumental role.'

Musgrove and Taylor investigated the attitudes of children to teachers in both primary and secondary schools. On the basis of short essays written by children on 'A Good Teacher' and 'A Bad Teacher', a number of scales were constructed as a measure of various qualities in teachers. A further sample of children were asked to rank the six statements in each scale in order of importance to them. Scales covered teaching, discipline and personality; manner and method of discipline; manner and method of teaching; teachers' personal qualities; and teachers' organizing abilities. As suggested earlier, all the children gave more weight to teaching rather than to personal qualities. It was interesting to note, however, that children in informal schools were more apt to be concerned with personal qualities than children in formal schools. Again, there was a striking difference between what the children felt and what their teachers felt. Teachers who were presented with the scales emphasized personal qualities more.

The authors point out:

> This enquiry highlights the discrepancy between children's notions
> of a good teacher and teachers' notions of a good teacher. Particu-
> larly if they were non-graduates, teachers placed great emphasis on
> the personal qualities of a good teacher; children at all stages placed
> emphasis on his teaching skills. . . .
> The contemporary emphasis on 'good personal relationships' in
> teaching, and on close and sympathetic contact with children, may
> actually interfere with the teacher's performance of his task as an
> instructor. . . .
> When 'expressive' relations are emphasized unduly, whether in a
> school or factory, 'instrumental' relationships may be impaired.
> Insistence on getting the job done might put at risk the friendliness
> between subordinates and those in authority. Too little friendliness
> between teachers and taught may well provoke resistances to learn-
> ing; too much concern with friendliness may mean that more diffi-
> cult tasks are never seriously attempted.

However, as David Hargreaves comments, we need to be cautious with
this kind of research. The children were operating a kind of identikit by
selecting among categories the most important. There is no reason, in
view of other evidence, to doubt the concern of children with efficient
teaching. However, the inquiry could conceivably mask the depth of
concern with human relations that teachers sense as being vital to classroom success. But this is a warning that could perhaps be taken with
earlier comments about the 'therapeutic' approach.

Nor has the Musgrove/Taylor research much light to throw on the
problem of social class—the young school leavers of *Enquiry 1* were all
working class. Could it be that the lack of stress on personal qualities
masks some degree of social unease? Other evidence suggests the difficulty that some children have in coping with the social demands of talking to or interacting with school adults. Particular skills are needed for
the pupil role in our schools—skills which may not be practised in all
homes. Conversely, teachers sometimes fail to read the signals of their
pupils. What is part of a different code of manners may be interpreted as
insolence or uncouthness. Teachers, too, need to acquire an understanding of the culture of their pupils if there is to be meaningful communication.

Recently, there has been rather more work on classroom interaction. It
is partly based on the sociological insights we have already discussed and
partly upon the work of social psychologists. For example, work on learning styles and creativity has served to stress the very different approaches
to learning that a teacher will meet among children. Haddon and Lytton
(1968) produced evidence to suggest that informal methods of teaching

in primary schools encouraged and developed divergent thinking abilities:

> The investigation has shown that the optimum development of divergent thinking abilities is related to a certain teaching approach. As to what lies at the roots of this relationship we can only speculate. But it would seem that it is based on the teacher's confidence in the child's ability to think adventurously and in new directions, which, in turn, will determine the child's estimation of himself and of his abilities. If the teacher can enter into the child's thinking, if she is prepared to let work develop in unexpected directions according to the child's needs and interests, if she can find and express genuine pleasure in the child's efforts, then self-initiated learning can be developed. It is in this climate that divergent thinking abilities are seen to flourish.

Other researchers have studied classroom activities in detail; they have analysed tapes and videotapes of teaching taking place and have endeavoured to develop categories to help them analyse the various kinds of interaction. Fairly typical of this approach is the work of N. A. Flanders (1968). The table on page 165 shows a set of categories used by Flanders for analysing the content of a lesson. The results, as perhaps the table itself suggests, show how frequently a lesson is dominated by the voice of the teacher. What Flanders argues is that this kind of analysis can be used as the basis of teacher training. The teacher is sensitized to what actually goes on and can be encouraged and trained to make more effective use of pupil expression.

Another piece of American work is by Bellack and Davitz (1963 and 1965). The analysis here took more note of the function of the language used in the various interplays recorded. The analysis looked at content, at the teaching significance of an utterance and at the feeling or tone. Various basic pedagogical moves were described:

> *structuring*: setting a context, launching or halting a phase of a lesson;
> *soliciting*: all moves requiring a student response;
> *responding*: the reciprocal of soliciting—a move usually made by a student;
> *reacting*: any modifying move other than above—i.e. the rating or assessing of a student response.

You will notice that the terminology, in particular the word 'move', is that of a game. Indeed, Bellack and Davitz feel that it is helpful to see what happens in a classroom in the light of a game with rules derived from the roles of the players. They note, too, how much the interchange

---

Teacher talk

Response

1.* Accepts feeling: accepts and clarifies the feeling tone of the students in a non-threatening manner. Feelings may be positive or negative. Predicting or recalling feelings are included.

2.* Praises or encourages: praises or encourages student action or behaviour. Jokes that release tension, but not at the expense of another individual; nodding head, or saying 'um hm?' or 'go on' are included.

3.* Accepts or uses ideas of students: clarifying, building, or developing ideas suggested by a student. As teacher brings more of his own ideas into play, shift to category five.

4.* Asks questions: asking a question about content or procedure with the intent that a student answer.

Initiation

5.* Lecturing: giving facts or opinions about content or procedures; expressing his own ideas, asking rhetorical questions.

6.* Giving directions: direction, commands, or orders to which a student is expected to comply.

7.* Criticizing or justifying authority: statements intended to change student behaviour from non-acceptable to acceptable pattern; bawling someone out; stating why the teacher is doing what he is doing; extreme self-reference.

Student talk

Response

8.* Student talk—response: talk by students in response to teacher. Teacher initiates the contact or solicits student statement.

Initiation

9.* Student talk—initiation: talk by students which they initiate. If 'calling on' student is only to indicate who may talk next, observer must decide whether student wanted to talk. If he did, use this category.

10.* Silence or confusion: pauses, short periods of silence and periods of confusion in which communication cannot be understood by the observer.

---

 * There is no scale implied by these numbers. Each number is classificatory; it designates a particular kind of communication event. To write these numbers down during observation is to enumerate, not to judge a position on a scale.

is dominated by teachers. 'The teacher-pupil ratio in terms of lines spoken is approximately 3 to 1; in terms of moves, the ratio is about 3 to 2.' In the lessons that were analysed, there was an overwhelming preponderance of utterances directly bearing on the subject matter of the lesson; perhaps everyone was conscious of the recording!

This kind of research is conscientious and seemingly detailed, but one is left, after reading it, with a marked feeling of unreality. There seems little sense of the complex interplay of a real lesson. And again, perhaps because so much of the work is American and based on high schools, it is the rather old-fashioned formal lesson that has been analysed. This is not to say that there is no value in looking for categories of analysis. Clearly, we could all benefit from understanding more of what is happening below the surface of classroom talk.

The work of Douglas Barnes in Leeds has seemed to many much more significant and hopeful. Like other researchers, Barnes secured recordings for analysis of a number of lessons. But the analysis was far more concerned with the nature and quality of the language used, what the language revealed about the conscious or unconscious assumptions of the teacher and what certainties or confusions may have lain behind the responses of pupils. So there is a concern for differentiating between open and closed questions, and for the teacher's success or failure in recognition of a pupil's move towards understanding, even if couched in language at some remove from the conventions of the subject.

Language, the Learner and the School (Barnes, Britton and Rosen 1969) is, in fact, an important book. Like all important books, it is a disturbing one as it forces the reader to look more closely at his own procedures and assumptions. There are too many examples of failure to communicate because a teacher has not made meaningful the language of the subject or has failed to understand the efforts of a pupil to come to terms (*his* terms) with a new concept. Far too often, the teacher, without even meaning to, has closed off a potentially useful discussion or merely sought a verbally correct response.

Like Bellack and Davitz, Barnes is, of course, only looking at formally structured lessons—but they still preponderate in our schools. The temptations are fewer in group and individual instruction but they are still there. It is worth noting, too, that Barnes has a background in literary criticism and is notaby sensitive to the nuances and directions of language. It is unfortunate that so much work in language by sociologists and psychologists lacks just this kind of sensitivity. Indeed, there is sometimes a clear ignorance of quite elementary linguistics. As for the style of so many research reports, one can only wonder at the quality of mind behind the work. Clarity of expression is always a mark of sound thinking though not all that is said clearly is worth saying.

There is still a great deal that we do not know about the teaching process. So far, the conventional processes of psychology have not taken us very far because the very techniques currently available are unsubtle and unrefined. It is more likely that we shall gain more from the work of those with some serious training in language study. In the meantime, not surprisingly, there are more insights to be found in the personal writing of concerned teachers and even in novels. A study, for example, of the English lesson in Barry Hines's (1968) *A Kestrel for a Knave* yields the most rewarding fruit for discussion and thought.

SECTION 2: READINGS

The readings for this final section take a somewhat different form. In the first place, they are mostly short. In the second place, a number of them come from one particular book—*How Children Fail* by John Holt (1969). Each one of the passages raises an issue about the work of the teacher. The passages, therefore, in conjunction with the text of the chapter, should be used as a basis for discussion—perhaps most usefully just after teaching practice.

Two other activities will be useful. Firstly, either record or get down on paper clear impressions of teaching practice experiences. Consider particularly what you feel were points of success and failure. This is excellent material for informal discussion. Secondly, secure tape recordings of work with children—a teaching session or a discussion group. Such material can be looked at in the light of what Douglas Barnes has to say. A self-help group of students is probably the best way to organize this kind of discussion.

1 From *Interpersonal Relations and Education*
Playing the system
There are, then, three laws to guide the pupil in learning the skill of pleasing teacher.

First law: *find out what pleases and displeases the teacher.*
Second law: *bring to the teacher's attention those things which please the teacher and conceal from him those behaviours which will displease him.*
Third law: *remember that it is a competitive situation. The pupil must try to please the teacher and avoid displeasing him more than other pupils.*

If this strikes you as containing at least a germ of truth, how does it work out in the classroom? Bring back memories of your own school days.

2 From *Culture and Education*
The teacher's task, then, is not to cause learning, but rather to control its direction. At the very least, he must use his powers of reward and punishment to commandeer and direct a process natural to the child, and

he must use his powers of explanation to ensure that the child learns understandings rather than misunderstandings. The teacher cannot arrest the learning process. This is the very foundation of his responsibility. When he teaches badly, the children do not merely fail to learn; rather, they learn, often all too well, what is undesirable.

3 From *Backward and Maladjusted Children in Secondary Schools*

In my own teaching life, there was Christina, a girl with an IQ of 127, who hated school because of the teachers' attitudes.

'They're horrible.'

'But why?'

'They interfere.'

'Tell me.'

'Well . . . mini skirts.'

'Yes?'

'Miss Richards makes us kneel on the floor. If the hem of the skirt—a school uniform skirt—does not touch the floor, she sends us home to change our skirt to a longer one. That's stupid. No one wears a skirt so long nowadays.'

'And what do you do?'

'We unroll the skirt from where we have rolled it up at the waist while she is watching. And then when she has gone away, we roll it up again.'

'That's disobedience.'

'Maybe. But she is interfering with our personal liberty. Everyone wears short skirts nowadays. She's an old frump with a dirty mind. Why should we be obliged to follow her fetishes?'

'You should follow school rules.'

'If rules are silly they shouldn't be allowed.'

'What do the other girls do?'

'The same as me. And there are hundreds of us. She might as well save her breath.'

'But if you have been told to do something which you have disobeyed. . . .'

'So what? I won't stay in their stupid school. I hate it, and I hate her. . . .' Christina's voice spluttered into silence, and her face became pink and hot.

'A mini skirt should not be enough to make you leave school. You are clever and could well go on and take A levels.'

'I hate the place. It's the atmosphere, and the attitudes. The teachers are bad mannered. For instance, suppose you're late for a class for a perfectly good reason, such as being let out late from another class because that teacher didn't hear the bell. You're hurrying so as not to be late for the next. You turn a corner and bump into a teacher who's hurrying, too. We're both wrong, but the teacher says, "Look where you are going, girl!" The teacher gives you a row, and you must stand and take it, politely. That's not fair. They have no right. We are not important to them. I know one instance isn't everything, but it builds up over the years. I want to leave. They might show good manners to us as an example. . . . They hate me, and I hate them.'

'Have you always felt like this?'

'Oh, no! I came to school wanting to do well. I always hurried to be on time. I got my white blouses all freshly ironed each day. I did my homework. But I found I couldn't please them. It was no good. So after a while I just thought "I don't care" and now I really don't. I really don't.' Christina's face showed her own surprise at what she was saying.

'Wouldn't anything change your mind?'

'Not now. I don't like people who think too much of themselves and are bad tempered. I like the work. The things to be learned are fine. It's the teachers I hate. If I stay on, I'll get to be like them. So I'm going to leave school.'

'What would you suggest if you were asked how to improve the school?'

'I would have teachers who liked children and didn't work out their grievances and dissatisfactions on us. I'd have cosy married women who had nice husbands and children and who were happy people—they'd be good teachers. They'd be nice to us.'

'What about the men teachers?'

Christina thought and answered carefully that there was no real difference between men and women teachers as far as the pupils were concerned. It was more a question of attitude. Nice teachers were good teachers. Bad tempered teachers were bad teachers. Liking, good manners and affectionate tolerance were the essentials. Christina made it clear that she did not want less discipline or easy work—school was for learning and hard work—what she wanted was courtesy and concern.

Christina did leave school at fifteen, the earliest possible time.

Has anything else gone wrong beyond what Christina articulates?

4 From *Work*
The next passage comes from an account by a teacher in a comprehensive school of the conditions under which he works. Do you feel that his complaints are justified? Discuss the attitudes to teaching and society that are implicit in this extract.

Streaming is a reflection of the general bureaucratic structure of the school. Just as the class divisions are hierarchical, so are the staff divisions. When I began at the school my status was low because I was new and only an ungraded assistant teacher. Now my position has improved because I have taught there several years and receive a special allowance. Yet I am still unimportant. Authority resides particularly with the headmaster, who is appointed by both the local authority and the school governors, his deputy and the two heads of upper and lower school, but also with the five heads of the main subject departments and the six-year masters—fourteen individuals in a staff of nearly eighty full and part-time teachers. This group functions in the orthodox bureaucratic manner (though their organizational theory is rather out of date, because they wish to supervise the minutest details of the projects they organize). Vast piles of paper spill out of their offices spelling out in minute detail the organizational procedures the staff are to follow and the boys are to conform with. Much of the staff's potential teaching time is spent filling in forms, collecting forms from the boys, and handing out letters for parents. This paper work doubles when a special event is due. The evening when the school is open for parents to visit, meet staff and see the work follows weeks of planning and special preparation. But the communication is generally a one-way passing down of what the 'authorities' in their wisdom believe to be good policy (and often it is). Committees of these 'authorities' proliferate, sitting on various matters such as examination entry and the use of visual aids in the schools. Full staff meetings are usually called to pass out information to the staff. Rarely is the democratic opportunity for comment or criticism from below given, so that frustration exists on the general staff level which is expressed in resentment, back-biting and unhelpfulness.

But one of the greatest contradictions between reality and school policy is revealed in the insistence of the latter in encouraging our working-class pupils to adopt a middle-class mode of behaviour and middle-class ideals. Emphasis is laid, especially in assemblies, on 'character training'. The boys are subjected to long sermons with such key phrases as 'honour of the school', 'self-control' and 'proper behaviour'. Infractions of the rules applying to wearing the school uniform are the subject of many sanctions; but it is not only dress: one fifth-year boy was suspended, just before his O level exams, for persistently wearing his hair long. Many of these restrictions appear petty, breed resentment and only help to confirm the opinion formed by numerous boys that school is alien to them and their point of view, and that their teachers do not really like them.

In fact some staff reactions confirm this. A small group, frequently the most vociferous, show their distaste for their job and pupils by various racial and reactionary, or intolerant assertions. Other staff view themselves as in transit and just moving through the school on their way to something better; usually the hope is to get into a grammar school. This means that only a small proportion of staff really believe in what they are doing and want to take an interest in the boys, and it falls to this group to carry out the real task of helping the boys to get to grips with educating themselves and opening their eyes on the world. I regard it as an obligation on a teacher to make a pupil question and query the world that impinges upon him, rather than encourage him to accept it gratefully or reproach him because he does not do so. The text on the wall of the junior school

I attended and which was built in 1855 still haunts many teachers with a middle-class orientation—'obey them that have the rule over you'. . . .

On one side of my classroom is a large window; another side holds the blackboard and the other walls have spaces for items to be pinned up. I use them for showing some of the boys' work; the rest can display information for the boys and my own exhibitions.

Unlike a primary-school teacher I teach only the one subject in this room and so cannot adequately relate what I am dealing with to other subjects. Boys come to me for a set period lasting forty or eighty minutes and then they move on. Just as I may see seven different classes in a day, so a particular pupil may be taught by seven different teachers for seven different subjects. No interplay exists between subjects, so lessons concerned with 'communications' like English, French, German, Art etc, are considered separately from one another. Even connections between the 'sciences' have to be inferred by the boys; and preparing for separate examinations called Mathematics, Physics and Chemistry reinforces this division between disciplines. Connections between History and Geography tend only to arise by chance; once, whilst we were talking about the 1917 Russian Revolution, a group of boys informed me with surprise that they were also studying Russia's geography. Furthermore they had not expected the two subjects to reinforce one another and give an added interest and meaning to the facts under consideration.

Thus I teach English in isolation and refer outside the subject to other areas when I can. Teaching English for me involves helping the boys to become 'articulate' in a broad sense—it entails giving them direction in acquiring the ability to express orally or by writing basic information, their opinions on various subjects, their own feelings or ideas; also I aim to help them understand, enjoy and perhaps evaluate all sorts of reading material; and finally I want to get them to see the use that can be made of books. These are wide and vague aims and when translated into reality in the environment of the school it is difficult to keep them in view.

In the classroom situation there is myself, the boys, the blackboard, their textbooks and exercise books. This is by no means a rich and varied educational environment and provides no adequate contrast to many of the boy's homes, especially as the books quickly become battered and defaced, the paint-work spattered and the general furniture chipped.

5 From *Growth through English*

Our first concern therefore is that teachers of English at all levels should have more opportunities to enjoy and refresh themselves in their subject, using language in operation for all its central purposes—in imaginative drama, writing and speech, as well as the response to literature. Teachers without this experience—who would never think of writing a poem, flinch at the idea of 'acting', and rarely enter into discussion of the profounder human issues in everyday experience—are themselves deprived and are likely in turn to limit the experience of their pupils. On the other hand, we were agreed that, just because language is so vital and pervading a concern, mature men and women can surprise themselves by the imaginitive power they suddenly realize they possess, given the right opportunity.

6 From *Young Teachers and Reluctant Learners*
The Hillview Project at the University of Bristol School of Education involved students meeting and developing personal relationships outside school with adolescents. These adolescents were not finding success in school, were working class and were almost certain to leave at the first opportunity. The book (Young Teachers and Reluctant Learners) *affords many valuable insights both into the lives and feelings of young people and the problems they present to many teachers. The two passages that follow give extracts from the journals of students and the comments of their tutors. How do you react—especially perhaps in the light of earlier discussion on the role of the teacher and role distance?*

When a teacher is insufficiently flexible to deal with the unexpected he will respond to the conflict this gives rise to in a number of ways. One of them is effectively to abdicate from all claim to authority. This degree of abdication is exceptional in the classroom, but because of the relatively unstructured nature of the Hillview project we came across a good many examples of it. On one occasion Miss Lucas had arranged to take her two boys back to her flat for the afternoon:

> As we did not have much time that afternoon we went first to the tower and planned to walk to the flat later. When I got to the tower they had squeezed themselves in (through the turnstiles without paying) ... they were uncertain what to do—whether to behave and do what I suggested or to disobey me deliberately. They decided on the latter, because they refused to come down the tower. They were not unpleasant and were quite cheerful—they merely sat at the top, smoking and talking, while I waited in good humour down below. Eventually they came down and we started off down the path. They had obviously decided, however, that they did not want to come to the flat and began to walk up another path.

What seems to us significant here is not so much the boys' behaviour or Miss Lucas's avoidance of confrontation with them, but rather her self-deception and inability to admit to herself that the situation was beyond her control. The phrase 'I waited in good humour' was surely a denial of the feelings of anger and rejection which would have been entirely reasonable at such a time. Indeed, Miss Lucas spoke rather more feelingly in discussion afterwards. Perhaps, like so many young teachers, she was unable to express her aggression openly at the time for fear that she might be more destructive than she intended. She was wise

172

not to go up the tower and attempt to drag the boys down; on the other hand, if she had let them know that she was angry no harm would have been done and the relationship might have been strengthened. It was clearly important that the boys should realize that she too had feelings. A reluctance to disclose personal feelings before children is rather common among teachers. Indeed the suppression of feeling sometimes seems almost one of the undeclared aims of the secondary school, going far beyond the restraint normal in our society. The recognition that anger or hurt or concern can be openly expressed in the relationship between teacher and child is vital if such a relationship is to have any authenticity. The young teacher cannot be confident in his authority if he is unable to acknowledge, even to himself, his real feelings.

The suppression of feeling in schools sometimes leads to that exercise of authority known as 'clamping down'. We may define this as an inflexible and aggressive overruling by the teacher of anything that stands in the way of what he sees as his purpose in the lesson. Such behaviour by the teacher is invariably accompanied by threats and by punishment, and completely blocks any opportunity for initiative on the part of the class. In such a situation there can be no genuine dialogue between teacher and child. There is no evidence in student journals or in what we have learned from discussion to suggest that this happened more than once or twice on the Hillview project. No doubt this can be explained by the size of the groups, the relatively unrestricted circumstances under which they met, and the absence of a structured curriculum. It does suggest though that, whatever the strains, it was possible for the relationship between student and child to be maintained. The students' feelings were engaged, and the relationship, although not always agreeable, was firm enough, we think, to help them acquire some insight into their own attitudes to the exercise of adult authority. . . .

7 From *Young Teachers and Reluctant Learners*

Mr Dash had taken two boys for the weekend to a friend's cottage and this is the account of the occasion he wrote in his journal:

Reg, Mike and I arrived at the cottage early; there was an air-gun there which the landlady said they could use if they brought their own pellets, so they couldn't wait to get their hands on it! One thing she had stipulated about its use however was that it should not be used on her goldfish. I forgot to remind them about this, and within an hour the goldfish was mortally wounded. Mike's comment was that he was only trying to make it move, which I thought as true as far as conscious reasons go. But on another level it was just another example of the incredibly compulsive and irrational way they behave sometimes; I suppose whatever warning I could have given them it would still have happened and they would have still felt compelled to do something which would endanger the goldfish! The next day, after this crisis was over, the gun was handed out again and the boys disappeared to shoot birds. The number of birds within shooting range however was limited, and the target soon became Reg, who came rushing into the house to the sound of pinging pellets. Mike came into the house shortly afterwards and started twisting Reg's arm which made him cry. What had caused these incidents? If I had hung around while they used the gun I suppose they would have behaved more sensibly, but not of their own accord. On both occasions I talked with them about what they had done. . . . Over the goldfish I was as philosophical as possible and pointed out that I was as embarrassed and ashamed as they were (I thought it pointless to add that killing was senseless because they could see that anyway); over the second incident all I could think of to say to Mike was that I didn't chase him with a gun just because I was stronger than him. No comment!

Mr Dash was an intelligent and thoughtful man, outgoing, friendly and positive. He was involved enough with the project to give up a weekend in order to take the boys into the country. He wanted to keep the occasion an informal one and so avoided any kind of preliminary discussions with the boys about how they should behave in the cottage. In his comment on his forgetting to warn them about the goldfish he expresses the opinion that, considering 'the compulsive and irrational' behaviour of the boys, something extreme would have happened whatever he had said or done. After the goldfish incident he did talk to them and obviously gave some thought to the most useful and constructive things to say, trying to relate his own and the boys' experience in a way that would be meaningful to them. However, what he said seems to have had little effect and the bullying incident follows. Mr Dash clearly knew that Mike was in the habit of victimizing the other boy, but seems not to have been able to use the opportunity offered by the weekend together to try to sort out the sources of friction. He once again avoided real discussion of the boys' behaviour and his last words 'No comment!' seems to suggest his own dissatisfaction with what he was able to achieve. Perhaps the most crucial sentence in his account is 'If I had hung around while they used the gun I suppose they would have behaved more sensibly, but not of their own accord.' It is as if he saw all intervention on his part as authoritarian, and for that reason invalid. If the boys could not behave well when left to themselves he was certainly not going to make them do otherwise. He sees no difference between the kind of support that an adult can give while children are working through gradual stages in their acceptance of responsibility, and the kind of adult behaviour which lays out all the rules from the top down.

It may be that Mr Dash had not yet resolved the conflict created by his own childhood experience of authority. It seemed that part of him wished to reject authority of any kind and yet, as he showed on other occasions, part of him had taken over without reflection the pattern of authority he had experienced. We have the impression that quite a few young teachers attracted to working with the more rebellious kind of child are in a similar position. However much they may have coped with their own problems of authority in their growth towards adulthood, when they are placed in a position of authority over children, they tend to suffer a reactivation of old conflicts.

8 From *Resources for Learning*
Lionel Taylor, a secondary school headmaster who became Director of the Nuffield Resources for Learning project, reflects on the aims of education in a confused and changing society. Is he right to believe that primary schools have especial advantages today?

Present shortcomings
It is impossible to define exactly the purpose of secondary education. We can state the general purpose of most trades in a straightforward way: the aim of the manufacturer is to produce goods at a profit, of the doctor to maintain his patients' health, of the barrister to win his clients' cases. But how do we complete the sentence 'The aim of the schoolmaster is. . . ?' Sometimes a master will say to a reluctant boy, 'My job is to see you get through your maths exam', and for a moment a distinct purpose emerges. Few would wish to suggest publicly that exam passing is even a first approximation to what secondary education is about, yet it is hard to do much better without being abstrusely philosophical or vague. We want all children to have the opportunity to cultivate their talents, develop their individualities, live life to the full, become good men and women, care for their neighbours, have a sense of duty, learn how to use their leisure (and be trained to work), be quick to respond to change (and hold fast to eternal values in a fast-changing world)—and so on and on.

At the other end of the scale schools concern themselves ardently with the picayune. 'Lavinia', a headmistress gravely begins her report, 'is noisy in the passages'. Headmasters pronounce upon the permitted width of trousers or length of hair and wonder how, short of an equation, to describe the sharpest curve allowed at the point of a shoe. This amiable confusion of the sublime and the ridiculous achieves a heady splendour each year on speech-day platforms where the ritual boasting of minor triumphs is followed by the attempt of some brave soul to reveal the Meaning of It All. At a lower level, in masters' meetings, a prosaic discussion about the best way to handle lost property will somehow reach the point when a master asks, 'but what are we aiming at in this school?' In the stupefied silence the only possible answer is 'just about everything.' It is not very helpful. The connection in schools between the ideal and the real seems as tenuous, if as enlivening, as the tip of the finger of God on the tip of the finger of Adam in Michelangelo's *Creation*.

Education then has little in common with limited and precise fields like business, medicine, the law. Its cares are as extensive as those of government and religion, and in consequence we try to squeeze into the school day a bit of everything. Whenever a new matter is recognized as a proper focus for general concern or public intervention, the demand grows for its inclusion in the curriculum. And how such matters multiply! Nothing is more important than personal relationships (what about marriage guidance from the fourth form upwards?) unless it be health (give them balanced meals, innoculations, a swimming pool). Our future as a nation depends on developing computers (add a bit more to the maths syllabus). Racial conflict will destroy us—unless the H-bomb, the motor car, drugs, environmental pollution, old age, get there first. So somehow there must be instruction in such matters. There is no end, it seems, to the things we ought to be doing.

Alas, the imperatives are now simply too many and too various, defying inclusion or coherence. Secondary education has become a bazaar for rival propositions: every adult from his memory, every parent from his heart, every taxpayer from his pocket, every employer from his need, reckons he has the right to speak his mind. Now boys themselves have suggestions to offer, and people will seek their opinions. The Schools Council recently conducted a survey among present and former schoolboys, and teachers and parents, on the importance of various aims of secondary education. The answers revealed a complete, a comic, disarray.

In truth, people expect far too much. The beleaguered schoolmaster, marking a pile of books or admonishing a boy for larking about, may be surprised at the reminder 'a teacher affects eternity; he can never tell where his influence stops', but the world at large has no doubt about it. The millenium, it seems, can only be ushered in through the schools. No wonder an American recently wrote an article on the teacher as 'victim of role inflation'.

The perplexities that afflict education in general are felt with particular sharpness in the secondary school. To see why, we should compare the task of the secondary schoolmaster with that of the primary teacher on the one side and the university or further-education lecturer on the other.

In the primary school what has to be taught is, paradoxically, both more clear and less precise than in a secondary school. Less precise because, with the eleven-plus in disrepute, standards are less closely defined and examined; more clear because the attitudes and skills are basic—not in the sense of being simple, but fundamental. If all preschool and primary learning were blotted from our minds we should be hampered indeed; not so with secondary schooling. Primary education is more important, secondary education more intricate and recondite.

Because the primary school deals with universals, it can convey them in a great variety of contexts. A teacher can, if she wishes, keep the context artificial. She can sit children at desks and say: 'We'll read in turn round the room', or 'I want you to copy some sentences from the blackboard', or 'We'll do some sums'; equally, though, in the current mode, she can devise all sorts of situations in which children are led to practise speaking, reading, writing, number skills, the organization of knowledge and the arts of expression. They can do so, for example, in pretending to shop; or through projects like 'Our Postman' or 'Ships'; by visits to the zoo or to museums; and so on. The primary skills are needed everywhere. You do not need to label them and isolate them—periods for this, periods for that. You can have what is called an 'integrated day'—throughout it a teacher can look after certain children and help them to learn as their interests and needs dictate, much as a mother does. Not only can subject boundaries be eroded, so can those between in-school and out-of-school activities. What is learnt in school can be practised everywhere: it is reinforced by daily experience. Sometimes, of course (whether wisely or not), unnatural skills invade the primary day. A recent example is the attempt to teach French from the age of eight upward. Here the teacher has an ally in the willingness—the gullibility if you like—of the young. Prep-school Latin masters have known this for decades and exploited it, setting their charges elaborate exercises in formal grammar in a dead language, knowing that a remarkable number will consider it simply an eccentric game.

9 From *Culture and Education*
Universal education—like universal military service—is inclined to expose the defects of society as an educative influence. In most societies the problems of the mental, spiritual and physical welfare of ordinary people are only seen clearly when they are brought into the school as a result of compulsory education.

Once such problems are made manifest, the school becomes a much more ambitious instrument of social control. Now to the selective function of education is added the function of providing something in common for all. All are educated and the school must dispense common culture as well as these specialized cultures which distinguish one group in society from another. It is no longer felt that growing up in society is an adequate general education. Instead of adjusting and elaborating the cultural situation, the school begins to play a fundamental part in the transmission of the central substance of the broad culture which links all men in society. The school has an important and conscious part to play, not only in helping children to become specialists—engineers, churchmen, scientists, 'gentlemen'—but also in helping them to become what all men are or ought to be: whole men, citizens, literate beings, mature individuals, and anything else recognized as relevant to anyone's education.

School is no longer a place where one learns literacy or academic subjects only. Increasingly there is a call for education to attack and remedy social and moral problems. The tasks of the school are elaborated and prolonged. The need for secondary education for all becomes recog-

M

nized since too many of the problems which are now proposed as the task of education cannot be tackled in early childhood.

To the expanding academic career or grammar school is added a secondary education intellectually less ambitious and vocationally less profitable. And at the same time the makers of social policy tend to ask the school to make good the deficiencies of society in transmitting everything from road-safety procedures to social morality, from toothbrush drill to cookery.

Interestingly, therefore, teachers begin to be educated as a specialist profession at the same time as schools are being asked to educate children simply as people. The teacher remains a product of the academic secondary education, and one who often owes an upward social mobility to his intellectual prowess. He often resents the non-intellectual tasks which are committed to him in the education of the average child. Ideally, I suppose, teachers should have a particularly intense training 'as people', but we do not really know how to give such a training.

You may care to make a list of all the objectives of school education you have now seen mentioned or heard. You will hardly be surprised at the length of the list. Which of these objectives would you support? What does your choice of objective imply about the personality and attributes of the teacher?

10 From *Education, Culture and the Emotions*
Professor Bantock is uneasy about some current attitudes to 'child-centred' education—attitudes perhaps assumed in some of the earlier extracts. Consider his criticism. What weight does it carry in your mind?

Thus it is right that, in teaching him, the child's powers and potentialities should be considered; this is the great benefit that child-centred education has bestowed on us. But the child himself does not, and cannot, fully realize what these potentialities are, because he can have no insight into the sorts of opportunities which the civilized life affords for their employment; and so that employment is not one the child can spontaneously come to. Careful nurturing, then, is necessary. Not only is it necessary to extend the range of the child's experience by presenting to him experiences which he is unlikely to encounter spontaneously but which are known to be valuable; it is also necessary to assist him to overcome the rebellious side of his nature which, as an observable fact, so often tends to jib at the self-denying discipline needed to master any complex human skill or knowledge. Let us use interest where possible, by all means; but it is unreasonable to assume that interesting stimulants can or should always be found to carry one over the drudgery which enters into all human acquirements. Many children, for instance, could benefit from learning to play a musical instrument. Is it reasonable to expect most children spontaneously to undertake the practice necessary for achievement? The benefits are remote; the scales and arpeggios are an all too immediate reality.

Furthermore, it is often necessary to protect the child, in our admass society, from influences which are likely to be cheapening and harmful. Child-centred theories tend to rest on the assumption of the natural goodness of man; the child should develop uncontaminated if only left to express himself rather than the equivocal values of his times. But, of course, no such isolation is possible; the child is subject to social pressure from birth. So, whether we think the child is conceived in sin, or comes trailing clouds of glory, the evil is still there to be combatted. It is part of the function of the school to bring to bear the more desirable and exclude the less desirable features of our heritage in order to serve the ultimate good of the child. Now our thinking about education has, in recent years, been much bedevilled by the use of a vague, imprecise vocabulary. Thus, we have tended to think that if we only provide the right conditions for fostering 'growth', or 'development', the precise definition of what sort of growth or of development towards what, can be left conveniently vague, or blanketed under some such formula as 'wholeness' or 'well-balanced personality'. A great deal of attention, in the development of child psychology, has been directed to the facts of the educational situation—how children learn, what incentives are necessary, involving questions of technique—but far too little to the values which this proliferation of techniques is concerned to serve. Our society in general lacks a widely accepted view of what can be allowed to constitute an educated person and the partial abdication of the teacher's function which child-centred education involves springs, to some extent, from an insufficiently positive faith that some things matter and that our children should have an opportunity to acquire them. How often, for instance, in child-centred infant schools, have I noticed children cutting out crude pictures from the cheaper type of glossy magazine in pursuit of some project which, I have been assured, has been spontaneously asked for by the class. And yet there is some reason to believe that, even thus early, children's sense of line and colour is being destroyed by these influences.

For, indeed, the reason for my criticism of child-centred 'teaching' lies in the belief that 'learning', whether it is the acquiring of knowledge, skills or taste, matters. A supine acquiescence in the notion that happiness is the ultimate value has led us to underestimate the importance of achievement, even at a temporary loss of personal content.

11 From *Dear Lord James*

It is often argued that in teaching it is experience that counts. From this comes the perennial staff room complaints about College of Education theorists and the uneasy belief that teacher education needs to be more practical and school based. Perhaps so, but how would you answer these comments?

Of the other external pressures which serve to reinforce and maintain the traditional assumptions of teacher education, the most important is that exercised by the NUT and more broadly by a whole range of opinion represented by practising teachers generally and headmasters in particular. This pressure can be seen within the colleges—usually emanating from the education departments—and at every level of the teachers' unions. It was recently given official backing by Edward Short (when Secretary of State). This pressure takes the form of a demand that the colleges lay much more emphasis on the practical elements in teacher education and that 'practising teachers' (a magic phrase) should be much more closely involved in the education of teachers; it springs from 'the narrow notions of professionalism and the excessive concern with the minutiae of the pedagogical process and method of teaching'. It is a reflection of the anti-intellectualism, the over-riding regard for experience, and the belief that good relationships at every level can provide answers to the most intransigent problems.

It may well be, of course, that practising teachers should be closely involved in the education of teachers—but in what capacity and to what end? If, as has been suggested, 'the [school] staff room is probably one of the most potent forces for conservatism in English education', the demand by teachers for a bigger say in teacher education is at least suspect. But whatever the case for or against, the disturbing factor is that teacher involvement—and the values it implies—are taken as a self-evident truth by the bulk of the staff in the colleges. Another truth held to be self-evident by tutors and by serving teachers is that all staff in the colleges of education should have had substantial teaching experience in schools. What a dismal view this implies of the educational needs of teachers, that a young graduate, who stimulates and opens the minds of students, is not making a greater contribution to the education and professional competence of student teachers than an ex-deputy headmaster who left schools fifteen years ago and hasn't read a serious book since! But then if experience is all you have, experience is what you value.

12 From *How Children Fail*
Teachers and schools tend to mistake good behaviour for good character. What they prize above all else is docility, suggestibility; the child who will do what he is told; or even better the child who will do what is wanted without even having to be told. They value most in children what children value least in themselves. Small wonder that their effort to build character is such a failure; they don't know it when they see it.

13 From *How Children Fail*
Practically everything we do in school tends to make children answer-

180

centred. In the first place, right answers pay off. Schools are a kind of temple of worship for 'right answers', and the only way to get ahead is to lay plenty of them on the altar. The chances are good that teachers themselves are answer-centred. What they do, they do because this is what they were, or are, told to do, or what the book says to do, or what they have always done. One ironic consequence is that children are too busy to think.

14 From *How Children Fail*

The other day a lady said for me, better than I ever could have said it for myself, just what is wrong with the whole school set-up. During this past vacation I visited a school that was still in session. It has the reputation of being very 'good' and 'tough'. The headmistress, who was very nice, asked me where I had taught. When I told her, she said with false humility, 'I'm afraid you'll find us very old-fashioned.' But she made me welcome, and particularly urged me to visit the arithmetic class of her fourth-grade teacher, who had been there for many years and was generally felt to be a jewel among teachers and the pride of the school. I went. Soon after I arrived the class began. The children had done some multiplication problems and, in turn, were reading answers from their marked papers. All went smoothly until, right after a child had read his answer, another child raised his hand. 'What is it, Jimmy?' the teacher asked, with just the faintest hint in her voice that this interruption could not really be necessary. 'Well, I didn't get that answer,' said Jimmy, 'I got ...' but before he could say any more, the teacher said, 'Now, Jimmy, I'm sure we don't want to hear any *wrong* answers.' And that was the last word out of Jimmy.

This woman is far ahead of most teachers in intelligence, education, and experience. She is articulate, cultivated, has had a good schooling, and is married to a college professor. And in the twenty years or more that she has been teaching it has apparently never occurred to her that it might be worth taking a moment now and then to hear these unsuccessful Jimmies talk about their wrong answers, on the chance that from their talk she might learn something about their thinking and what was making the answers come out wrong. What makes everyone call her a good teacher? I suppose it is the ability to manage children effortlessly, which she does. And for all I know, even the Jimmies may think she is a good teacher; it would never occur to them that it was this nice lady's fault that they couldn't understand arithmetic; no, it must be their own fault, for being so stupid.

15 From *How Children Fail*

John Holt comments on a characteristic of the inmates of prison camps. Like The Good Soldier Schweik they put on an air of amiable foolishness. They retain a shred of the human dignity of resistance by acting stupid:

Does not something very close to this happen often in school? Children are subject peoples. School for them is a kind of jail. Do they not, to some extent, escape and frustrate the relentless, insatiable pressure of their elders by withdrawing the most intelligent and creative parts of their minds from the scene? Is this not at least a partial explanation of the extraordinary stupidity that otherwise bright children so often show in school? The stubborn and dogged 'I don't get it' with which they meet the instructions and explanations of their teachers—may it not be a statement of resistance as well as one of the panic and flight?   .

I think this is almost certainly so. Whether children do this consciously and deliberately depends on the age and character of the child. Under pressure that they want to resist but don't dare to resist openly, some children may quite deliberately *go stupid*; I have seen it and felt it. Most of them, however, are probably not this aware of what they are doing. They deny their intelligence to their jailers, the teachers, not so much to frustrate them but because they have other and more important uses for it. Freedom to live and to think about life for its own sake is important and even essential to a child. He will only give so much time and thought to what others want him to do; the rest he demands and takes for his own interests, plans, worries, dreams.

16 From *How Children Fail*

The fact is that we do not feel an obligation to be truthful to children. We are like the managers and manipulators of news in Washington, Moscow, London, Peking, and Paris, and all the other capitals of the world. We think it our right and our duty, not to tell the truth, but to say whatever will best serve our cause—in this case the cause of making children grow up into the kind of people we want them to be, thinking whatever we want them to think. We have only to convince ourselves (and we are very easily convinced) that a lie will be 'better' for the children than the truth, and we will lie. We don't always need even that excuse; we often lie only for our own convenience.

Worse yet, we are not honest about ourselves, our own fears, limitations, weaknesses, prejudices, motives. We present ourselves to children as if we were gods, all-knowing, all-powerful, always rational, always just, always right. This is worse than any lie we could tell about ourselves. I have more than once shocked teachers by telling them that when kids ask me a question to which I don't know the answer, I say, 'I haven't the faintest idea'; or that when I make a mistake, as I often do. I say, 'I goofed again'; or that when I am trying to do something I am no good at, like paint in water colours or play a clarinet or bugle, I do it in front of them so they can see me struggling with it, and can realize that not all adults are good at everything. If a child asks me to do something that I don't want to do, I tell him that I won't do it because I don't want to do it, instead of giving him a list of 'good' reasons sounding as if they had come down from the Supreme Court. Interestingly enough, this rather open way of dealing with children works quite well. If you tell a child that you won't do something because you don't want to, he is very likely to accept that as a fact which he cannot change; if you ask him to stop doing something because it drives you crazy, there is a very good chance that, without further talk, he will stop, because he knows what that is like.

We are, above all, dishonest about our feelings, and it is this sense of dishonesty of feeling that makes the atmosphere of so many schools so unpleasant. The people who write books that teachers have to read say over and over again that a teacher must love all the children in a class, all of them equally. If by this they mean that a teacher must do the best he can for every child in a class, that he has an equal responsibility for every child's welfare, an equal concern for his problems, they are right. But when they talk of love they don't mean this; they mean feelings, affection, the kind of pleasure and joy that one person can get from the existence and company of another. And this is not something that can be measured out in little spoonfuls, everyone getting the same amount.

In a discussion of this in a class of teachers, I once said that I liked some of the kids in my class much more than others and that, without saying which ones I liked best, I had told them so. After all, this is something that children know, whatever we tell them; it is futile to lie about it. Naturally, these teachers were horrified. 'What a terrible thing to say!' one said. 'I love all the children in my class exactly the same.' Nonsense; a teacher who says this is lying to herself or to others, and probably doesn't like any of the children very much. Not that there is anything wrong with that; plenty of adults don't like children, and there is no reason why they should. But the trouble is they feel they should, which makes them feel guilty, which makes them feel resentful, which in turn makes them try to work off their guilt with indulgence and their resentment with subtle cruelties—cruelties of a kind that can be seen in many classrooms. Above all, it makes them put on the phoney, syrupy, sickening voice and manner, and the fake smiles and forced, bright laughter that children see so much of in school, and rightly resent and hate.

The alternative—I can see no other—is to have schools and classrooms in which each child in his own way can satisfy his curiosity, develop his abilities and talents, pursue his interests, and from the adults and older children around him get a glimpse of the great variety and richness of life. In short, the school should be a great smörgåsbord of intellectual, artistic, creative, and athletic activities, from which each child could take whatever he wanted, and as much as he wanted, or as little. When Anna was in the sixth grade, the year after she was in my class, I mentioned this idea to her. After describing very sketchily how a school might be run, and what the children might do, I said, 'Tell me, what do you think of it? Do you think it would work? Do you think the kids would learn anything?' She said, with utmost conviction, 'Oh, yes, it would be wonderful!' She was silent for a minute or two, perhaps remembering her own generally unhappy schooling. Then she said thoughtfully, 'You know, kids really like to learn; we just don't like being pushed around.'

No, they don't; and we should be grateful for that. So let's stop pushing them around, and give them a chance.

REFERENCES

ALTMAN, E. (1967) The mature student teacher *New Society* 28th December

ASHLEY, B., COHEN, H. and SLATER, R. (1967) Why we are teachers *Scottish Times Educational Supplement* 12th May

BANTOCK, G. H. (1967) *Education, Culture and the Emotions* London: Faber

BARKER LUNN, J. (1970) *Streaming in the Primary School* Slough: NFER

BARNES, D., BRITTON, J. and ROSEN, H. (1969) *Language, the Learner and the School* Harmondsworth: Penguin

BELLACK, L. and DAVITZ, J. R. (1963, 1965) *Language of the Classroom* Teachers College Columbia University

CLEGG, A. and MEGSON, B. (1968) *Children in Distress* Harmondsworth: Penguin

DIXON, J. (1967) *Growth through English—The Report of the Dartmouth Seminar on the Teaching of English* Birmingham: NATE

DOUGLAS, J. W. B. (1964) *The Home and the School* London: MacGibbon and Kee

DUTHIE, J. H. (1970) *Primary School Survey* Edinburgh: Scottish Education Department

FINLAYSON, D. S. and COHEN, L. (1967) The teacher's role *British Journal of Educational Psychology* 37, 2, 22–31

FLANDERS, N. A. (1968) Interaction, analysis and inservice training *Journal of Experimental Education* Autumn, 37, 126–133

FLOUD, J. and SCOTT, W. A. (1955) Recruitment to teaching in England and Wales *The Reader*

HADDON, F. A. and LYTTON, H. (1968) Teaching approaches and the development of divergent thinking abilities in primary schools *British Journal of Educational Psychology* 38, 3, 171–180

HANNAM, C., SMYTH, P. and STEPHENSON, N. (1971) *Young Teachers and Reluctant Learners* Harmondsworth: Penguin

HARGREAVES, D. (1967) *Social Relations in a Secondary School* London: Routledge

HARGREAVES, D. (1972) *Interpersonal Relations and Education* London: Routledge

HINES, B. (1968) *A Kestrel for a Knave* London: Michael Joseph

HOFSTADTER, R. (1964) *Antiintellectualism in American Life* London: Cape

HOLT, J. (1969) *How Children Fail* Harmondsworth: Penguin

HOY, W. K. (1968) The influence of experience on the beginning teacher *School Review* 76

JACKSON, B. and MARSDEN, D. (1962) *Education and the Working Class* London: Routledge and Kegan Paul

JACKSON, B. (1964) *Working Class Community* London: Routledge and Kegan Paul

KEDDIE, N. (1971) 'Classroom knowledge' in Michael Young (ed) *Knowledge and Control* London: Collier-Macmillan

KOUNIN, J. S. (1967) An analysis of teachers' managerial techniques *Psychology in the Schools* 4, 3, 221–228

LACEY, C. (1970) *Hightown Grammar School* Manchester: Manchester University Press

LIEBERMANN, (1956)

McDOWELL, D. (1971) 'The values of teacher education' in T. Burgess (ed) *Dear Lord James* Harmondsworth: Penguin

MEAD, M. (1951) *The School in American Culture* Cambridge, Massachusetts: Harvard University Press

MUSGROVE, F. and TAYLOR, P. H. (1969) *Society and the Teacher's Role* London: Routledge

PETRIE, C. (1972) *Backward and Maladjusted Children in Secondary Schools* London: Ward Lock Educational

SCHOOLS COUNCIL (1968) *Enquiry 1: Young School Leavers* London: HMSO

STENHOUSE, L. (1967) *Culture and Education* London: Nelson

TAYLOR, L. C. (1971) *Resources for Learning* Harmondsworth: Penguin

TURVEY, S. G. (1969) in R. Fraser (ed) *Work: Twenty Personal Accounts* Harmondsworth: Penguin

READINGS

1 HARGREAVES, D. (1972) *Interpersonal Relations and Education* London: Routledge and Kegan Paul

2 and 7 STENHOUSE, L. (1967) *Culture and Education* London: Nelson

3 PETRIE, C. (1972) *Backward and Maladjusted Children in Secondary Schools* London: Ward Lock Educational

4 TURVEY, S. G. (1968) in R. Fraser (ed) *Work: Twenty Personal Accounts* Harmondsworth: Penguin

5 DIXON, J. (1697) *Growth through English* Birmingham: NATE

6 HANNAM, C., SMYTH, P. and STEPHENSON, N. (1971) *Young Teachers and Reluctant Learners* Harmondsworth: Penguin

8 TAYLOR, L. C. (1971) *Resources for Learning* Harmondsworth: Penguin

10 BANTOCK, G. H. (1967) *Education, Culture and the Emotions* London: Faber

11 McDOWELL, D. (1971) 'The values of teacher education' in T. Burgess (ed) *Dear Lord James* Harmondsworth: Penguin

12–16 HOLT, J. (1965, 1969) *How Children Fail* London: Pitman; Harmondsworth: Penguin

Index

Winnicott's theory of
  development of 20, 25–8
sex-appropriate behaviour 58
sex-linked roles, emergence of
  58–9
sexual intercourse, adolescents
  and 106
Skinner, B. F. 11
social class
  and attitude to adults 69–70
  and attitudes to school 108–13
  discrimination based on 160–1
  and family network patterns
    107–8
  influence on language 16–18,
    23–4, 62–8, 110–11
  influence on school progress
    62–8
  influence on sex-appropiate
    behaviour 58
  influence on social learning 10
  of teachers 147
*Social Relations in a Secondary
  School* (Hargreaves) 108
Socialization
  four critical concepts of 17
  readings in 34–43
  studies of 12–14, 16 *et seq.*
  of teachers 150–1
soma, in infant's emotional
  development 26
speech *see also* language
  arrival of, in infant 57
  origins of 31–4
Spitz, R. A. 25, 28–9
staffroom
  hierarchy, 151, 152
  mediocrity norm 153
stage-specific behaviour 19
Staines, J. W. 117
Swift, D. F. 110
symbolic cognitive mode 60, 61
symbolic representation 61

target behaviour 11, 18
Taylor, L. C. 154

Taylor, P. H. 161–3
teachers
  aims compared with
    therapists' 71–2
  background and motivation of
    148–9
  and class control 155–7
  consensus norms 153
  and counselling skills 77
  and emotionalism 76
  extracurricular activities 152
  hierarchy and status 151–3
  pupils' idea of 147, 160, 161–3
  relationship with pupils 158–63
  responsibility, limits of 157–8
  role of 82, 149–51, 157–9
  and timetable 154
  training 77, 151
*Teaching Disadvantaged Children
  in the Preschool* (Bereiter and
  Engelmann), reading 43–4
therapist
  aims compared with teacher's
    71–2
  teacher as 157–8, 163

Unattached, The (Morse), reading
  125–8

voting, adolescent 107

Wilson, John 70
Winnicott, D. W. 20, 25–8
Wiseman, S. 66–7
word utterances, study of 13–14
Work (ed. Fraser), reading 169–71
working class
  mothers' views on language
    and learning 62–4, 66
  teachers from 148
working-class children
  absence of labelling 19
  discrimination between
    middle-class and 160–1
  and family network 107
  lack of preparation for school
    73